WORLDLY POWER

WORLDLY

The Making of

POWER

The Wall Street Journal

Edward E. Scharff

BEAUFORT BOOKS PUBLISHERS/NEW YORK

Grateful acknowledgment is made for the use of the following:
    Direct quotations from The Wall Street Journal reprinted by permission of The Wall Street Journal, Copyright © by Dow Jones & Co., Inc. All rights reserved.
    Quoted material from Origins of The Wall Street Journal, 1880–1902, Copyright © 1961 by David R. Jones. Reprinted by permission of the author.
    Quoted material from A Proud Profession, Copyright © 1981, by William F. Kerby. Reprinted by permission of the publisher, Dow Jones-Irwin. All rights reserved.
    Quoted material from A Pride of Prejudices, Copyright © 1967, by Vermont C. Royster; published by Alfred A. Knopf. Reprinted by permission of the author.
    Quoted material from The Great Bull Market: Wall Street in the 1920s, Copyright © 1968 by Robert Sobel. Reprinted by permission of the publisher, W. W. Norton & Company, Inc.
    Quoted material from The Wall Street Journal: The Story of Dow Jones and the Nation's Business Newspaper, Copyright © 1982 by Lloyd Wendt. Reprinted by permission of the publisher, Rand McNally & Company.

LIBRARY OF CONGRESS CATALOGING-IN-PUBLICATION DATA

Scharff, Edward E.
    Worldly power.

    Bibliography: p.
    Includes index.
    1. Wall Street journal—History.   I. Title.
HG4910.S3   1986   071'.47'1   85-26741
ISBN 0-8253-0359-1

Published in the United States by Beaufort Books Publishers, New York.

Designed by Irving Perkins Associates

Printed in the U.S.A.   /   FIRST EDITION

10   9   8   7   6   5   4   3   2   1

To Louise, for her happy whistling.

Contents

ACKNOWLEDGMENTS

WHEN I FIRST started work on this book in 1981, I was struck by how little had been written about *The Wall Street Journal*. Except for the occasional magazine article over the years, there had been no book chronicling the newspaper's past by anyone outside Dow Jones & Company. I was in for a bigger surprise when I visited Dow Jones headquarters in lower Manhattan and confronted the company's "archives." They consisted of a small pile of yellowed news clippings and some crinkled correspondence from a few early employees. The whole of them might have fitted easily into a shoe box or two. Later, I came to realize that the company's indifference to its origins had been somewhat deliberate. Bernard Kilgore, the man who forged a great newspaper from the ashes of the 1930s, was not merely unconcerned with the newspaper's earlier days, he was positively determined to eradicate their spirit—the old-boy system that had nearly destroyed the paper, along with the rest of Wall Street, in the aftermath of the great crash.

Most of this book, then, is based not on written material but on conversations with scores of *Journal* employees, present and past. With few exceptions, those I contacted were eager to tell me whatever fragments of company history that they knew—though the task of separating fact from mythology was sometimes difficult. Those who have toiled at the *Journal* over the years are a large and singularly proud group whose enthusiasm for the newspaper does much to explain its unparalleled success. Many of those who consented to interviews might not wish to be named, but collectively their help was indispensible. And then there are a few to whom I owe special thanks: William F. Kerby, Kilgore's right-hand man and his successor as publisher of the *Journal*, put up with my questioning for the better part of two days, though he had recently completed his own book of memoirs, *A Proud Profession*, which was, of course, an invaluable source; Vermont Royster, another survivor from the old days, was similarly helpful; David R. Jones, one of the so-called young "geniuses" who went to work at the *Journal* in the mid-fifties and is now national editor at *The New York Times,* gave me access to his 1961 master's dissertation, *Origins of The Wall Street Journal, 1880–1902,* which contains material from witnesses to the early days who are now deceased.

I also owe thanks to Lawrence Armour, Dow Jones's chief of corporate communications, who arranged interviews with key corporate executives and also provided interesting insights. Dow Jones's archives were considerably enhanced in 1982 with the publication of an official company history by Lloyd Wendt. My research was entirely independent of Mr. Wendt's, except for two documents whose contents were unavailable to me elsewhere and for which his book was the only source. One was a letter from Kilgore to Ed Cony describing his feelings upon taking over for K. C. Hogate. The other was an unpublished manuscript by William L. Moise on the life of Clarence W. Barron, which contains some otherwise unrecorded details about Barron's relationship with his wife.

In addition, there were many who lent encouragement, sometimes more. I am indebted to my agent, Charlotte Sheedy, to Enid Klass, who was dogged in pursuit of illustrations, to my friends at The Writers Room in New York City, to Robert Klein, Marshall Loeb and William S. Rukeyser of Time, Inc., as well as to Eric Kampmann and Susan Suffes of Beaufort Books. Ordinarily, throwing a bouquet to one's publisher might seem perfunctory, but in this case the sentiment is real. Finally, I have my wife Louise to thank. Her contribution went beyond words.

Edward E. Scharff
Old Greenwich, Connecticut
November 14, 1985

Prologue

IN THE AGE of video, it seems a little strange that the most popular newspaper in the country is a pictureless sheet of unrelieved gray, a visual throwback to the nineteenth century that has little news of sport, criminal mayhem, or most other subjects that are regular fare for most mass media. *The Wall Street Journal* is nothing less than a modern communications miracle, by far the greatest publishing success of the postwar era. In 1985 it sold some two million copies a day, five days a week, putting it far ahead of any other U.S. newspaper or magazine that could claim much influence with important leaders. And the *Journal*'s readership is the cream of American society, with an average household income of $107,800 a year in 1985 and an average net worth of $767,800. Wealth aside, it is hard to imagine anyone of standing in business or politics *not* reading the *Journal*, for as much as any one publication can, it sets forth the intellectual agenda for the nation, particularly in the area of economics.

Given the *Journal*'s place as, arguably, the most powerful publication in the United States, it also seems curious that not many people—even among journalists—know who really runs it and its parent, Dow Jones & Company. The truth is that the people in charge like things that way. They like casting themselves and their reporters in the role of good company men who might be equally at home working for IBM or General Motors. They quietly disdain the egomaniacs and prima donnas whom they suspect of dominating the by-lines in such newspapers as *The New York Times* and *The Washington Post*. The men who run *The*

Wall Street Journal—and it is still very much a man's world—are smart
and self-confident, yet they are careful not to exhibit the usual newsman's swagger. It frustrates nearly all of the reporters who work there,
but the men who run *The Wall Street Journal* abhor the journalistic cult
of personality of the Woodward-and-Bernstein variety.

One explanation is that the *Journal,* as it evolved during and after
World War II, was a newspaper of shy, skeptical Midwesterners who
distrusted the Eastern sophisticates at uptown papers like the *Times* and
the *Herald Tribune.* Practically none of them went to Ivy League schools,
and nearly all of them would have felt ill at ease in tony New York
social circles. They stayed in their offices downtown, declining to serve
on the charitable boards that form much of Manhattan's social nexus.
They even lived in out-of-the-way places—principally Brooklyn
Heights—instead of on Central Park West or the East Side. They wore
unprepossessing business suits without a hint of tweediness, and the
New York literary crowd paid them no account whatever.

The other reason for the *Journal's* aloofness is its special vulnerability
as the nation's financial paper of record. In some respects it behaves
like an arm of government, an extension of the Securities and Exchange
Commission. When the law requires the private sector to disclose its
activities, there is little alternative but to tell *The Wall Street Journal,* and
this fact gives the newspaper a quasi-monopoly on certain essential information. Such a privileged position requires *Journal* employees to uphold unusual standards of decorum. Every now and then, however, a
Journal reporter's normal worldly appetites for fame, fortune, or glory
get out of hand, threatening to wreck the whole enterprise. When that
happens, the men at the top must beat back the flames and then renew
their resolve to keep the newspaper as chaste as the piano player in a
whorehouse, which is sometimes an apt description of the newspaper's
role. One October day in 1983, for instance, a thirty-four-year-old reporter named R. Foster Winans struck a deal on a Long Island golf
course with a stockbroker named Peter Brant. Winans, who was paid
somewhat less than $32,000 a year—not much money by New York
standards—to write a stock market column called "Heard on the Street,"
would give Brant advance information about the contents of those columns in exchange for some of the trading profits. Brant, whose annual
earnings were more than a million dollars, would eventually gross about
$900,000 in fraudulent trading profits and pay Winans and his ho-

mosexual lover a mere $31,000. Why did Winans risk utter ruin for such paltry remuneration? There were three reasons, Winans later testified at his own trial on fraud and conspiracy charges: He was "financially pressed" at the time; he was "intellectually curious" to know if his little column could indeed generate large profits; and he was magnetically drawn to the aura of wealth that surrounded Brant. "He had this very romantic life-style. He was wealthy beyond my imagination," said Winans. Indeed, he continued, the whole scheme boiled down to "an opportunity to be around him, get to know him, be his friend."

Winans, who was convicted and sentenced to a year and a half in prison, was, in a perverse way, a victim of the same worldly temptations to which the *Journal* caters daily—greed, envy, and egotism. His disgrace, the *Journal*'s first public scandal in recent memory, was not without precedent. There had been other times when the newspaper had had to cast out those who committed sins of personal glorification or self-indulgence, though never before had there been documented illegality. The problem was that as the years went by, the *Journal* would have to work harder and harder at enforcing a kind of institutional monasticism, for it became more and more difficult for people there to resist the normal human desires when the newspaper itself was so inordinately prestigious, powerful, and prosperous. It was perhaps a little miraculous that a scandal like the Winans incident did not occur more often.

CHAPTER 1

"The *Right* Stockholders Knew"

THE WALL STREET JOURNAL was born of the Gilded Age, the decades after the Civil War when manufacturing was displacing farming at the heart of the American economy. It was an era of pure laissez-faire. J. Pierpont Morgan, Jay Gould, and other titans decided the fate of the nation, while the government obligingly kept out of the way. The capital of the United States unquestionably was Wall Street, unencumbered by laws or regulations save those of supply and demand. Everything had its price, including accurate information.

The Street spawned numerous "bucket shops," illegal brokerages—betting parlors, really—which were infested with tipsters, flimflam artists, and sharpies selling infallible ways to beat the market. They had ample business opportunity because nearly everything in the financial district was a subject for rumor and conjecture. The big corporations provided virtually no information at all, not even about their annual profits. There were some state laws requiring that companies report their earnings, but not necessarily to the public. Secretiveness was more or less expected. "Wall Street and its captains ran the stock market, and they and their friends either owned or controlled the speculative pools," wrote stock market columnist Oliver Gingold, who arrived on the Street at the turn of the century. "The speculative public hardly had a chance. The *right* stockholders knew when to buy and sell. The others groped."

The financial press quickly became part of this system. By dint of its ability to inform the financial establishment and mislead everyone else, it acquired extraordinary power. "The influence of a money article on a line of stocks is so great," observed Wall Street operator Matthew Hale Smith in 1871, "that if a favorable notice can be secured for a handsome check, it is regarded as well laid out."

The best newspapers tried to discourage their reporters from bribe-taking, but, as *The New York Times'* great financial editor, Alexander Dana Noyes, recalled: "Such rules were perhaps in those days honored more often in the breach than in observance." Financiers lavished gifts and favors upon the reporters not just at Christmastime, but whenever a stock-rigging pool or a major consolidation of companies was in the works.

Among the earliest Wall Street news agencies was one begun in the early 1870s by John J. Kiernan, an affable Irishman who collected information from incoming steamers and gave it to his messenger boys for distribution to subscribers up and down the Street. Kiernan, something of a glad-hand politician, made his office a welcome spot for idlers and gossips from around the town. "The average output of an average day by the Kiernan News Agency about fitted a sociable holiday," recalled one of its veterans.

In 1880 Kiernan hired two earnest young reporters from New England, Charles H. Dow, twenty-nine, and Edward D. Jones, twenty-five, ambitious men who would not long be content with the lazy ambience of the place. Dow was the more distinguished of the two, then and always. Tall and imperturbable, marked by a slight stoop and a grave expression, Charles Dow came from a farm family in Sterling, Connecticut, where he was born in 1851. At twenty-one Dow went to work for the respectable *Daily*

Republican in Springfield, Massachusetts. Three years later he went East to Rhode Island and caught on as a reporter with the prestigious *Providence Journal.*

The turning point in Dow's career evidently was the summer of 1879, when the *Journal* sent him out West by train and stagecoach to report on the great gold and silver strikes around Leadville, Colorado. He cabled back:

> Everywhere that men dug, they came to silver ore. Men sprang from poverty to affluence in an hour. It was an entirely new thing. . . . The ignorant laborer dug his post-hole and emerged to daylight a millionaire.

What really turned Dow's head was not so much the subterranean treasures as the company of observers in which he found himself, the representatives of Wall Street potentates, "the "Tilden-Havemeyer combination; the Cooper-Hewitt clique, the Griswolds and the Barnum interests." Within the year Dow left Providence for Wall Street to seek work as a reporter on mining stocks.

Dow was soon joined there by his friend Edward Jones, an impatient, fiery-tempered redhead. Jones had been born in Worcester, Massachusetts, in 1856, but there is little known of his early life. He entered Brown University with the class of 1877, then dropped out after his junior year to work for three different Providence newspapers in as many years.

In 1882, after just two years with Kiernan News Agency, Dow and Jones discussed starting a rival news service. Dow worried about their lack of Wall Street savvy and asked railroad magnate Collis P. Huntington for advice. "Go ahead," said Huntington. "Nobody else knows anything about the stock market." They started their new business with a third Kiernan defector, Charles M. Bergstresser—the "company" in Dow Jones & Company. The three men set up shop in the basement of 15 Wall Street, the same building where John Kiernan did business, next door to the New York Stock Exchange.

It was a small room, down a flight of dingy stairs and behind a public soda fountain. Like the Kiernan agency upstairs, Dow Jones & Company was engaged in delivering dozens of news bulletins up and down Wall Street each day. Haste was of the essence, for financial news begins to sour the moment someone hears it and decides to act.

In the beginning Dow and Jones were the news service's principal leg men, making the rounds of the brokerage houses, banks, and uptown hotels, then scurrying back to 15 Wall Street to fire off their bulletins, most of them about railroads and crop conditions. Bergstresser copied down the news from Dow and Jones in longhand, making twenty copies at a time by pressing an ivory-tipped stylus onto a flimsy book of yellow tissues interspersed with carbon paper. The messenger boys grabbed the tissues and ran.

The following year Dow Jones began sending copies of its bulletins to a nearby job printer, who compiled them into the *Customers' Afternoon Letter*. The Dow Jones bulletin service cost about $15 a month, but people willing to wait for their news could get the *Afternoon Letter* for $1.50 a month. By 1885 Dow Jones had its own press at 71 Broadway, and on July 8, 1889, the *Afternoon Letter* was rechristened *The Wall Street Journal*, four pages measuring 20¾ by 15½ inches and selling for two cents a copy.

The little newspaper was not much to look at. It was no more than the type from the news bulletins assembled in chronological order, along with some stock and bond listings and a few other odds and ends—the occasional sporting or political event. The front page, which would go largely unchanged for forty years, consisted of four columns, the outer two given over to gaudy brokerage advertisements and the middle two packed with news briefs. Anyone reading the *Journal* from start to finish would get a tedious, blow-by-blow account of the day's business without benefit of editing. In the first issue, for instance, readers were treated to a juicy nonfinancial plum in column two of the front page:

> The Baltimore American puts up a bulletin that there is a rumor to effect that Kilrain has won and Sullivan's backers are holding the wire to hedge on bets.

This was in reference to perhaps the diciest boxing match of the century: John L. Sullivan defending his heavyweight crown against Jake Kilrain in the last bare-knuckle championship ever fought. Since all of the states had outlawed bare-knuckle boxing, no one was saying where the match was being fought.

In the third column of the front page, readers got an additional tidbit:

> Press, Cincinnati—It is reported here from a reliable source that Sullivan and Kilrain were fighting at 11:45 a.m. The contest was a long one and Sullivan was having the best of it.

But anyone who had money on the fight ought to have kept reading. Not until they turned the page would they have seen the following:

> The Boston Globe has an unconfirmed rumor that Sullivan won in 9 rounds.

> Baltimore American reports Sullivan knocked Kilrain out in the 8th round, winning the fight.

> Private advices just received confirm the Baltimore American special statement that Sullivan whipped Kilrain in 8 rounds.

All stories, no matter how consequential, received the same piecemeal treatment for many years. In 1898, for instance, on the eve of the Spanish-American war, the *Journal* covered the President's address to Congress on the Cuban situation this way:

THE PRESIDENT'S MESSAGE

> Washington special—President's message contains between six and seven thousand words.

> Washington special—President's message reached Capitol at 12.05.

> Washington special—President's message laid before the Senate at 12.07.

And so on.

Not for several decades would *The Wall Street Journal* amount to much more than a stock and bond trade sheet. Analysis was rare and criticism of the financial community almost nonexistent. The newspaper's commentary upon the Panic of 1893, for instance, might stand as a parody of stock market journalism throughout the ages:

> In sizing up the situation as it exists for the moment, and in assigning the principal causes which have brought about the recent heavy declines in the market, one of the most active and prominent brokers in the Street said last evening that, as a matter of course, the primary reason for the weakness in the market was to be found in the increasing want of confidence in the financial situation.

Dow Jones & Company flourished simply because its news service proved faster and more reliable than the others. The newspaper, still a sideline business, grew steadily, reaching a daily circulation of 7,000 by the late 1890s. It also had plentiful advertising. Sometimes the brokerage ads took up four-fifths of the front page. Inside were advertisements for Canadian Club Whiskey, Lord & Taylor's Department Store, C. G. Gunther's gentlemen's furrier, the Hotel Marlborough's one-dollar table d'hôte dinner, and Ripan's Tabules (" 'I suffered for years with indigestion. After eating I could only get relief by lying on my back. . . . I have found Ripan's Tabules a Godsend.' "). And on November 14, 1898, the *Journal* brought out its first morning edition, explaining to readers that the 3:15 p.m. deadline for the final afternoon edition had precluded a comprehensive list of closing stock and bond quotes.

The most interesting element of the early *Journal* would prove to be the front-page editorials introduced on April 21, 1899, under the heading "Review and Outlook." The editorial writer was Charles Dow himself, and his essays over the following three years became stock market classics, the basis for what would become known as the Dow Theory, which is to technical stock market analysis what Freudian Theory is to psychiatry. The professorial Dow did not serve up any of the stupefying graphs or jargon that would come to characterize the market technician. Rather, he attempted to take the mystery out of stock price fluctuations by relating them to human nature. His explanations were never too much for the uninitiated. He wrote:

> The market is always to be considered as having three movements, all going on at the same time. The first is the narrow movement from day to day. The second is the short swing, running from two weeks to a month or more; the third is the main movement covering at least four years in its duration.

Dow's explanations of stock market behavior were elegant in their simplicity. On the impatience of the average investor, he wrote:

> Nobody who plants corn digs up the kernels in a day or two to see if the corn has sprouted, but in stocks most people want to open an account at noon and get their profits before night.

Or, in his most famous description of the market dynamic:

> In the game called the tug-of-war a score of men, an equal number being at each end of a rope, pull against each other to see which party is stronger. In the game called stock exchange speculation, the speculators are at liberty to take sides and the side which they join invariably wins because, in stock exchange parlance, "everybody is stronger than anybody." When everybody takes hold on the bull side, the market goes up very easily, but, as it goes up, one after another lets go until the advance halts. Meantime those who have let go sometimes go round and take hold on the other side.

The most enduring of Dow's accomplishments was no doubt the index of twelve leading stocks, mostly railroads, that Dow Jones began keeping as early as 1884, and which Dow often cited in his columns as the single most useful tool in deciphering the market. Almost from the beginning there were complaints that the stocks in the Dow Jones index were not an adequate representation of the whole stock market, so the newspaper expanded its index to twenty stocks. Complaints persisted, and in 1896 the *Journal* began publishing two separate indexes, one for railroads and one for industrials. The twelve industrial stocks, a clue to the underpinnings of the economy then, were listed as "Sugar, Tobacco, Leather preferred, Cotton Oil, Cordage preferred, Rubber common, Chicago Gas, Tennessee Coal and Iron, General Electric, Lead, American Spirits, and Laclede Gas."

The early *Journal* was part of a profound revolution in communications. Between 1850 and 1880 the number of American newspapers had doubled, to about 850. By 1900 their number had more than doubled again, reaching 1,950. Behind this great burst of the journalistic enterprise lay the first quantum advances in information technology since Gutenberg. In 1815 the greatest news story of the century—Wellington's victory at Waterloo— took four days to reach London, only 240 miles away. Then, in 1844, Samuel F. B. Morse opened the first intercity telegraph wire between Baltimore and Washington. Suddenly, instantaneous transmission of information was possible almost everywhere.

At its founding the *Journal* had a private wire to Boston, as well as telegraph correspondents in Washington, Philadelphia, Chicago, Pittsburgh, Albany, and London. In 1892 it acquired a telephone, a typewriter, and, most important of all, a Mergenthaler Linotype. The revolutionary Linotype machine did away with most manual typesetting, tripling the speed at which newspapers could turn out lead. "We are now able to receive a short statement of news, turn it into type, put it on the press and give out 100 neatly printed copies in about three minutes," the *Journal* boasted to readers on July 5, 1892.

The *Journal* hired its first woman, a Miss Egan, to attend its new telephone and typewriter. Miss Egan got the job, one employee recalled, because "Dow thought that the presence in the office of a lady might help to restrain the vivid varieties of . . . profanity to which Jones, under stress of business, would occasionally give way."

The first telegraphic news ticker had been introduced in 1867 by the New York Gold Exchange, but its capacity was severely limited. It printed only the fluctuations in gold prices. One of Thomas A. Edison's early achievements was an improved ticker that was capable of printing forty words per minute across a broad page, like a typewriter. Though the machine was still clumsy and unreliable, John Kiernan began installing it for some of his customers in the early 1890s. Its guts consisted of a large clock mechanism that was powered by a ninety-six-pound weight. As the weight descended to the floor, the clockworks turned and drove the keys. Every thirty minutes an office boy had to rewind the weight by hand. Not for another decade did a mechanic get around to adapting the device to an electric battery.

At first Dow Jones scoffed at Kiernan's machines, but the news ticker was clearly a great improvement. For all the progress in the speed at which news could be gathered and put into print, a serious lag remained in disseminating it. No matter how fast the messenger boys ran, the last customers on their routes still got their news last, a very real handicap. The great virtue of Kiernan's ticker was that it spat out the bulletins simultaneously all over Wall Street.

When Kiernan retired in 1897, Dow Jones & Company acquired his ticker manufacturing business, the Printing Telegraph News Company, and began offering its technological wonder to their own customers. The company set a price of $30 a month for a combined ticker and messenger service, for the ticker still did not work fast enough to deliver all the news. *The Wall Street Journal* cost extra.

Edward Jones grew weary of the business, selling his interest in it to his partners in 1899. Still only forty-two, Jones would work for a succession of brokerage houses and return to journalism briefly at *The Daily News Record,* before dying of cerebral hemorrhage in 1920. The newspaper he had helped to found would take note of his passing with a three-paragraph item on page seven headed, "Edward D. Jones Dead." Charles Dow, always the senior man in the company, died much earlier, in 1902 at the age of fifty-one. The next day's *Journal* was bordered in black and filled with tributes. *The Wall Street Journal,* the obituary said, was "essentially Dow's creation and Dow's work."

Dow apparently had run a newspaper that was somewhat more honest than the Wall Street environment in general. Said one of the editor's old cronies: Dow "ran through the thousand and one temptations that beset men of his calling without a blemish on his character." Nonetheless, his conduct would hardly measure up to modern standards of probity. Dow never earned more than $7,500 a year from Dow Jones & Company, but he supplemented his earnings with investment profits, and from 1886 to 1891, he even held a seat on the Stock Exchange, executing orders for the Irishman Robert Goodbody, who would start his own brokerage as soon as he had become naturalized.

Much of the financial advertising in the *Journal* was placed to buy the newspaper's silence, according to William Peter Hamilton, who later became its editor. Moreover, the early partners of Dow Jones & Company had no reservations about trading on privileged information. Oliver Gingold, who often ran their buy and sell orders over to the Goodbody office across Broad Street, recalled: "They all went in for a little mild gambling—all on margin. I don't think anyone ever thought of paying cash."

The partners evidently did try to discourage the reporters from taking bribes, but top pay was only $18 a week for a job that took from 7 a.m. to 6 p.m., six days a week. "It was not considered really reprehensible, except by a faithful few . . . to accept calls of stock from manipulating syndicates," said Hamilton. "It need hardly be said that corruption of that kind did not stop with the reporter."

Charles Dow, who had been seriously ill for months, had arranged to sell the company for $130,000 to the man who had been Dow Jones' Boston correspondent since the *Journal*'s inception. His name was Clarence Walker Barron, as exuberant a man as Dow was dour. Under his ownership the *Journal* would lose much of the restraint it had had under Dow.

Barron—C. W., as he liked to be called—was a man of exaggerated proportions. The most striking thing about the man was his girth. Barron weighed three hundred pounds in his prime, though he stood just five-foot-five. So fabulous was his expanse that he had to wear a leather harness beneath his vest to keep his belly from meandering as he moved. Obviously a man of voracious appetite, the publisher kept bon-bons and salted nuts before him at all times and ingested multi-coursed meals that would have put Rabelais to shame. One assistant recounted a typical Barron breakfast: juice, stewed fruit, oatmeal, ham and eggs, fish, beefsteak, fried potatoes, hot rolls and butter, coffee with cream.

Barron's excesses went well beyond food. He demanded personal service at all hours and for all manner of reasons. He was attended night and day by a team of two or three male secretaries. So long as he was awake and not otherwise engaged, Barron would dictate thoughts and questions to his secretaries in an unceasing, staccato stream, and because of his obesity, Barron never slept more than a few hours a night. He would dictate over supper, in the barber's chair, or at stool. He would dictate from the bathtub, with his nose and his navel forming twin peaks above the soapy water, and he would still be dictating long after he had climbed into bed.

With these secretaries Barron showed a strong sadistic streak, boasting openly about the rate at which he could drive them to quit. Indeed, virtually none of them lasted in the job beyond two years. In addition to the endless hours that Barron forced them to work, the men had to perform indescribable chores, like helping the publisher to relieve himself. On Barron's frequent train trips, one of the secretaries was entrusted with a hatbox containing his special bedpan, for Barron was far too large to squeeze into a cramped railroad toilet. Once, on a train in Europe, Barron began shouting, "Bring the hatbox! Bring the hatbox!" The startled secretary grabbed the all-important box and thrust it at his boss. But upon opening it, Barron found not the object of his immediate desire, but an ordinary silk top hat. "Damned fool!" he shouted angrily. "Wrong hatbox, wrong hatbox!"

Despite his grotesque physique, Barron had an almost mystical conviction that he would live to be one hundred. (Against all odds he would live to seventy-three.) Two or three times a year, he journeyed to Dr. John H. Kellogg's renowned Battle Creek Sanitarium in Michigan, where the health food pioneer would help him shed a few pounds. Then Barron would repair to the East or to Europe and gleefully gain them all back again.

Forty-six years old at the time of Charles Dow's death, Clarence Barron was the very picture of an American capitalist. He had a handsome, distinguished look and wore an elegantly trimmed beard. He lived in a baronial mansion in Cohasset, Massachusetts, with eighteen telephones, including one in his bathroom. He was commodore of the Cohasset Yacht Club and loved to swim off his great yacht *Hourless,* with a couple of the ever-present male secretaries swimming along to push him back into the boat when he had had enough. In New York he lived in a suite at the Waldorf-Astoria, where he hung out with friends like John W. ("Bet-you-a-million") Gates, the fabled speculator; E. H. Harriman, the railroad magnate; Hermann Sielcke, the king of coffee futures; and Harry F. Sinclair, a principal in the Teapot Dome scandal. Like his friends, Barron loved to play the stock market, though he was hardly in their league financially.

A lifelong devotee of Horatio Alger novels, Barron also pontificated like a great capitalist. He bullishly asserted that the grand tycoons of his era were performing divine work. "There is not a single reason why this great continent should not enjoy a continuance of vigorous, healthy, booming business," he said in 1920. "We have only to furnish the necessities of life, which we possess in superabundance, to the rest of mankind in order to receive into our own life the wealth, the luxury, the comforts, the things artistic, which can make the American working man a prince and a capitalist." Barron, a convert to the obscure Lutheran sect of Emanuel Swedenborg, was also something of a religious fanatic. "The greatest gauge of all is the spiritual progress of the people," he insisted. "When there is not right thinking, disaster lies ahead."

Barron was born in 1855 in Boston's North End. His father, nicknamed "Honest Henry" Barron according to C. W.'s brief autobiographical notes, was a teamster who worked about the Boston wharves. Barron grew up in working-class Charlestown but with the help of family friends, was permitted to attend Boston's more polished English High School, where he won prizes for two essays entitled "Transcontinental Railways" and "Civil Service Reform."

Determined to be a newspaperman from the age of fifteen, Barron apprenticed himself to a Boston court reporter in order to learn shorthand. He would later write: "I think it is a great mistake to give the shorthand field over to girls. I think it is the best training for young men in practical life, far ahead of Greek or Latin. . . . I have followed the practice in my different offices of employing the best stenographers available and developing them into newspaper men. Many of them have graduated or fallen into banking fields and the way of wealth."

Barron's first brief newspaper job was with *The Boston Daily News,* and his shorthand gave him his first scoop. Covering a lecture by abolitionist Wendell Phillips, Barron discovered that he was the only reporter present who could get the radical reformer's rapid-fire oratory down on paper. He later claimed that his lengthy story, "Wendell Phillips on Finance," sold out the edition and was reprinted.

Moving to *The Evening Transcript,* Barron began writing about local business matters. "One day I reported to my superiors that it was absurd to give the quotations of Boston securities and every transaction, yet never give the news under the fluctuations; that I believed there was a news item every day in State Street that might be picked up," said Barron in his notes for a never-completed autobiography. "I was asked to annex that to my daily duties. I said, 'Give me my whole time for the new project.' My request was granted.

" . . . I thus established the financial section of the paper. The result was unexpected. The *Transcript* was already taken by everyone; yet in a few weeks the *Transcript* circulation increased fifteen percent."

Nonetheless, Barron soon fell out with the *Transcript* over an article about Henry Villard, the German-born journalist and railroad promoter. "I had denounced Henry Villard's Oregon Transcontinental scheme. I spoke of him as 'Visionary Villard,' " Barron recalled. As it happened, Villard had married Fanny Garrison, the daughter of Wendell Phillips' abolitionist ally William Lloyd Garrison. And among Garrison's strongest backers was a man whose business partner was also president of the *Transcript.* Such things will happen in Boston.

Barron decided to strike out on his own with a news service. For a dollar a day, businessmen could subscribe to his bulletins, handbills like those of Dow Jones that were run through the streets of Boston by a couple of messenger boys at the rate of twenty to thirty a day. In 1887, when Barron was thirty-two, he began a newspaper that carried the same name as his bulletin service, *The Boston News Bureau.* As with Dow Jones' *Customers' Afternoon Letter* in New York, Barron's paper consisted of each day's bulletins printed in chronological order. There was no advertising, and if the bulletins did not reach the bottom of the page, the extra space was left blank.

Before long the ambitious Barron was calling his newspaper "The Financial Bible of New England" and signing on as the Boston correspondent for Dow Jones to help establish his name in Wall Street. In 1896 he started *The Philadelphia Financial Journal,* a carbon copy of the Boston paper. In 1902 he completed his sweep of the country's three most important cities by buying Dow Jones & Company and *The Wall Street Journal.*

Actually Barron did not buy Dow Jones; his wife did. Barron was as ingenious at squandering money as he was at making it, and at the time of Dow's death, he apparently was broke. Jessie Waldron Barron, his spouse of two years, seems to have put up the meager $2,500 cash down payment when her husband could not. She also acquired the stock in her own name. Clarence Barron would not own a single share of Dow Jones for another decade.

Mrs. Barron had been a well-to-do widow running a respectable Boston boardinghouse, when Barron, her tenant of fourteen years, proposed marriage in 1900, agreeing to adopt her two girls, Jane and Martha. At his death Barron would leave his publishing companies to Jane—her sister, Martha, had died—and Jane Waldron Bancroft would beget a matriarchy that would prove an inestimable blessing for Dow Jones & Company. *The Wall Street Journal* would be almost the only major American newspaper owned by a family that did not feel compelled to install its heirs as publishers and editors, which may be the most succinct explanation as to how the *Journal* came to be the most successful newspaper in the country.

For the moment, though, Barron's family took absolute control of the company. Mrs. Barron left her husband behind in Boston—their marriage seems to have been celibate—and moved into the Waldorf, assuming full command of Dow Jones & Company. For several years the business grew and prospered, probably because Charles Dow had bequeathed her a group of bright and able newsmen. Mrs. Barron's first editor was the erudite Thomas F. Woodlock, a classics scholar at the University of London, who had come to New York seeking his fortune. Under Woodlock the _Journal_'s circulation rose steadily from about 7,000 a day to an estimated 11,000. And when Woodlock resigned in 1905, apparently after an argument over business policy, Mrs. Barron replaced him with another holdover from the Dow era, Sereno S. Pratt.

The newspaper changed little. Its front page became a bit more tidy, but the contents remained turbid. And as Woodlock, Pratt, and others drifted away, the newspaper gradually deteriorated, as did the rest of the business. Barron, who as yet took no personal part in running the _Journal,_ sent his son-in-law, Hugh Bancroft, to straighten things out. Bancroft, a patrician lawyer, evidently hated the task. In 1911, with the _Journal_'s circulation and advertising revenues in sorry decline, he resigned and went home to become chairman of the Boston Port Authority.

As last it was clear that Barron would have to take matters into his own hands. In March 1912 he made his first appearance in the _Journal_ newsroom, kicking office furniture and pounding his cane to command attention, said a contemporary, whose remarks are included in the authorized company history. " 'He berated them all for their sins and mistakes and told them he intended to straighten them out, at once. They could obey him or they could get out.' "

Whatever his eccentricities, Barron got results. Under his stewardship for the next sixteen years, the _Journal_'s circulation rose from about 7,000 to 18,750 in 1920, to 52,000 for a brief period in 1928. Its physical size swelled as well—from four pages a day to twenty or more—and the newstand price went to seven cents, versus two cents for _The New York Times._ At Barron's death a new Barron newspaper, _The Wall Street Journal Pacific Coast Edition,_ was planned. Besides making commercial progress, Barron linked the _Journal,_ once and for all, to his news services in Boston and Philadelphia, and installed correspondents in most important American cities.

Both Barron and his newspaper were capable of soaring pomposity. "Knowledge is power—also profit," he would say. "Learn how to read, how to interpret, how to weigh the news." The real truth, of course, was that Wall Street insiders, including Barron himself, were the only people who knew which stocks to buy and sell, and Barron did not seem to print that sort of information. At the same time, editorials in Barron's newspaper became much more strident. Under Woodlock and Pratt, the newspaper had carried on in the restrained, scholarly manner of Charles Dow, even supporting Teddy Roosevelt's trust-busting, to the dismay of Wall Street's establishment. But after 1908, when William Peter Hamilton became the chief editorial writer, the *Journal* tended to reflect Barron's own views. The Kiplingesque Hamilton wrote daily sermons in support of free-market capitalism, and Barron approved so heartily that he bestowed upon his editorialist the simple but lofty title "editor" of *The Wall Street Journal.*

Hamilton was nothing if not dogmatic. "You can't write a fifty-fifty editorial," he told an interviewer. "Don't believe the man who tells you that there are two sides to every question. There is only one side to the truth." Of the 1920 Democratic Convention that nominated James M. Cox to run against Republican Warren G. Harding, Hamilton wrote:

> It is in the public interest that all our cranks, soreheads and anarchists should get together so that we may count them in a constitutional way and estimate the real extent of the forces of disease they represent.

And of the United States' officially recognizing the government of the U.S.S.R. in 1925:

> In any real sense of the word as civilized people understand it, there is no government in Russia to recognize. The gang which has made government there impossible has its hand against all men.

Gradually Hamilton's militant moralism reached the news columns as well. A series of articles in 1922 about the history of organized labor concluded:

> Whatever benefits organized labor has conferred on its mem-
> bers, these benefits have been obtained at an incalculable cost
> to the rest of humanity. . . . The history of the movement in
> this country is one of the most sordid records of humanity.

A side column, "Tips on Amusements," would carry smug,
thumbnail assessments of Broadway culture:

> "Desire Under the Elms"—Interesting to those who care for
> Rural degeneracy.
>
> "What Price Glory"—War play notable for its profanity.
>
> "White Cargo"—Picturesque degeneration of the white man
> in West African climate.

As the Barron era wore on, the *Journal* became increasingly
defensive of its familiar world and hostile to all manner of social
change elsewhere, be it the Soviet Union or midtown Manhattan.
It was particularly defensive of Wall Street, flying into rage at
the suggestion from any quarter that the Street might benefit
from some sort of outside regulation. "Wall Street has steadily
raised its ethical standards," Hamilton insisted. "For the self-ap-
pointed bodies which would try to regulate Wall Street and
everything else, I have neither use, space nor sympathy."

Actually Barron knew enough of Wall Street's shady side to
try to impose ethical standards upon his staff. He forbade the
reporters to trade in stocks they wrote about, but they ignored
him, and for good reason. Barron himself was notorious for ordering up stories that promoted certain companies whose stock
he owned. True or not, it was rumored among the men that to
put a juicy tidbit on the Dow Jones news ticker without giving
Barron a chance to call his broker was a firing offense.

Clarence Barron's career was just working up steam when he
took over the *Journal*. After putting Dow Jones & Company back
on its feet, he became a globe-trotting financial pundit, an adviser
to Presidents, and a confidant of industrial potentates. Often
Barron accompanied Pennsylvania Railroad president William
Wallace Atterbury aboard his private car. As the two men rode
from town to town, the business leaders in each place would come,

hat in hand, to answer their questions about local commerce there. Barron swaggered through Europe, lecturing, interviewing, and counseling finance ministers and monarchs. Some of the articles he wrote were published as books: *The Audacious War* in 1915; *The Mexican Problem* in 1917; *War Finance* in 1919; and *A World Remaking* in 1920. In the process Barron acquired a modicum of celebrity for himself and his newspapers. In 1921, at his son-in-law's suggestion, Barron started a new weekly newspaper for investors called *Barron's*.

Barron also founded one of New York's more successful advertising agencies, Doremus & Company, after discovering how much profit other ad agencies were realizing through the financial "tombstone" ads that invariably ended up in Barron's publications. Barron named the new firm for an office functionary, Harry Doremus, who owned no part of it. Wall Street legend has it that Doremus grew thoroughly discontent in Barron's employ and left two years later to start a rival ad agency with the same name. Barron immediately crushed him, telling firms up and down Wall Street that to do business with the upstart Harry Doremus was the surest way to be locked out of all Barron's publications. C. W. Barron was no man to be trifled with.

Doremus was not the only one who disliked working for Barron. The financial news tycoon also loved to needle the news staff. Every morning one of Barron's beleaguered male secretaries would carry a long list of Barron's nettlesome questions to the Dow Jones general manager, Kenneth C. Hogate. A memorable example from the mid-twenties: "How much steel is consumed in the manufacture of women's corset stays?" Hogate would farm these questions out to the reporters as the day's first order of business, knowing that C. W. would soon be on his back for the answers.

One day Barron sent Hogate a list of some 120 questions of the corset-stay variety. By nine that morning Barron was on the phone from his yacht in Florida wanting to know if the answers were ready. Hogate protested that his reporters had scarcely had time to get to work on them. Thereafter, Barron would call Hogate every thirty minutes to check on the reporters' progress and complain that he was growing impatient. At the third or fourth

call, Hogate finally broke: "C. W., I can't take this nonsense any
longer. I quit." Stung, Barron insisted that Hogate come down
to Miami and resign in person. Hogate hung up on Barron, called
his wife, Anna, in Scarsdale, and told her to start packing for
Florida.

Though Clarence Barron was accustomed to abusing his employees, Kenneth Hogate was no ordinary flunky. The two had
something very much like a father-son relationship. The first
thing that struck people about Hogate—familiarly known as
"Casey"—was that he was obese, just like his boss. He weighed
three hundred pounds, more sometimes, though he, at least, was
over six feet tall.

The second thing one noticed about Hogate was his uncommon
affability, which had always made him something of a prodigy.
The son of a weekly newspaper editor in Danville, Indiana, the
cherub-faced Hogate had been editor of the newspaper at
DePauw University, then had gone on to a job at *The Cleveland
News and Leader*. Within months Casey Hogate had moved on to
the more prestigious *Detroit News*, telling editor Malcolm W. Bingay that he was twenty-eight and had a full twelve years of newspaper experience behind him. In fact, he was just twenty-one.
Hogate later confessed the lie to Bingay, but it made no difference. Bingay named him city editor when he was only twenty-
four. This was an important job, for the automobile industry was
in its heady adolescence, and Detroit was America's newest boom
town.

Barron had heard Hogate's name from Walter P. Barclay,
managing editor of the *Journal,* whom he had sent to Detroit in
1921 to see about opening a news bureau there. Soon afterward
Barron was passing through Detroit himself, probably en route
to Battle Creek. He took one glance at the portly young Hogate
and beamed with satisfaction. "If I had ever had a son," Barron
announced, "he would have looked just like you."

Hogate left the *News* at once to become Barron's man in Detroit.
The next year the *Journal* publisher brought him to New York,
and the year after that Barron demoted Barclay and made Hogate managing editor. Hogate was hard-working and obviously
talented, but there were other reasons for his rapid ascension

that were far less tangible. "I talked to Hogate for ten minutes and it seemed I had known him always," someone once commented to Barron.

"Yes," said the old man without pause. "You knew his heart was right."

Despite his closeness to Barron, Hogate was determined to quit. He and his wife took the long train ride down the Florida coast, finally reaching Miami. At the dock they stepped aboard Barron's yacht. It pulled away without warning and steamed out to sea, where the crew anchored within sight of land.

There Barron and Hogate sat staring at one another, hour after hour, neither of them saying a word. At last Hogate cleared his throat and said: "C. W., I'm quitting. That's final."

"No, you're not," said Barron, who then retreated to his cabin and began writing notes to Hogate and summoning Anna to deliver them.

Finally Hogate opened the cabin door and said to Barron: "Turn this thing around for Miami, or I'll jump off and swim."

But minutes later Hogate heard the boat's engine stop cold. Climbing to the deck he saw Barron and the yacht's captain pulling away in a lifeboat. Several hours later the launch returned, piled to the gunwales with intricate Turkish rugs, a peace offering for Mrs. Hogate. In a fit of contrition, Barron had walked into a store and bought all of its inventory. Hogate, who eventually took over the company, would tell this story to friends and shake his head with a smile: "How could you quit a man like that?"

Barron was perhaps fortunate to breathe his last on October 2, 1928, a year before the great crash that would make a mockery of his pontifications. At seventy-three he fell into a coma at Dr. Kellogg's sanitarium, apparently because of an overworked liver. His last words, whispered to a hovering secretary were: "What's the news?"

It would take some years before Barron's executors could untangle his estate. They found that Barron had had numerous brokerage accounts, some in his name alone and others in partnership with men like Harry Sinclair. In some cases Barron had unintentionally sold a stock short in one account—betting that it would go down—while holding a long position in the same stock in another account.

Barron had played so fast and loose with the market that he had no recollection of what he owned and what he didn't. In his final years he had also spent money at the impressive rate of some $500,000 a year, taking money from his businesses without telling anyone. When his estate was finally liquidated, acquaintances were shocked to learn that Barron's net worth was only about a million dollars, a pittance considering his far-flung enterprises. His executors, however, were relieved. They had begun to fear that the old man might actually have died a pauper.

CHAPTER 2

"Hang On to Your Shekels"

IN THE LATE 1920s young Ivy League graduates arrived at *The Wall Street Journal* in much the same way that Nick Carraway came to the bond business in *The Great Gatsby*, by way of an introduction from a well-connected relative. Dick Cooke, a Princeton man, said he began work at the newspaper on October 13, 1927, after an all-night poker game. His ticket of admission: a word of introduction to Kenneth C. Hogate, the general manager of Dow Jones, from his uncle Harry Bliss, a power at Merrill Lynch. "I had no great ambition. I just thought that in three or four years I would make enough to retire and then do whatever I wanted," said Cooke. He would not exactly strike it rich, as it happened.

Reporting for work at 44 Broad Street, Cooke found a small, drab second-floor newsroom staffed by finicky men in stiff white shirts. It was a humdrum scene: reporters working quietly at their telephones; a large, circular copydesk rimmed by studious-looking pencil editors. But one corner of the floor bustled with activity. This was the domain of the Dow Jones news ticker, and its sovereign was Eddie Costenbader, a gruff, imposing man who sat between the ticker typists and a telephone operator named Florie.

Costenbader was usually barking at one of his assistants, wanting to know when some piece of news would materialize or where exactly some reporter was at that particular moment. A good percentage of the sentences he uttered began: "Where the hell is . . . " During particularly heated moments, like the issuance of a dividend by U.S. Steel, Costenbader would turn from the telephone and yell to his wire operators something like: "Eleven dollar extra steel dividend!" and then Florie the telephone operator would scream even louder: "Eleven dollar extra steel dividend!" in case anyone hadn't heard, and then there would be a general chorus of cries: "Eleven dollar extra steel!" until the excitement drained away a few seconds later.

Like many of the new hands, Cooke was marched around the block to the New York Stock Exchange building and shown into what was called the comparison room, where a Dow Jones news ticker sat side by side with the competition, the New York News Bureau wire. Cooke's job was to read both news wires as they clattered along, looking for big stories—an extra dividend being the hottest scoop imaginable. When something of note came over the wire, Cooke would reach for the open phone line to Costenbader's desk and tell his boss who had the story first, Dow Jones or the New York News Bureau, nicknamed "Tammany," though no one knew why. If Dow Jones was scooped by as little as fifteen seconds, it was considered a sound defeat. Thirty seconds' lag meant that the Dow Jones reporter was in for trouble, and a full minute's lag could well cost him his job.

Reporters, of course, went to great lengths to avoid defeat. They would sit outside a corporate boardroom during an important meeting and wait for a company spokesman to emerge with the expected announcement. Then they would race for the telephone as if their lives depended on it. If there was a convenient window overlooking the street, one reporter might wave his handkerchief to a confederate in some prearranged code. The man waiting at a phone booth below was supposed to know, for example, that two waves meant "No extra dividend" or that four waves meant "Merger not approved."

Some firms, like the giant American Can Corporation at 230 Park Avenue, showed their contempt for the reporters' rat race by refusing to let them use company telephones. In such cases the reporters from Tammany and Dow Jones would often have a gentleman's agreement to take the same elevator down from the twelfth floor and enter telephone booths in the lobby simultaneously, but such agreements were breached whenever possible. The Dow Jones reporter might have a friend at American Can with a desk on the eleventh floor. While the Dow Jones man pretended to abide by the terms of the Tammany truce, a confederate would race down the fire stairs to the friend's telephone and score a two- or three-minute victory over the unsuspecting competition.

The way to win favor at Dow Jones was with such triumphs on the ticker. The newspaper was still something of an afterthought—for two reasons. The first was that the *Journal* had no real competition. Morning and afternoon the newspaper covered stocks and bonds, little else. The newspaper most closely resembling it was the equally dull *Journal of Commerce*, which specialized in commodities and shipping news. The other reason for the news ticker's paramount importance was that it still made far more money than *The Wall Street Journal*. The ticker, linked to almost every major brokerage in the country, was Dow Jones' lifeblood, and as far as most young reporters were concerned, Eddie Costenbader was the man to please.

Life as a Dow Jones reporter was somewhat grubby and not very demanding of a man's intelligence. Speed, accuracy, and efficiency were wanted, not imagination, literacy, or a grasp of economic subtleties. And yet it was a much sought job. The scent of wealth was in the air. Though salaries were modest—a new copydesk hand might earn $50 a week—the staff was immaculately turned out, some with fresh boutonnieres in their lapels. One reporter arrived for work each day in a chauffeur-driven limousine. Another had a sixty-acre horse farm in New Canaan, Connecticut. When *Journal* editors called him at home, the servant who answered always asked if they wanted "the main house or the stables?" Nearly everyone had fantasies of making a fortune on the side—including C. W. Barron.

The financial press was an intimate part of the thriving Wall Street community, none more intimate than the reporters and editors of *The Wall Street Journal,* the favorite neighborhood paper. What drew most young men to the *Journal* was an open secret having nothing whatever to do with the fabled fun of the news business or the romance of the rolling presses. Newspapermen and radio newscasters were privy to inside information that could practically guarantee profits in the stock market. In addition, they were paid—sometimes handsomely—to work in conjunction with speculative rings and stock syndicates. Easy money was all around.

There had always been stock manipulators and shady dealers on Wall Street, but in an earlier time they had at least been considered scurrilous. The Wall Street establishment, the big, aristocratic banking houses like J. P. Morgan & Company, and Kuhn, Loeb had shunned "speculators" like Jesse Livermore, "Bet-you-a-million" Gates, and the Durant brothers, the riverboat gamblers of the period who made their fortunes by betting on stocks they cleverly manipulated. But as the twenties wore on, the great speculators took hold of the public imagination, giving Wall Street a romance that the stuffy banking houses most definitely lacked. And after 1924, when the market began to rise without interruption, the image of the successful speculator became an essential ingredient in selling stocks to middle-class America. It was the old rags-to-riches fantasy at work: every man a potential millionaire. And the larger the speculators loomed in the public eye, the more inclined the staid Wall Street establishment was to go along with them, even to mimic them a little.

In the ebullient air of the late twenties, Wall Streeters were busy forming investment pools and syndicates—polite names for what were, in effect, schemes to swindle the stock-buying public. The general idea was for pool members to buy up shares of some stock quietly, then to bull up the price with rumors and flourishes of publicity. As more buyers jumped in and prices rose, the pool members would sell off their shares at a fat profit. Masters of the stock-rigging art—Jesse Livermore was the greatest—could create something approaching melodrama on the Stock Exchange ticker by buying a bit here, selling a little there, and then buying a little more a few minutes later, working the stock steadily upward in a way calculated to give goose bumps to the rubes outside Wall Street. Once the syndicate unloaded its shares and walked away from the ticker, the fun ended. Thousands of investors were stuck with the losses.

There was nothing illegal about such schemes, however unethical. The Wall Street establishment and the *Journal* were constantly defending the financial community's conduct, arguing with much bluster that while there were some shady operators around, just as in any free marketplace, Wall Street was still run by solid citizens who could police their less scrupulous associates far better than any outsiders.

Ironically, as the great bull market of the twenties gathered steam, few people really wanted government regulation. Rather than shying away from a stock because it was rumored to be rigged, the public would rush to get on the bandwagon, always assuming that they could cash in and get out before the price of the stock caved in. It was a great game of musical chairs, a vast chain-letter scheme in which those who got in early made profits, while the many thousands who got in later took losses. No one on Wall Street, indeed, no one who was playing the market anywhere, wanted an end to it because everyone liked to think of himself as an insider. The stock market kept swelling to new highs. Almost any cause for public elation would set off a stock rally, even Lindbergh's solo flight from New York to Paris or another of Babe Ruth's home runs. And people kept plowing more money in.

Clarence Barron and *The Wall Street Journal* had begun the era as outsiders, wanting to know—like everyone else—what J. P. Morgan and Jay Gould were thinking. Gradually Wall Street had become more egalitarian. Everyone seemed to qualify as an insider of sorts. The place was no longer a rigid aristocracy, but more a school for scoundrels. Now it was *assumed* that a reporter in the financial district was allied with some syndicate or other. Otherwise, what was he doing there? Up and down Wall Street, people knew that reporters from all the big newspapers could be bought. The financial district was governed by its own unwritten set of laws.

Under Clarence Barron *The Wall Street Journal* cast itself more and more in the role of Wall Street's public defender, as Congress grew wary of the Street's unregulated business practices. The newspaper had once adopted a statesmanlike tone: "There is a greater and a lesser Wall Street," Sereno Pratt had written in 1907. "The greater Wall Street, whatever may be said of the lesser, stands for fair dealing . . . for uncompromising hostility to jugglery and manipulation."

But in the twenties William Peter Hamilton's arrogant editorials were ever vigilant in defense of Wall Street prerogatives: "Not so many years ago, or perhaps about the time when the politician had been cruelly deprived of the privilege of traveling on the railroads for nothing, Wall Street seemed to live in a state of continual apology," wrote Hamilton in 1928. ". . . It was not thanked if the great enterprise which it financed and promoted, whose stock it distributed was successful. It was blamed for incompetence and dishonesty anywhere. . . . But Wall Street does not apologize nowadays."

The Wall Street practice that made Congress most suspicious of all was the unrestricted extension of credit to brokerage customers. Brokers' loans—or "call money"—obviously helped fuel speculation, driving the market to dizzying levels. Practically anyone who knew a broker by name could buy stock on ten percent margin—a one-dollar down payment for every ten dollars' worth of stock. And on Wall Street brokers would simply "carry" a favored customer. The buyer made no down payment at all. It was assumed that the market value of the stock would rise, enabling the customer to pay off his broker's loan with profit to spare. Few people considered what might happen if the stock went down because, for true insiders, that was rarely a problem.

In 1920 the brokerage industry had only a billion dollars' worth of call money, or loans to customers, outstanding. But the figure began to mount steadily, reaching $2.5 billion in 1926; $3.5 billion in early 1928; $6 billion in January 1929; and, in October 1929, more than $8.5 billion. There are no records showing how many ordinary, middle-class Americans held stock in 1929 or how much of it they owned. The call money figures stand amid the rubble as one of the few statistical reminders of how the great crash must have devastated the public.

After 1924 the market turned irreversibly bullish. Speculation grew, as more and more people bought stock with brokers' loans. As a result the interest rate on call money began to climb, reaching twelve percent by the end of 1928. Such an extravagant rate of return made the brokers' loans themselves an attractive vehicle for investment, particularly for the so-called investment trusts (big, public investment pools equivalent to the modern mutual funds), which had to keep large amounts of their holdings in "safe," liquid form.

The resulting situation might have been laughable had it not been so explosive. A broker would lend money to a client, enabling him to buy stock or, perhaps, shares in a large investment trust. The investment trust would put part of the new capital into stocks and the rest into brokers' call money returning twelve percent interest. The call money would go back to brokers, they would lend it out to more customers, and the cycle would repeat itself. Demand for various kinds of investments kept growing, along with the speculative fever. As a result the call money rate increased, as did the value of the investment trusts lending out the investors' money through the brokers. As stock market historian Robert Sobel observes in his account, *The Great Bull Market:* "It resembled nothing more than a dog chasing his own tail."

There were many who viewed the call money situation warily. Congressional skeptics introduced a flurry of bills to restrict brokerage loans. In addition, the Federal Reserve Board tried to dampen the flames by wrenching interest rates higher, but this only seemed to make more call money available. Investors seemed as eager as ever to borrow, regardless of interest rates.

The Wall Street Journal, public spokesman for the red-hot securities industry, pooh-poohed all Congressional meddling. Said the *Journal* in March 1928:

> People who know nothing about credit, surplus bank funds, collateral, call loans or anything else germane to the question profess to be terrified when the Stock Exchange loans attain

the figure of $4 billion or more. They talk of a "pyramid" of speculation, forgetting that the pyramid is the most stable form of all building with the broadest possible base. . . . Nothing can be so easily liquidated in this country as the speculative position in stocks.

This was a point the *Journal* would make again and again. In July of the following year, for instance, it would ridicule the Senate Finance Committee for investigating stock market credit systems, insisting: "If the country were being robbed of the credit it needed and could use, the fact would first be reflected in the level of common stock prices."

At the start of 1928, the Dow Jones Industrial Average stood at about 200, twice as high as it had been in 1924. The market roller-coastered for the first six months of the year, finishing just where it had started—with the Dow around 200. But in the last half of 1928, the market exploded. The Dow Jones average shot up fifty percent and ended the year at an even 300. In a characteristically taciturn State of the Union address, President Coolidge told Congress: "I regard the present with satisfaction and anticipate the future with optimism." The *Journal's* elation was less restrained. Its January 1, 1929, editorial said: "Unless [the stock market] has lost its proverbial power of prophecy, it bespeaks much future as well as present prosperity."

By July 1 the Dow Jones average had reached 333, and the *Journal* noted: "Conditions financially and commercially were never sounder than now." On July 8 the paper rejoiced: "Some traders are so bullish they have stopped naming tops for certain stocks and are saying they never will stop going up." And a week later, with the Dow at 346, the paper gushed: "The market is too big, the country is too big and industry too well stabilized to be influenced by isolated bearish developments."

This was the summer of which Bernard Baruch would later say: "When beggars and shoeshine boys, barbers and beauticians can tell you how to get rich, it is time to remind yourself that there is no more dangerous illusion than the belief that one can get something for nothing."

The Dow Jones average hit the lofty 380 mark in late August, and *The Wall Street Journal* cheered on. "The outlook for the fall months seems brighter than at any time in recent years,"it said. The market grew still more frenzied in early September, when the New York Stock Exchange created an additional 275 seats, selling them at the breathtaking price of $625,000 each.

Then, in late September, the first inevitable cracks appeared. Faith in the bloated market began to wane. Stock prices fell abruptly for a few days. The *Journal* soothingly diagnosed the problem as "a major advance temporarily halted for technical readjustment." In October the market faltered again. On the tenth some stocks dropped by twenty or thirty points, and the cracks in the market facade were spreading. Some stocks rallied, though, and within a few days the *Journal*—reflecting Wall Street's inexhaustible bullishness—was sounding the horn once again:

> A week ago you heard all over the Street pessimistic forecasts as to the future of the market. You read in a number of newspapers comments to the effect that we were in a major bear market.
>
> Stocks are now 10, 20 and 30 points above where they were a week or so ago and optimism again prevails.

The market continued declining ominously on Monday, October 14, and slid all week, before suffering a sharp setback in the half-day trading session on Saturday. On Monday, October 21, six million shares traded in a wave of pessimism. Still the *Journal*'s comment remained upbeat:

> There is a vast amount of money awaiting investment. Thousands of traders and investors have been waiting for an opportunity to buy stocks on just such a break as has occurred over the last several weeks, and this buying, in time, will change the trend of the market.

The market did rally on Tuesday, but it fell sharply again on Wednesday the twenty-third, when paper losses mounted to $4 billion. One stock, Adams Express, tumbled a full ninety-six points.

On October 24, Black Thursday, stocks plummeted, as an unprecedented 1,676,000 shares changed hands in the first half hour of trading. By 11 a.m. the market was reeling with $9 million in paper losses. Stock Exchange officials closed the visitors' gallery because some of those watching had become hysterical with screaming. That afternoon representatives of the biggest banks— J. P. Morgan & Company, Chase National, Guaranty Trust, and First National among them—hurriedly raised a pool of $20 million to $30 million with which to bolster the market. They appointed Stock Exchange vice-president Richard Whitney as their agent. Whitney, the epitome of a Harvard-educated Wall Street aristocrat, strode assuredly onto the trading floor and asked for the price of U.S. Steel, then bought a huge block of it. He paced from one trading post to another, buying large blocks of other stocks in a commanding voice until it was at last apparent to everyone that the Wall Street establishment was sounding its trumpet.

The market steadied, but only temporarily. By Monday prices were sinking further. Brokers hastily called in loans from clients whom they had been "carrying." The *Journal* finally acknowledged: "It was a panic, a purely stock-market panic, of a new brand." And yet it was not so serious, the paper went on to say, because whereas past panics had been caused by tight money, or business or crop failures, this one had no apparent cause other than "the market itself. . . . The storm has left no wreckage except marginal traders forced to sell at a loss." The "marginal traders," it neglected to say, meant practically everyone whose name was not Morgan, Rockefeller, or Mellon.

The next day was Black Tuesday, October 29, the day the bottom fell out. In the first half hour of trading, 3,260,000 shares traded. By day's end the Dow Jones Industrial Average had retreated to 260, 120 points lower than on September 3. It was a day without equal, the worst in market history, with people selling stock so frantically that the Stock Exchange ticker fell two and a half hours behind in reporting the prices. Coincidentally, it was also the biggest stock market story that *The Wall Street Journal* would ever have to report. The paper gave the story a prominent place on the front page, but the headline was among the greatest understatements in journalistic annals. It read: "Stocks Steady After Decline."

The market rallied that Wednesday after Richard Whitney reappeared on the floor to announce that due to a "paperwork backlog," the market would close after a brief session Thursday and remain shut until Monday. A resounding cheer went up. The situation seemed under control now. "We have had panicky stock markets in the past, many of them," the *Journal* consoled, "and stocks have always come back ultimately, the good ones always reaching new highs." The next day it offered this good-humored assessment:

> Many small marginal traders who were worrying a few weeks ago over the heavy taxes they would have to pay as a result of profits on the long side are now worrying because they won't have any taxes to pay.

Readers would have been much better off with *Variety*, the show business newspaper. Its headline: "Wall Street Lays an Egg."

The newspaper to which young Barney Kilgore came that summer was caught up in the frenzy. Reporters were up to their necks in broker loans, some boasting of making paper profits of $8,000 to $10,000 in a single day. One Harvard graduate told a senior editor that his account at Hayden Stone was now worth more than half a million dollars. "What should I do?" he asked half rhetorically. "I'd get out," was the sage reply. The reporter ignored the advice, of course, and within a few months wound up more than $200,000 in debt.

But Kilgore was unlike most young men at the *Journal*. He was a small-town Midwesterner of middle-class Scottish stock, about as far from the sophisticated Ivy League set as one could get. The thought of playing the market hardly occurred to him. He took a job with *The Wall Street Journal* because he was enamored of newspapers and New York seemed to hold out infinitely more possibility than Indiana. That was all.

Kilgore was twenty, a handsome fellow with wavy brown hair

and an air of maturity well beyond his years. He had just graduated from DePauw University, a Methodist college in Greencastle, Indiana. He grew up in nearby South Bend, the son of Tecumseh Kilgore, a plain-spun school superintendent and sometime insurance salesman. Though soft-spoken and modest, Kilgore had quickly been marked as a genius at college. A scholarship student, he hardly seemed to study, yet he made Phi Beta Kappa with ease. He was editor of both the school newspaper and the yearbook, as well as a regular in the debating society and the dramatics club. One weekend, envying his roommate's typing ability, Kilgore taped a keyboard chart on the wall in front of him and sat down to teach himself, pounding away on a borrowed typewriter until he had perfected a rapid, three-finger style that he would use for the rest of his life. He decided to teach himself to play the piano, too, because boogie-woogie tunes were in demand at fraternity parties. In his quiet way Kilgore was as affable as he was brilliant. As the newspaper editor Kilgore was the only student permitted to keep a car—an old Model-T Ford—but he shared it liberally, charging five cents a ride to those who had the money and rescinding the fee for anyone who didn't. He was already afflicted with a disconcerting nervous twitch that tugged his head down toward one shoulder every so often, but that aside, Kilgore never seemed frenzied or even in a hurry.

Kilgore had gone to DePauw with the idea of becoming an engineer and possibly adventuring in South America. But then his roommate, Charles Robbins, fell in love with campus newspaper work and talked Kilgore into trying out for *The DePauw,* published three times a week. Kilgore set his heart on journalism and switched his major from engineering to political science.

Robbins graduated a year ahead of Kilgore and wrote job-seeking letters to newspapers all over. He finally landed a $25-a-week job as a police reporter for *The Indianapolis Star,* but in March 1929 he got a letter from Kenneth Hogate of *The Wall Street Journal,* a DePauw alumnus, offering him a copydesk spot at twice the pay. That June Kilgore wrote a similar batch of letters, then went off to work in a Des Moines bakery owned by the father of a girl whom he was courting. Within weeks he, too, had a letter from Hogate, and he dropped the girl for the *Journal* copydesk.

Kilgore would not stay in New York very long. In the buoyant optimism of the times, Hogate had decided to go ahead with the new Pacific Coast edition of *The Wall Street Journal* as envisioned by Barron. Though *The Boston News Bureau* was still publishing, this was to be the first edition of *The Wall Street Journal* printed outside Manhattan. Kilgore was young, unattached, and, in his words, "easy to ship"—in short, a natural choice to help man the new copydesk in San Francisco.

The first issue of the new edition appeared on October 21, eight days before the stock market debacle. On November 1, two days after the crash, the ever-optimistic *Journal* proclaimed in New York: "The sun is shining again, and we will go on record as saying good stocks are cheap." Kilgore, however, still a month shy of twenty-one, had written to his father, Tecumseh, with uncanny wisdom: "Put up a storm door to keep the wolf out, and hang on to your shekels."

Back in New York the stock market crash and its aftermath had devastating effects on *The Wall Street Journal* that Kilgore could hardly have foreseen. William Peter Hamilton, the abrasive editorialist and Wall Street's stalwart defender, died on December 9 at age sixty-three. There was not much forewarning. In early December the stress of the past few weeks suddenly began to show on Hamilton's face. He took ill, and after a few days' convalescence at his home on Pierrepont Street in Brooklyn, Hamilton contracted pneumonia and died.

It was a wrenching loss for the newspaper. Hamilton's strident editorial voice was the essence of the *Journal* in most readers' minds. Casey Hogate memorialized him: "Almost a gentleman of another day was William Peter Hamilton," and he promised that Hamilton's "virile" style "will not be lost from the editorial columns of *The Wall Street Journal* because it has become too much of the warp and woof of the paper itself." Nonetheless, much of the *Journal's* gumption died with Hamilton. Hogate immediately took the "Review and Outlook" column off the front page and buried it deep inside, where most newspapers had the good sense to put their editorials.

As for the living, many large fortunes had suddenly vanished, and with them the illusion of endless prosperity. Like some tribe of primitive Indians, the men at the *Journal* and elsewhere on the Street continued to believe that the Great Spirit would soon return to the stock market, but the Dow Jones indexes kept on sinking. Three years later the Industrial Average would stand around 60, less than one-fifth of what it had been in early October 1929. Faint hope remained, but for the most part, men walked about with an air of dazed detachment and ennui.

Reporter Oliver Gingold—originator of the term "blue-chip stock"—had amassed a fortune before the crash, but unlike most he had seen boom times come and go, having been around the *Journal* since 1900. Every six months or so, Gingold would sell off half of his winnings and put the proceeds into government bonds. He was on a European cruise in October 1929, and there was nothing he could do except follow the news. His stocks were decimated along with everyone else's. Gingold's government securities, however, would help keep him in Park Avenue splendor until he died in 1966 at age eighty-two.

The *Journal* reporter who seemed to take the crash hardest was the dapper Connecticut horse breeder. For weeks afterward, or so the story went, he wandered around the office moaning that he did not even have sufficient money for lunch. "For God's sake," someone finally snapped, "from now on you'll have to learn to live off your salary like the rest of us."

"Salary!" the reporter is said to have exclaimed, pounding himself on the forehead. "Oh, my God, I forgot about that!" Bounding up to the business office, he collected more than six months' back pay. He had been making perhaps $125 a week, but until the market collapse, that had seemed too petty to bother with.

Oddly, within a few months the crash began to look like an isolated incident. Stocks recovered a little, and neither the wave of bank failures nor the vast unemployment lines of the Depression were yet in sight. On March 7, 1930, President Hoover declared: "All the evidence indicates that the worst effects of the crash upon unemployment will have been passed during the next sixty days." But the misery was just beginning.

The Wall Street Journal's circulation fell swiftly in the Depression that followed. From a high of 52,000 in 1928, it would dip below 28,000 in the 1930s. The number of pages would also fall—from twenty-four or twenty-eight pages in the twenties to only twelve or sixteen in the early thirties. Often there was not much for the reporters to do because Wall Street itself was comatose. Many of the younger fellows worked at perfecting their squash games and had time to reflect upon how lucky they were still to be employed. Miraculously the *Journal* stayed open, though pay cuts were frequent.

Still the paper would rally to the defense of Wall Street as the occasion demanded. Both houses of Congress were now determined to regulate the securities industry. Lengthy hearings ensued to determine the real reasons and the real villains behind the crash. There was a major bill sponsored by Senator Carter Glass of Virginia and Congressman Henry B. Steagall of Alabama that would, among other things, force Wall Street banks to choose between traditional banking and investment banking—the lucrative business of underwriting and selling new securities. The *Journal* had a new editorial writer now, or rather it had resurrected an old one. Thomas F. Woodlock, an early partner of Dow Jones and the paper's editor from 1902 until 1905, had returned after a succession of brokerage jobs and a term on the Interstate Commerce Commission. Like Hamilton, who had once been his protégé, Woodlock was a weighty intellectual, an ardent free-enterpriser, and no shrinking violet when it came to expressing his views. On April 14, 1932, Woodlock took aim at the Glass-Steagall Bill:

> There are those who are moved to wrath by the thought that a group of intelligent speculators prey continuously upon the "public" and amass enormous gains. . . . There are those who cannot endure the sight of autonomous securities markets beyond the control of legislatures, bureaucrats, and, in fact, of courts.

Meanwhile the Senate Banking and Currency Committee was

beginning its two-year hearings on stock exchange practices that would finally result in creation of the Securities and Exchange Commission—"the policeman at the corner of Broad and Wall." The hearings, orchestrated by Ferdinand Pecora, an energetic young staff attorney, would rivet the country's attention, uncovering much of the chicanery that had been Wall Street in the twenties. "Far from being an impartial forum for the free play of supply and demand, as pictured by its authorities," Pecora later wrote, "the exchange was in reality neither more nor less than a glorified gambling casino where the odds were heavily weighted against the eager outsiders."

The hearings got under way on April 11, 1932, and the first witness was Richard Whitney, now president of the New York Stock Exchange. Whitney sat in the witness chair for two weeks answering questions about routine operations of the stock market with condescending simplicity, and stonewalling any question that hinted at Wall Street's shady dealings. In exasperation Peter Norbeck of South Dakota, chairman of the hearings, began berating Whitney for his intransigence. "There isn't a person in this room who does not know what 'rigging' is, and I shall not attempt to explain it to the man who knows more about the market than anyone else in the country," the Senator yelled.

Woodlock labeled Norbeck's ranting "solemn piffle," in an April 23 editorial, declaring: "Whatever the Senate committee investigating the New York Stock Exchange may or may not reveal before its foreshadowed demise, Chairman Norbeck's angry outbreaks while the president of the Exchange was on the stand Thursday were nothing more or less than a confession of the committee's failure to date to prove against the Exchange its presumption of guilt."

The *Journal*'s arrogance faded the next Tuesday when Congressman Fiorello La Guardia, the future New York City mayor, made a surprise appearance before the Senate committee to report the results of a separate probe that his House Judiciary Committee staff had conducted. Entering the room with the diminutive La Guardia were two bulky assistants carrying a large steamer trunk stuffed with scrapbooks of newspaper articles, canceled checks, and other documents. Whenever a stock was to be rigged, La Guardia testified, the market insiders had retained a "high-pressure publicity man" whose job was to plant phony newspaper articles touting the stock in question. Reporters published prewritten stories under their own by-lines in exchange for cash or options to buy the stock they were touting at an artificially low price.

La Guardia produced batches of canceled checks given to his committee by one such publicity man, A. Newton Plummer, who had turned government witness after being caught in an illegal swindle by police. The Congressman described "campaigns" to hype the stock of Savage Arms Corporation in 1924 and produced a check for $140.50 signed by Plummer and endorsed by William J. Gomber.

"W. J. Gomber?" Senator Norbeck gasped. "Isn't he employed by *The Wall Street Journal,* which is panning this committee for this investigation?"

La Guardia nodded. Gomber was in fact the man who wrote a well-read daily column called "Broad Street Gossip" on page two of the *Journal.* He had also been involved in the second Savage Arms deal, as evidenced by a check for $209 that he had taken from Plummer.

"And here is a check for $268," La Guardia continued. This one bore the endorsement of Richard Edmondson, who wrote the *Journal*'s "Abreast of the Market" column. Both Gomber and Edmondson had also taken checks from Plummer when he was working for a pool that rigged Pure Oil Corporation stock in January 1925. The *Journal* and its sister publication, *The Boston News Bureau,* had also printed Plummer's phony stories about Indian Motorcycle Company when its stock was rigged in 1923. This was only the tip of the iceberg, La Guardia explained, and in order to make his point, the Congressman recited the names of only a handful of the reporters whose endorsements appeared on the checks.

Within moments details of La Guardia's testimony in Washington clattered across the news ticker in New York. Edmondson hung over the newsroom machine with a taut expression on his face. When the machine printed out his name, Dick Edmondson put on his hat, walked out the door, and was not seen again for years. Bill Gomber neither left nor was fired. He simply sank from a highly visible job to more and more anonymous positions. Later, in the depths of the Depression, Edmondson was allowed to return to an anonymous spot on the *Journal* copydesk. Often he and Gomber sat there side by side, heads bowed and working soundlessly, former star columnists who bore the full weight of the paper's humiliation.

There was plenty of shame to go around. The new Securities and Exchange Commission was set up in 1933, and Wall Street came under scrutiny of a sort that it had long resisted. The most vivid proof that the old order had fallen came in March 1938, when rumors abounded that Richard Whitney, who had so gallantly represented Wall Street in its darkest hour, was in some sort of legal difficulty.

One morning the telephone rang on Eddie Costenbader's desk. The ticker czar picked it up and began writing notes with a fury. With sweat trickling down his face, Costenbader stood and gestured wildly to a young assistant managing editor, William F. Kerby. Cupping a hand over the mouthpiece, Costenbader told Kerby that he had a man on the phone who claimed to be Richard Whitney. He ordered Kerby to call Whitney's office on another line to verify that it was the great man himself talking to Dow Jones.

As he relates the incident in his memoirs, Kerby dialed Whitney's brokerage house, identified himself, and asked to speak to Mr. Whitney. Whitney's secretary confirmed that, indeed, her boss was speaking with Dow Jones's Mr. Costenbader at that very moment, and Kerby went back to Costenbader to whisper that he was positive it was Whitney on the phone.

"Thanks, Mr. Whitney," said Costenbader, hanging up. "Break! Break! Richard Whitney confesses to fraud," he hooted at the Teletype operator. Whitney, the very symbol of Wall Street integrity, was on his way to the federal prosecutor's office to confess that he had embezzled customers' securities, a crime for which he would spend three years and four months in Sing Sing. He had phoned Dow Jones with the story first, as if to do one last favor for a friend from the old days, when a few strong men ruled the world of Wall Street.

CHAPTER 3

"Dear George"

KENNETH CRAVEN HOGATE had a Midwesterner's instinctive distrust of nearly all things Eastern. He confided as much to W. S. Gilmore, his editor at *The Detroit News,* before boarding the train for New York in 1922. Hogate was twenty-five then and full of ambition, far more so than his baby face and portly physique hinted. No doubt New York was the right place for him to seek wealth and power, especially with Clarence W. Barron's obvious fondness for him. But Hogate told his old boss that he doubted that he had sufficient interest in financial affairs to be Barron's protégé. More important, Hogate confessed to a strong feeling that he was meant to live his life in the Midwest, the world of his father, Julian DePew Hogate, editor and publisher of *The Hendricks County Republican,* near Indianapolis. Detroit at least seemed a part of the same spiritual landscape as central Indiana. The burgeoning automobile industry had not yet erased peoples' farm-bred virtues—honesty, diligence, and lack of pretense.

Hogate, like most upward-striving Middlewesterners, was Republican. His conservatism, however, was born of solid Hoosier independence, not of the rank and privilege that made most Wall

Streeters hostile to the slightest whiff of political change. Hogate felt he would never be as comfortable on Wall Street as Barron. He did not quite trust these fellows from wealthy old families and fancy schools—even though he would have to hire a good many of them as favors to the important men he wanted to please.

In the early thirties Hogate would surprise Wall Street associates by endorsing the creation of a Securities and Exchange Commission, an idea that the old guard was resisting with all its might. Had Barron still been living, he would certainly have gone along with them. Even more surprising, Wall Street forgave Hogate for the betrayal. The men on the Street thought enough of Hogate to name him to a committee studying internal stock exchange reform, and later he was even considered a candidate to preside over a much chastened New York Stock Exchange.

Casey Hogate made friends everywhere. The man's innate good humor and generosity were overwhelming. While shooting to the top of Dow Jones, he would become mayor of Scarsdale, then one of New York's ritziest suburbs, and at his weekend farm near Pawling, New York, he would socialize with celebrated neighbors like Thomas Dewey, Lowell Thomas, and Franklin D. Roosevelt.

Hogate hated the New Deal and opposed nearly everything F.D.R. did, but he considered the President a friend and a neighbor. When Roosevelt was first elected President in 1932, Hogate sent out a memo to his editorial staff saying that they could criticize the new President's policies to their hearts' content but never could they attack the man personally. The President obviously valued the friendship as well. He sometimes called Hogate from the White House for a telephone chat, knowing full well that the publisher would jovially take him to task.

Once in the late 1930s, F.D.R. phoned Hogate and asked him to organize a softball team to take on his own squad, called "The Nine Old Men." The game took place one summer weekend near the Roosevelt home at Hyde Park. Late in the contest Roosevelt sent braintruster Rexford Tugwell to the mound against Hogate, who could swing the bat with surprising skill despite his overweight. Hogate smashed Tugwell's first pitch way beyond the outfield, then slowly lumbered to first base and could go no far-

ther. The President immediately yanked the pitcher, then turned
in his wheelchair to needle the baserunner: "Mr. Hogate, they
tell me that you have to hit a home run to get to first base." Said
a rattled but respectful Hogate: "Mr. President, that is the way
it is with a businessman under the New Deal. He has to hit a
home run to get to first base."

Hogate advanced at Dow Jones more rapidly than anyone
could have expected. Within a year after his move to New York,
Barron made Hogate managing editor of the *Journal.* Three years
later, in 1926, he became vice-president of Dow Jones & Company, and in 1928, general manager and chief operating officer.
Hogate ran Dow Jones while C. W. Barron trotted around the
globe, interviewing captains of industry, inspecting architectural
digs in Egypt, consulting with ministers and monarchs, including
Kaiser Wilhelm.

Then in October 1928 Barron died. His tangled estate passed
into the hands of his daughter Jane, and the job of sorting
through it all fell to her husband, Hugh Bancroft, who now became president of Dow Jones. At forty-nine, Bancroft seemed
an ideal man for the job, a handsome Boston patrician who had
graduated from Harvard at seventeen and Harvard Law School
at twenty-one. He had been district attorney for Middlesex
County, president of the Cohasset National Bank, and chairman
of the Boston Port Authority, and, off and on since 1905, he
had worked for his eccentric father-in-law's financial news empire.

Bancroft and Barron had a rocky relationship over the years.
Barron doted upon his daughter Jane but treated her erudite
husband with contempt. Bancroft must have felt deeply ambig-
uous about working for his father-in-law's companies; he wandered off to other jobs a number of times, but always he came
back. Finally, after twenty-three years, Bancroft was president
of the news empire, forever free of C. W. Barron's prickly temper. Then a year later the stock market crashed, leaving Dow
Jones & Company and the other Barron properties nearly as
scarred as Wall Street itself. The United States fell into deep
depression, as did Hugh Bancroft himself. Acquaintances said
he looked increasingly distraught, not up to facing the problems
confronting his companies.

As the Barron publications and wire services rapidly lost business, Hugh Bancroft backed away from them, retreating more and more to his summer home in Cohasset, where he spent much of his time forging tools in the blacksmith shop he had set up for his hobby. He left Dow Jones & Company, *The Boston News Bureau,* and the family's other properties in the hands of Casey Hogate. In 1932 Bancroft officially retired, though his name continued to appear atop the *Journal* masthead. On October 8, 1933, Bancroft, fifty-three, died in his blacksmith shop. The next day's *Wall Street Journal* attributed the death to a heart attack, noting that Bancroft's health "had been poor for several years." Acquaintances believed Hugh Bancroft had committed suicide.

The fate of *The Wall Street Journal* and all the other Barron properties was now in the hands of Jane Waldron Bancroft, who owned or controlled some ninety percent of the stock. Among *Journal* reporters speculation was that Bancroft's widow would fold not only the fledgling *Pacific Coast Edition,* but quite possibly the money-losing *Wall Street Journal* itself. Only Eddie Costenbader's news ticker seemed safe, for the indispensable wire service still turned a profit.

Jane Bancroft surprised everyone. An earthy woman whose three children were nearly grown, she met with Casey Hogate after her husband's funeral and asked him to save what he could of C. W. Barron's dwindling empire. "I want you to do what's best for the company," she told Hogate. "Don't you and the boys worry about dividends."

Hogate, still just thirty-six, had been wrestling with the problems of the *Journal* and the other properties for some time—ever since the crash, in fact, when he had taken the stridently pro-Wall Street editorials off page one and tried to make the *Journal* look more respectable. Still, the *Journal* was beset with the same cancer as Wall Street. Circulation had dwindled from a 1928 high of 56,000 to less than 30,000. Not many people wanted to read about stocks and bonds in the depths of the Depression. Hogate was too cautious a man to make radical moves, but obviously the newspaper would have to change in order to survive.

The managing editor of *The Wall Street Journal* was Cyril E. Kissane, a small, moon-faced man with a bowler hat and a stubby mustache, who, like Governor Dewey, resembled the groom atop a wedding cake. Cy Kissane was Hogate's man, but unfortunately Hogate was no infallible judge of talent: Kissane seemed to be a man of serious limitations. He had grown up in Brooklyn, graduating from St. John's College there, and then had worked his way up through the New York News Bureau, the financial pages of *The Brooklyn Eagle, The New York Herald,* and, finally, *The Wall Street Journal,* where he had covered the leather industry for several years before being named city editor. Hogate, a confirmed workaholic, admired Kissane's dogged habits and plucked him out to be managing editor, the top spot on the paper.

Kissane's lack of worldliness was more than a joke among staff members; it was a cross to bear. Indeed, in the Washington bureau Kissane reportedly was simply and succinctly referred to as "Stupid," as in "What does 'Stupid' want today?" Kissane was so oblivious to geography west of the Hudson River that he once sent a wire to his man in Detroit asking him to "please stop by" the office of a man in St. Paul that afternoon. Once, he cabled Charles Robbins in Cincinnati, saying that he was coming through town and wanted to sample some Southern fried chicken. Robbins recalled driving his boss across the Ohio River into Kentucky farm country, where they passed a field of grazing cattle. "Those are fine cows," the managing editor observed.

"No," corrected Robbins, an Oklahoman, "those are steers."

"What's a steer?" inquired Kissane, ever the intrepid leather reporter.

Cy Kissane was known for holding good stories out of the newspaper until their news went stale. Among his notions of what constituted a really hot item, however, was almost anything that first appeared in Walter Winchell's gossip column. This could be a problem, since Winchell's column was notorious for plugging stocks on the wispiest of rumors. Early in the Roosevelt era, when F.D.R.'s popularity was all but overwhelming, Winchell's column offered a ridiculous rumor that the President was about to resign. Kissane duly cabled the Washington bureau demanding the story at once. The cable went to William Henry Grimes, the rough-and-tumble bureau chief, who turned purple with rage when he read it, according to Bill Kerby. Grimes is said to have aimed a kick at his typewriter stand that smashed the machine against the opposite wall.

With Bancroft dead and the *Journal* sinking, Casey Hogate finally concluded that Kissane would have to go. The *Journal* needed a real newsman, not someone reared in the insular, self-dealing world of Wall Street. In Hogate's mind, this automatically left out virtually every experienced news hand in New York. Almost by default Hogate went down to Washington and offered the jobs to Grimes, Washington bureau manager since 1923 and the sort of newsman that *Journal* men in New York had not seen before.

Grimes was a gruff, irascible country boy from Bellevue, Ohio, who wore his ill-fitting clothes wrinkled and askew. He had briefly attended Western Reserve University in Cleveland, but his real diploma came from the fiercely competitive Washington bureau of United Press. The *Journal* hired Grimes in 1923 to take over its own paltry Washington bureau, which then consisted of one man, John Boyle, a longtime retainer whose main chore was telegraphing a few figures from the daily Treasury Department statement. Boyle's office, Grimes discovered, was under his hat.

Even before the New Deal made Washington a critically important news town, Grimes turned *The Wall Street Journal* bureau into a true presence, hiring four additional men to help him get news from the Federal Reserve Board and the Interstate Commerce Commission that could not be found in other newspapers. As a former wire service man, Grimes gave the *Journal* a touch of professional cynicism that it badly needed. At times Grimes' behavior was a little too testy for the *Journal*. Once, Grimes interviewed the Secretary of the Treasury from a pay phone at the National Press Club and got so angry at the Secretary's dissembling that he yanked the telephone out of the wall.

Except with a typewriter Grimes was all but incomprehensible. He spoke in a hoarse whisper, rarely completing a sentence. Subordinates had to fill in the elipses that punctuated his thoughts. Once, in New York, he stormed into the newsroom and yelled at a young desk hand: "What are you doing about the gold situation?"

"Well," stammered the subeditor, unaware that there was much going on in gold, "we don't have anything in the works."

"Well, you damn well ought to have something," snapped Grimes, marching off. The terrified deskman turned to a colleague, Vermont Royster, and asked: "What the hell is he talking about? What 'gold situation?' " Eventually Royster remembers, someone worked up the nerve to call Grimes and ask what he had in mind. "Hell, if I knew what was going on I'd tell you," Grimes snorted. Then he hung up.

Grimes had qualities that the *Journal* sorely needed: toughness and principle. The toughness was especially obvious. One reporter went to Grimes' office to ask for a raise. Opening the door softly, he saw the fiery-eyed managing editor actually jumping up and down on his hat. The reporter retreated without a word, never summoning the courage to ask Grimes about the incident.

The new managing editor decisively killed off the *Journal's* afternoon edition—the original—after sales had dwindled to a few thousand. Instead he created two additional morning editions and moved the final deadline for news copy from a gentlemanly 6 p.m. to a more professional 11:30 p.m. He shifted the responsibility for deciding how news stories would be played on inside pages from the composing room foreman to a newsroom editor, which was where it belonged, and he ordered the deskmen to really edit copy rather than just hunting for misspellings and small factual errors.

It was in matters of principle, however, that Grimes made the most significant changes. The *Journal* had never been scrupulous about differentiating between news and business employees— the most fundamental division in publishing. At any high-quality newspaper, the news and advertising departments remain blissfully ignorant of one another's activities as a way of ensuring the integrity of the news copy. Since the days of Dow and Jones, however, the Dow Jones messenger boys and reporters had hustled advertising and subscriptions while they made their rounds. In the old days it had been difficult at times to distinguish between front-page news and front-page advertising. On Saturdays a whole page-one news column was given over to the market musings of Goodbody & Company, the brokerage where Charles Dow had been a partner. During the 1920s particularly, the distinction between news and advertising was all but meaningless. The information printed in the news columns might have been placed by some broker or pool operator just as though it were paid advertising, except that no one bothered to inform the reader.

Now Grimes separated news from advertising once and for all. He decreed that henceforth not even the *Journal*'s own admen could set foot inside the newsroom. He was equally tough on public relations men, close cousins to the advertising profession. Grimes' contempt for PR men was absolute. When one of his friends left a newspaper job to become public relations officer of a government agency, recalls Kerby, Grimes could only conclude: "There must be some flaw in his character which I didn't detect."

Once the head of an advertising and public relations firm reportedly confronted the managing editor in his office and tried to make him publish a news story based on a bank's press release. The PR man slyly reminded Grimes that his agency also handled a second bank's advertising account, which contributed substantial revenues to the financially strapped *Journal*. Grimes was indignant and threatened to call the other bank and inform its president that the PR man was trying to use his account as leverage to get a story printed about a competitor. The PR man left abruptly.

As a final step Grimes forbade his reporters to trade in any stock they wrote about. Now, when a reporter handed in a story, he had to sign a mimeographed form attesting that he owned none of the stocks mentioned. The staff was understandably furious. Most Wall Street journalists had come there to play the market, not just write about it. In good times at least, their contacts in the brokerage community had been worth far more to them than their salaries. But Grimes began firing the violators, and the other hardened malcontents quit. Before long *The Wall Street Journal* newsroom became chaste as a convent, with Bill Grimes acting as mother superior. He had given the newspaper some qualms, if not much quality.

The Wall Street Journal, still losing money, remained very much incidental to the operation of the Dow Jones News Service, which was what paid the bills. Indeed, the news service remained strong enough that Dow Jones still hired messenger boys to deliver bulletins up and down Wall Street each half hour for finicky customers who did not want one of the noisy ticker machines in their offices.

Much of Casey Hogate's time went into drumming up new ticker business to keep Dow Jones & Company afloat. He rightly surmised that, for financial news at least, there was a growing vacuum outside New York, even in the face of the Depression. Hogate tapped energetic young reporters whenever he could find them to man new bureaus around the country. He did not want more Eastern Ivy Leaguers, though. He did not really trust them. Instead Hogate tried to bring some honest Midwestern faces into Dow Jones & Company. The Dow Jones president would hire almost any young man from his alma mater, DePauw, who had decent credentials and sufficient gumption to ask for a job. Hogate "prefers youngsters from western colleges," noted *Time* magazine after a 1934 interview, "because he thinks they have a sharper news sense."

Charles Robbins, Barney Kilgore's roommate, was one of the first Hogate hired from DePauw. Robbins was quickly dispatched to the Midwest, where he found that Hogate had been right about the country's appetite for financial news.

In Robbins' first post, Cincinnati, Procter & Gamble was by far the biggest business in town. The Ivory Soap maker was run by the imperious Colonel William Cooper Procter, son of the company founder. Procter apparently hated the press with all his soul, a trait not uncommon among business executives then and now, and until the *Journal* came to town, he had managed to duck reporters. Just as Robbins arrived, a reporter for *The Cincinnati Enquirer* wrote a well-researched story saying that Procter & Gamble was about to raise its stock dividend. Just to spite the newspaper, Colonel Procter ordered his board of directors to vote down the higher dividend.

At first Robbins also had trouble cracking Procter & Gamble defenses, he remembers. The treasurer of the company, Herbert French, ordered him out of his office, saying that P&G was just a Cincinnati soap maker, that it had no interest in New York financial matters. Then New York came to Cincinnati in the person of "Sell 'Em" Ben Smith, one of the legendary market bears of the 1920s. "Sell 'Em" Ben acquired his nickname one dreary

October day in 1929 when he gleefully called out to assistants on Wall Street: "Sell 'em. Sell 'em all." Like Jesse Livermore and the other bear raiders, Smith took aim at a company whose stock he thought was inflated. By selling shares short he put himself in a position to make a fortune if the stock went down. Then he personally orchestrated a run on the stock to make sure that it plunged.

This time Ben Smith had his eye on high-flying Procter & Gamble. His plan, Robbins learned from a brokerage source, was to dump a few thousand shares of P&G stock on an already jittery stock market in hopes of starting an avalanche. In those days most people still held their stock on thin margin, having borrowed from their brokers to buy in the first place. A sharp break in the price would force them to sell stock in order to cover the brokers' margin calls. And as such people sold, the stock price kept falling, adding to the number of margin calls and thus forcing more and more people to sell. The only way to avert panic in the stock was to convince the public to ignore Smith's initial dumping of P&G shares.

Charles Robbins said he called Herbert French again and offered a deal. In exchange for a proper interview with Colonel Procter, he said, he would try to foil Ben Smith's stock raid. Procter accepted the deal within minutes, and Robbins hurried over to his office at Fifth and Walnut to ask the executive about such matters as sales, earnings, inventories, and the prospects for an extra dividend. Procter was obviously uncomfortable with his first press interview. He answered Robbins' questions cryptically, though he did concede that his soap business was still bubbly. The interview went out on the news ticker and appeared on the front page of the *Journal* the next day, Robbins recalled, along with details of Ben Smith's intended raid. Smith had to abandon the attack, of course, and a few weeks later, at P&G's annual meeting, Colonel Procter eyed the young *Journal* reporter and muttered, "Robbins, thanks." The financial press had its first foothold in Cincinnati.

Robbins represented the *Journal* in several Midwestern cities during the late twenties and the thirties. He was clearly on his way up at Dow Jones, until he ran afoul of William Henry Grimes' new set of rules. Like other men of the pre-Grimes era, Robbins took it upon himself to represent Dow Jones in the broadest sense. One night in 1939 Robbins recalled, he took Casey Hogate out for a long, bibulous dinner in Chicago. Hogate told the reporter that he wanted the *Journal* to grow from a stock and bond newspaper into a more general business paper. Robbins said he agreed with his boss, adding that he felt the business department should try to woo corporate advertising, in addition to the usual tombstone ads from investment banks and brokerages. In fact, Robbins remembered boasting, he was sure he could snare some big corporate ads himself without much trouble. Soon afterward Robbins was in St. Louis, where he called upon Edgar Queeny, head of Monsanto Chemical. Robbins said he suggested that Monsanto take out an advertisement in the *Journal,* and Queeny had his ad department draw up a contract on the spot.

When Grimes got word that one of his newsmen had sold advertising space, he went through the ceiling. "You've got to get rid of Robbins," he reportedly told Hogate. "I won't have him." As Robbins tells it, Hogate called him to New York and told him apologetically that, while he would not permit Grimes to fire him, Robbins would have to choose between a job as a reporter and a job on the Dow Jones business side. Thoroughly miffed, Robbins quit to join the advertising department of *The New York Times.*

Back in the early thirties, while Robbins' career at Dow Jones was still galloping ahead, his DePauw chum, Barney Kilgore, was making his mark in San Francisco, where he had been since the autumn of 1929. *The Wall Street Journal Pacific Coast Edition* was not so grand as it sounded. It was a much different, much thinner product than the Eastern newspaper. For the most part it contained news of California companies, along with a few reprints from the New York paper. Circulation never grew beyond about 3,000. In fact, as the Depression wore on, a large percentage of the so-called subscribers stopped paying for the newspaper. Paid up or not, subscriptions were never canceled for fear that Hogate would see the precipitous drop and kill off the *Pacific Coast Edition* once and for all. "That western rat hole," Hogate reportedly called it, insisting that he would not increase the *Pacific Coast*

Edition's subsidy from the news ticker's profits. The *Pacific Coast* staff often had to forgo salary and simply divvy up whatever meager amount of cash was in the till.

Probably no amount of editorial tinkering could have propped up the *Pacific Coast Edition*. The basic problem was the same as in the East: The country's economy was prostrate. So grim was the situation that Kilgore wrote a joke headline, which, he declared, could run with any story in the paper. It read: "Giant Firm on the Rocks."

Though circumstances could hardly have been less propitious, Kilgore's personal career flourished. He rose from a lowly spot on the copydesk to the job of news editor in two years. As always in his life, Kilgore seemed to have time on his hands, no matter how much work he took on. In addition to performing editing chores, he began to write an occasional column for the little *Pacific Coast Edition* that was altogether different from anything the *Journal* had ever printed.

Both in California and in New York, *The Wall Street Journal* was written for financial experts, men in narrow specialties who spoke a jargon so opaque that often not even the reporters understood what they were saying. Bill Kerby, working the copydesk in the mid-thirties, recalls nearly choking on some of the stories he had to edit. One said that the world price of cotton had risen the day before due to the effects of something called the "Bombay straddle." He asked a more experienced deskman for an explanation, but the man pleaded ignorance, so they went to the senior commodities reporter, who had written the story. He couldn't explain the Bombay straddle to them either. Kerby put in a call to an international cotton investor, who said that cotton speculators in Bombay had devised a system for buying cotton in New York and London, selling it in Bombay and Tokyo, and conducting their transactions in a complex mélange of foreign currencies. The point was to hedge against the unpredictable fluctuations in various currency and commodities markets. Furnished with this reasoned explanation, Kerby went back to the reporter and demanded to know why he had written his story in such incomprehensible jargon. Said the reporter: "It's written only for the trade." So was the rest of the newspaper.

Kilgore's new column appeared without a by-line and was called "Dear George—." It took the form of an epistle to an uncomprehending friend, perhaps a son in his freshman year at college. The column was an attempt to explain arcane financial subjects in clear, straightforward English. Barney Kilgore had a talent for explaining the inexplicable. He would write:

> Dear George
> You will recall that I told you foreign exchange rates—i.e., the value of one currency in terms of others—were determined within certain limits by supply and demand for foreign funds. These certain limits, in the case of currencies based on gold, are the points at which it becomes cheaper to ship the gold itself than to buy credit abroad.

The editors had always assumed that their highly sophisticated readers already had a grasp of matters like foreign exchange. But the readers' response suggested otherwise. Letters poured in asking the "Dear George" column to address myriad subjects of puzzlement, and when the letters were all counted, they numbered over three hundred, better than ten percent of the *Pacific Coast Edition*'s total readership. Such popularity was too valuable to waste. "Dear George" was soon appearing on the editorial page of the New York edition as well.

The column still ran without Kilgore's by-line. In fact, almost no one got a regular by-line in the *Journal* except the esteemed editorialist Thomas F. Woodlock and the Washington bureau manager, Grimes, whose name appeared on most Washington stories whether he wrote them or not. The purpose of by-lines in that era was to build the reputations of one or two recognizable names, thus making them familiar figures. Younger newsmen labored in anonymity, believing that their chance for fame lay ahead.

In late 1932 Kilgore was called back to New York to write his "Dear George" column three times a week. Still not fully occupied, he began writing articles for the front page on broad topics like banking and accounting or the implications of the country's money supply. He was becoming the *Journal*'s first economics correspondent, and his by-line soon appeared alongside those of the more senior Grimes and Woodlock.

By now Hogate had his eye on Kilgore. The publisher had an idea for a front page column called "What's News" that would give the major stories of the day in crisp, one-paragraph summary form. Hogate urged the column upon Grimes when he became managing editor in early 1934, suggesting that Kilgore be recruited to write it.

Kilgore took an enormous leap into celebrity that March. At one of President Roosevelt's frequent deskside press conferences, a question arose as to the technical difference between two alternative methods of paying the controversial "soldiers' bonus" to World War 1 veterans. "Read Kilgore in *The Wall Street Journal*," Roosevelt responded, saying that the columnist had had "a good piece" on the issue. At another press conference not long afterward, F.D.R. was asked about a complex Supreme Court decision on the National Industrial Recovery Act. The President's advice to the assembled newsmen: "Read Kilgore."

Back in New York the *Journal* gushed with delight. The next day's headline crowed: "President Tells Reporters to Read Kilgore Article." After that it was only a matter of time until Kilgore went to Washington to cover the deeds of his best-known fan. Early the next year, Kilgore became Washington bureau chief. At twenty-six he was running the *Journal's* most important operation outside New York. With the staff of twelve that Grimes had built, *The Wall Street Journal* Washington bureau was the second largest in town, bigger than that of any out-of-town paper except *The New York Times*. The *Journal's* circulation hovered around 30,000, and the reporters had to accept occasional pay cuts and "Scotch weeks"—mandatory vacation without pay—but it was a prestigious assignment.

Barney Kilgore was Casey Hogate's kind of man—a bright Hoosier from DePauw without an ounce of Eastern affectation. Yet Kilgore was a mass of contradictions, even as a young man. He never seemed brash or self-aggrandizing, true, but he pushed himself forward nonetheless. He was reserved, always clearing his throat and straining against that damned nervous tick in his neck. He fought it endlessly, bracing his pectoral muscles in a battle that could leave him looking pale and exhausted by the end of the day. In every other sense he seemed the calmest of men, with a deep reserve of energy.

Put into a room full of important people, Kilgore often as not slinked into the background. In later life, after he had transformed the newspaper into a communications miracle, he would usually introduce himself as being "with *The Wall Street Journal*." Kilgore never interrupted, even when he thought the speaker was talking nonsense. And when he himself was interrupted in mid-sentence, he stopped and listened. Nonetheless, he always seemed to have the last, quietly convincing word.

Kilgore's men looked on him with reverence. He was too much of a man's man to be described as saintly, but if there were flaws in his character, no one around him seemed to notice them. What Kilgore had, besides intelligence and humor, was the knack of leadership. He commanded respect by almost never pulling rank, by making people beneath him feel useful and appreciated. Vermont Royster, who came to work in Washington in 1936 as a glorified copyboy, saw in Kilgore a combination of self-possession and self-effacement bound together with extraordinary maturity. "I thought of him as an old man," Royster recalls. "He was all of twenty-eight." Royster did see a glint of boyhood in Barney Kilgore. In a corner of his Connecticut Avenue bachelor apartment, the bureau chief kept an elaborate miniature railroad, immaculate in detail. Kilgore told Royster he had spent weeks handcrafting a tiny taillight for the Pullman car. And when Kilgore showed the train off for friends, his eyes seemed to widen a bit with pride and delight.

Washington provided Kilgore's first brush with pack journalism, the curious phenomenon that occurs when numerous reporters converge on the same big story—in this case the New Deal. Like businessmen who give lip-service to the virtues of competition without actually wanting any for themselves, reporters in a group may talk like adversaries, but they end up writing much the same thing. There is safety in a crowd.

Kilgore rarely succumbed to this mentality, perhaps because he had risen at the *Journal* by writing about business and economics problems in a manner that was so novel that he simply had no competition. In any case, he seldom got entangled in the sorts of minor stories that faddishly divert the attention of the press corps for months on end. He was good at looking beyond the mere politics of the Social Security Act, for example, and dispassionately reporting on the larger questions. He would write:

> The time to find out whether the life preserver is made of cork or cast iron is before the time comes to use it, not when an emergency develops. And the mere fact that everyone on the boat is in favor of life preservers is an irrelevant consideration.

Or, on the practical effects of F.D.R.'s massive public works programs:

> As the result of certain parts of the New Deal program, a lot of people are developing something that resembles what the psychologists would call conditioned reflexes. They hear one thing and think immediately about something else.

> For instance, take flood control proposals. If you shout "flood control" at the nearest public utility stockholder he jumps about three feet. That's because he thinks "cheap electricity" and "government yardsticks" instead of "flood control." His reflexes, so to speak, have been trained to connect these ideas automatically.

Kilgore was remarkably resourceful. Riding along on Presidential campaign trains in 1936, he began passing out cards to people in each community and asking them to jot down their reactions to the candidates' speeches they had heard. However unscientific the method, it was possibly the first time any reporter had used public polling in covering an election campaign.

To the surprise of old friends, Kilgore immediately set out to become a social success in Washington, apparently convinced that social acceptance was vital to attaining real professional status there. He frequented parties at the Press Club, where he pounded out his boogie-woogie tunes on the piano as he had in college. Soon he acquired a cook and began inviting important people to dinner parties. At these parties he would usually choose a hostess from one of several appealing women friends, most of them secretaries whom he had met on his rounds. Kilgore never seemed at a loss for pretty girls.

In the bureau there was much speculation as to which of these damsels Kilgore would marry. He surprised them all in October 1938 by marrying the beautiful and refined daughter of a Greencastle, Indiana, dentist, Mary Louise Throop. He had met his wife at a DePauw alumni reunion. After the marriage Kilgore's dinner parties became still more frequent. They included guests like Robert Taft, the conservative senator from Ohio, and White House columnists Robert Kinter of the *New York Herald Tribune* and Joseph Alsop. They were journalists, young Congressmen, and second-tier government people, the kind who generally made the best news sources. Kilgore treated social life as though it were part of his work, and it paid off. He was the first *Wall Street Journal* man ever admitted to the Gridiron Club, the Washington newspaper fraternity's most exclusive institution. He would fret for years that no other *Journal* men had been admitted.

As a bureau administrator Kilgore was usually relaxed. When he trusted people, he delegated great responsibility, which explains why he himself always seemed to have extra time on his hands. Typically Kilgore would not appear in the *Journal*'s National Press Building office until mid-afternoon. Then he would sit down to write his own stories, read staff files, and offer suggestions. After deadline Kilgore might accompany his men upstairs to the National Press Club bar, where a shot of Virginia Gentleman sold for a quarter. More often, a bottle of whiskey and a deck of cards would appear on Kilgore's desk, and the bureau hands would ante up for a game of rummy called "Coon Can." The card game was more than a diversion, it was a propaganda session. Barney Kilgore had ideas about the newspaper business, and he was looking for converts.

In the beginning the talk was desultory. Kilgore would muse about the possibility of a national newspaper—a daily that went coast to coast, as weekly magazines did. He was dreaming, of course. In 1935 the logistical problems of such a venture were unthinkable. But if such a thing were possible, what would it look like? Perhaps sports would be the glue that held it together. The weekly *Sporting News,* published in St. Louis, might be the perfect prototype for a national daily. But on second thought sports were essentially regional, Kilgore concluded. People in New York wanted to read about the Yankees and the Dodgers. Just a couple of hundred miles away, they cared only about the Red Sox and the Braves. So a national newspaper probably would have to be about business and the economy. Those were the only things that were really the same all over. *The Wall Street Journal* might be as good a vehicle as any for a coast-to-coast newspaper, although the name was not much good. Since the words "Wall Street" were now anathema to most Americans, anyone who wanted to make the paper national would probably want to change the name to something that emphasized business over finance—something like "World's Work."

But the main thing, Kilgore would say while someone was shuffling the cards, was that a businessman in Portland, Oregon, had to be reading the same newspaper as the businessman in Portland, Maine. That was where Dow Jones had erred with the *Pacific Coast Edition.* A newspaper was either interesting and useful to people or it wasn't, and what was interesting and useful to businessmen in one place had to be interesting and useful everywhere. No one needed a lot of little regional newspapers about local business conditions when so many big regional papers already were in place. What they needed was a national daily newspaper about business that treated the entire United States as though it was one great business community, because most business problems were not confined to city and state boundaries.

Kilgore's insight was extraordinary in the mid-1930s, a time when air travel was still for the wealthy and the adventurous, when America was still a land of hometown permanence. Not for another ten or fifteen years would people start to trade in their hometowns like used automobiles—three years in Atlanta, two in Chicago, four in Houston—all for the good of IBM or some other corporation. Americans of all classes mostly grew up, worked, raised families, and died in the same community. The country was divided into infinitely small components by geography, race, religion, ethnicity, trade, and social standing. The idea of a national business community seemed a bit farfetched. Why should anyone on the Atlantic seaboard feel much in common with someone on the West Coast? And yet Henry Luce's *Time* magazine had been flourishing for a decade, reporting general news with style and wit. And Luce's newer publication, *Fortune*, was treating business news in a sophisticated, literate manner that Kilgore envied. Why not a national newspaper?

Not all of Kilgore's musings took the form of office card games. He wrote memos to Casey Hogate almost every day, bombarding the publisher with ideas, observations, and criticisms. One of Kilgore's pet peeves was that the *Journal* seemed to have become a clipsheet for other publications like *Fortune* and *The Kiplinger Washington Letter*. Time and time again, he complained, these publications appeared to snatch interesting news items from the inside pages of the *Journal*, then rewrote them in more spritely English or else expanded them into full-length magazine articles. Kilgore suggested that the *Journal* make better use of its short news items, too, by combining the best of them into a newsletter on the front page. The result was the weekly "Washington Wire" column, an instant hit with the readers. At first Grimes wanted the column to run on the editorial page, not page one. But Hogate liked the "Washington Wire," and so it appeared out front every Friday morning.

It was a valuable lesson for Kilgore. Thenceforth, he did most of his lobbying with Hogate, the publisher, rather than Grimes, the managing editor. Grimes was a cautious man who considered the newspaper's health too precarious to tinker with. Hogate at least was willing to listen. Kilgore's main message: Despite its puny size, the *Journal* had to start acting like a big-time newspaper; otherwise it never would outgrow its trade paper reputation.

Grimes seemed to be aware of the problem. He had pushed the *Journal*'s two European correspondents, Charles Hargrove in Paris and George Ormsby in London, to include some political analysis in their dispatches, previously limited to strict financial reportage. As a result Ormsby went to Berlin in 1936 and wrote about the strange goings-on under the young Nazi regime there. But Ormsby's stories went awry. They were heavy on Adolf Hitler's economic plans and inattentive to his awesome military buildup and the cultural upheaval that was under way.

As Hitler's shadow lengthened, the need for more broad-minded European coverage became obvious. Still Grimes clung to the plodding, financial approach. On March 12, 1938, Hargrove reached Berlin and learned that the German army had marched into Austria the day before. Hitler had immediately silenced the press; the outside world did not know about the quiet invasion. Hargrove, an Englishman, had a friend at the British Embassy smuggle out his short dispatch in a diplomatic pouch. The cable reached *Journal* headquarters in New York, where Bill Kerby, Grimes' assistant, says he added background material and dummied the story into the lead position on page one—an impressive scoop for the little paper. But Grimes looked over the story and rejected it. "Not the *Journal*'s type of story," he reportedly murmured, ordering it condensed into a single paragraph for inclusion in the "What's News" column. By happenstance, though, Casey Hogate was wandering through the newsroom, and strolling up to the news desk, he picked up Hargrove's story and read to the end. "Just the sort of thing we need more of," he declared.

The story ran on page one. Kilgore phoned Kerby from Washington the next morning to congratulate him. The *Journal*'s big story was the talk everywhere. "How did you wangle that one past Brother Grimes?" he asked.

Kilgore himself was constantly testing Grimes' limits, trying to see how much really interesting fare he could pack into the paper without running afoul of the managing editor. Though the country's intelligentsia was increasingly preoccupied with the prospect of war, the *Journal* had paid scant attention to the War and Navy Departments, except to report on the dollars and cents of big defense contracts with private industry. In 1939 Kilgore assigned Vermont Royster, now a reporter, to write a series of stories describing how long it would take to make a World War I battleship ready for duty again.

One of Royster's stories dealt with the laborious process of manufacturing battleship armorplate. When the story appeared, says Royster, the Navy was surprisingly upset. It charged that Royster, a Naval Reserve officer, must have availed himself of classified information while performing weekend duty. In truth Royster says, he had taken the "sensitive" details from the *Encyclopaedia Britannica*—a telling indication of how little military technology had advanced since World War One. But the more important point, so far as the *Journal* was concerned, was that Kilgore's bureau was now putting effort into stories that were only marginally about business. The real subject was military preparedness, a matter of vital interest to everyone, businessman or not.

Such attempts were a drop in the bucket. The newspaper's financial straits grew worse every year. By the end of 1940, circulation was a dismal 32,000. Most days the *Journal* was only twelve or fourteen pages long. Dow Jones & Company's total profits for the year came to $69,000 on revenues of $2 million, and that was only because of the news ticker.

The explanation was not that Wall Street was hurting. In fact, things were looking up there, with the flight of European capital and preparations for war. The real problem with the *Journal* was its irrelevance. The nation's attention was riveted on Europe. What people wanted to know was whether the United States would be drawn into war and, if so, could it beat Hitler? Meanwhile, the *Journal* was pelting readers with cotton prices and corporate earnings. A typical *Journal* defense story would begin: "The Navy Department yesterday sought to buy 3,550,000 pounds of copper but received bids for but 2,100,000 pounds."

As with the 1929 crash, the *Journal* had no idea how to handle a really important story. A discouraged Casey Hogate wondered how much longer he could keep the *Journal* alive. Something had to be done.

CHAPTER 4

Drunk with Possibilities

IN THE FALL of 1940, Casey Hogate took Bill Grimes aside and, in the kindest words possible, told the bluff managing editor that he would soon be replaced by Bernard Kilgore, sixteen years his junior. Grimes was not entirely surprised, for he had watched Kilgore steadily gaining Hogate's confidence over the last few years.

Grimes seemed to have fought an endless succession of rear-guard battles against Kilgore. Most of them centered on the same question: What sort of newspaper should they publish? Kilgore kept pushing for a greater variety of subjects, apparently forgetting that the *Journal* was a newspaper for and about Wall Street, not a substitute for *The New York Times* or the *Herald Tribune*. Grimes was an old soldier of the Depression, wary of innovation, especially when the *Journal's* position was so precarious. Moreover, he was a veteran of United Press, the real infantry of the news business. A man who comes up through the wire services tends to believe that people buy newspapers for news, not for pretty writing or circumspection. Wire service men are addicted to deadlines, committed to giving readers the latest information humanly possible. Kilgore showed a decided preference for what wire service men derisively call "thumb-suckers," stories that are heavy on background and interpretation but light on hard, breaking news.

Hogate thanked Grimes for his seven years as managing editor. There was no question that he had made the paper more solid and respectable, no question that the readers put more trust in it now than in 1933. The trouble was that the readers kept falling away; the paper was slipping deeper and deeper into the red. The *Journal* was on the verge of collapse. There was nothing much to lose by giving Kilgore a chance, and there was everything to lose by leaving things as they were. Kilgore had some novel ideas for boosting circulation, and if they didn't work . . . well, the newspaper was apt to fold anyway.

The *Journal* staff was formally notified of Kilgore's promotion on February 14, 1941, but by then it was already an open secret. Hogate's memo said that within a few days William Henry Grimes would take over the editorial page as "editor" and Kilgore would succeed him as "managing editor," the real boss of the *Journal*. There would be other personnel changes as well. "While this seems a sizable change," Hogate's note concluded, "all the personalities are well and favorably known to the entire staff, and everyone affected . . . is in hearty approval."

This last falsehood was forgivable, for Grimes had stepped aside graciously, burying whatever bitterness he felt and trying to be content in his new role as editorial writer. In truth Grimes would never quite approve of Barney Kilgore's ideas and would never stop grumbling about them. But with time Grimes' complaints would take on a fatherly tone, and complain as he would, no one ever doubted his loyalty to Kilgore and *The Wall Street Journal*.

Most of the other older men at the *Journal* disliked Barney Kilgore—at least in the beginning. One taste of the brassy, less businesslike newspaper that Kilgore was trying to push on them, and they knew that their staid old readers were going to choke, too.

Kilgore held a meeting of *Journal* editors and reporters to outline the major changes he had in mind. Kilgore could be an impressive speaker, spontaneous and funny, but that was when he felt he was among peers, people who shared his ideals and his vision. That was not the case now, and he cleared his throat tentatively, strained to control his nervous tick, and spoke in a soft voice just a little above a whisper. He began by saying that he had gone to some outside newspaper people for advice. They had pointed out that the hugely popular *Reader's Digest* was perfectly written for someone with an eighth-grade education. *Time* magazine, he continued, was written for people with a bit more sophistication, with a high school education, perhaps, or a year of college. *Harper's* was aimed at people with a couple of years of college or a bachelor's degree. But, said Kilgore, "They haven't found anyone with enough education to read *The Wall Street Journal.*" Even a fellow with three doctoral degrees in law, accounting, and finance could not read the paper, written as it was for a handful of specialists at Lehman Brothers and J. P. Morgan & Company. Indeed, there was some doubt as to whether even those people could understand what the *Journal* said.

From now on, Kilgore said, *The Wall Street Journal* would make a fetish of simplicity. "You mean that we're supposed to write *down* to our readers?" an incredulous reporter reportedly asked. "No," said Kilgore, "just write simply enough so that people can understand." A *Journal* story had to satisfy its sophisticated readership, but it also had to be clear enough not to discourage neophytes. "Don't write banking stories for bankers," he ordered. "Write for the banks' customers. There are a hell of a lot more depositors than bankers."

Kilgore's second dictate: The *Journal's* subject matter had to be broadened. "Brokers are nice people," he said. "There just aren't enough of them to keep a first-class newspaper afloat." Henceforth, the *Journal* would cease to be a newspaper about stocks and bonds. It was now a newspaper about everything involved with earning a living and spending money, the things that preoccupied most people.

Next, the *Journal* was going to be a *national* newspaper, a daily paper for people all over the country. There was no such thing as a business story that was important to San Franciscans but not New Yorkers. Businessmen's deepest concerns had nothing to do with geographic boundaries. Therefore, if a story lacked universal interest, it did not belong in either the Pacific Coast or the New York edition. From now on those two editions would be as similar as technology allowed.

Finally, he said, a story on the front page of *The Wall Street Journal* had to be distinctive, unlike anything that people were accustomed to seeing on page one of the *Herald Tribune* or the *Times*. The *Journal* should be every businessman's second newspaper. It could never displace the hometown newspaper in primacy, so it would have to be written with the understanding that readers already knew about the important news developments of the previous twenty-four hours.

To be honest, Kilgore was not sure what kind of story he wanted for his front page. He did not want routine articles about humdrum business developments—a story, for example, about a meeting between steel executives and government officials that said, "Government and industry agreed yesterday that the steel supply problem is being solved." He wanted articles on broad topics written simply and absorbingly. "Just write what you think is damn good reading," he instructed.

No one had the slightest idea what Kilgore was talking about. Since the late nineteenth century, when the American newspaper began to come into its own, news writing had emerged as a distinct form—in the same sense that the novel and the sonnet were distinct writing forms, though news was, of course, a good deal more restrictive. But just as with the sonnet, the rules of news writing strongly colored the content.

The form that all newspapers adopted was called the "inverted pyramid," still very much the dominant form in which news is written for radio, television, and newspapers today. As every cub reporter learns, the rules of the inverted pyramid are simple: Put all of the latest, most salient facts at the beginning, then flush out the article with background and quotations from bystanders in descending order of importance. That way an impatient reader gets the latest news in the briefest, most economical fashion. The first paragraph of the standard news story contains the "Five Ws"—Who, What, Why, Where, and When. Example: "The St. Louis Cardinals yesterday combined home-run hitting and strong pitching to whip the New York Yankees, six to two, in the first game of the World Series at Sportsman's Park." A reader who stops there still gets the essentials of the outcome; if he continues reading, he gets only lesser facts: who the pitchers were; what the winning manager said after the game; what the weather was like.

Besides brevity the inverted pyramid offers at least the appearance of objectivity, an important asset in the early part of the century, when most newspapers were trying to escape the image of yellow-sheet journalism. The compactness of the inverted pyramid helped filter out the reporter's personal opinion and forced him to redirect his energies toward getting facts right, for the public was learning to distrust sensationalism. Indeed, these advantages were so evident that by the turn of the century nearly all major newspapers had adopted the inverted pyramid style.

But the inverted pyramid also had serious limitations, the greatest being that it stifled thoughtful discussion of current issues and inhibited the reporter from expressing an informed point of view—no matter how well versed he was in the subject matter. The standard news article simply holds a magnifying glass to isolated incidents without attempting to analyze, evaluate, or place them in the context of related social trends. That is why the average newspaper still reacts to a major event—say, a Presidential assassination attempt—as if no one has heard the news, even though the entire world has already heard it from radio and, indeed, watched it actually happen on television. The morning paper pretends that the event is still news to people because its instinct is to celebrate the event, pressing it upon the reader's consciousness and inviting a visceral reaction. Only on some obscure inside page will the newspaper take the space to ask larger questions such as: Why did such a terrible thing happen? What should be done about this? By enlarging the event, without regard for subtlety or context, the inverted pyramid invites readers to make two-dimensional judgments. The event was either good or bad; the suspect is either guilty or innocent; the political candidate is a rogue or a hero. The shades of gray essential to intelligent debate are lost.

Kilgore deepened the confusion by declaring that a front-page story no longer needed to contain the words "today" or "yesterday." If news could not be defined as the very latest available information, then what was it? Said Kilgore: "It doesn't have to have happened *today* or *yesterday* to still be news to someone who hasn't heard about it." Thus did Kilgore effectively discard the inverted pyramid and all that went with it. He and his men would create a new form to define the shape and content of their articles, a new form that would have a lasting effect on journalism. This new form, as it evolved, consisted of thesis and counter-thesis, and its strength lay in allowing readers to focus on the merits of an argument rather than on the details of one particular event. The typical *Journal* story begins with a thesis about some problem sweeping America, plaguing the auto industry, or stirring up trouble in Europe. Then comes the evidence: two or three paragraphs of example, statistics, or quotations from informed people. Next comes the counter-thesis, a paragraph that says something like: "To be sure, not everyone considers this issue to be a real problem." The rest refines the original thesis and explores broad consequences.

The *Journal*'s news form evolved into something ideally suited for a contemplative audience and for enlarging the news into something verging on current history. Where news previously had been limited to things that happened yesterday or this morning, it was now apt to be something that had been going on for a long time but without being called to anyone's attention. The new form made all sorts of innovations possible. For example, it would lead the *Journal* to invent the so-called "round-up" story, summarizing the mood of money lenders or the price of housing around the country, and it would lead to the "trend" story, a story recognizing that a change in the collective behavior of ordinary people was just as surely "news" as any official government decree.

Moreover, it was a form that encouraged people to keep reading, not to stop after the first paragraph or two, as most did with the inverted pyramid. And as the world became more complex, as television and radio began to give people more and more of their news about what happened today and yesterday, more and more newspapers would begin to emulate the *Journal*'s style, realizing that it was the only way to offer their readers something additional. Indeed, the *Journal* story form was perhaps the prototype for television news documentaries, and it would alter the style of virtually all other news media as well.

All of this lay ahead, of course. The essence of what Kilgore did in the beginning was to discard the old and make way for something new. For *The Wall Street Journal,* and for the news industry in general, it was a momentous step.

The *Journal* staff's reaction to Kilgore was more sullen than mutinous. It was as if someone had suggested that they try writing their stories in Swahili, for the inverted pyramid had been instilled in them from the day they had first touched a typewriter. Jobs were still scarce enough that no one dared confront Kilgore directly, but there was much cruel mimicry of his facial tick, and snide remarks were whispered everywhere. The resistance reportedly was worst in the corner of the room where Eddie Costenbader and his right hand, Eddie O'Keefe, held sway over the news ticker, shouting their orders in thick Jersey City accents. The ticker was still responsible for keeping Dow Jones & Company afloat, so Costenbader had reason to fume that Kilgore was shifting the reporters' energies away from the most important chore, feeding his tape service. As in the old days, the *Journal* remained a way of recycling information that had first appeared on the ticker. There was obviously much wisdom in leaving the priorities of the system intact.

Kilgore made no bones about it. He was waging a war with the ticker for the hearts and minds of the staff. He was not so much blind to the needs of the news service as he was drunk with the possibilities of what the *Journal* could become. Eventually he won people over to his side, not with bullying, but with infectious enthusiasm, as well as his extraordinary talent for making people feel indispensable. His quickest converts were younger men like himself, many of them from Hogate's favorite recruiting source, DePauw University. Among the DePauw men in New York there was Buren McCormack, a talented rewrite man, Bill McGaughey, "Cactus" Mahoney, Maynard Lemon, Perry TeWalt,

Robert Bottorff, and, of course, Kilgore himself. Eventually the upper ranks of Dow Jones would become so crowded with DePauw men that others would see them as a clique. In part they were a clique, but, more important, they were a remedy for the narrow East Coast provincialism that had ensnared the *Journal* for years, and Kilgore would welcome other talented men to his team wherever he could find them.

From the start Kilgore found that most of the older men could no more write to new specifications than chickens could fly. They wrote their stories, and then Kilgore and his men rewrote them. The *Journal* was surely the most heavily rewritten newspaper in history, as it still is. Kilgore used some of his young allies almost as ambassadors, sending them to the back of the newsroom to pry useful information out of the older men as though they were interviewing some reluctant news source. The younger reporters would ferry the information back to the rewrite men, who would use it to produce a totally different kind of story from anything the older reporters might have willingly produced. One youngster, Tom Wise, recalled being dispatched to the back of the room to question a veteran *Journal* reporter named Harry Rohs. Rohs knew practically everything about the U.S. tire industry but was so inarticulate on the subject that he might have had trouble explaining it to Harvey Firestone himself. Adopting an air of beatific innocence so as not to offend, Wise asked Rohs to tell him just how they went about making a tire from start to finish. "Oh, for God's sake!" said Rohs, shaking his head in disgust.

Kilgore's closest ally turned out to be Bill Kerby, Grimes' former top assistant and one of the few men not from DePauw who would rise to a top position at Kilgore's newspaper. Among the hardest things Grimes had had to do after learning of Kilgore's promotion was telling Kerby that he would probably lose his place as assistant managing editor and revert to being a reporter. Kerby had evidently been like a son to Grimes.

Kerby, an agreeably shy man of thirty-two, took the demotion in stride. Secretly he acknowledges, he had been rooting for Kilgore and had sneaked some of Kilgore's prize story ideas onto the front page by pretending not to know that Grimes opposed them. Kerby felt he could get away with such subterfuge in part because his friendship with Grimes went back a long way. He was the son of Frederick Monroe Kerby, a correspondent with Scripps Newspapers in Washington and New York and a long-time golfing buddy of William Henry Grimes. Back in 1928 Grimes and the elder Kerby had discussed Bill's interest in newspapers, Kerby relates in his memoirs, and Grimes had offered the boy a summer job in Dow Jones' Washington bureau after his sophomore year at Michigan. Bill Kerby had worked for Grimes the next summer, too, and in September Grimes had assured him that a permanent job would be waiting after he graduated.

The offer had vanished with the stock market crash, but Kerby had landed a $35-a-week spot as a dictation typist in the Washington office of United Press, Grimes' old stomping grounds. There the crisp and efficient Kerby soon worked his way into a plum job covering Capitol Hill, where he stayed until Grimes finally brought him to Casey Hogate's attention in 1933. Hogate hired Kerby over lunch one day in the House of Representatives' members' restaurant, where members of the working press and their guests were welcomed. According to Kerby's memoirs, Hogate had ordered himself a second portion of the restaurant's special seafood pie—a heaping concoction of creamed lobster, crab, oysters, shrimp, and filet of sole, topped with baked mashed potatoes and garnished with two extraordinary ounces of beluga caviar. Then, despite the unmistakably Atlantic bent of his appetite, the Indiana-born Hogate had let Kerby know that he was making an exception by hiring an Easterner, offering the diffident young man a starting salary of $55 a week.

Kilgore picked Bill Kerby and Buren McCormack as his first and second lieutenants, telling them that for the front page he wanted a flow of stories that were useful, interesting, and amusing. It would not be enough to produce better versions of the same stories other papers had, he insisted. "Grimes tried that, and it didn't work." Kilgore's advice to Kerby: "Hook 'em with an intriguing mystery lead and keep sinking in more hooks as you go. . . . The easiest thing in the world for any reader to do is to stop reading."

With Kerby and McCormack apparently writing or rewriting

almost every page-one story, the *Journal* made an abrupt change, taking on a tone that could sound both authoritative and bemused. Of the government's new defense-oriented housing priority system, the paper would report: "A defense worker at Ketchikan, Alaska, has a better chance of getting a new house built than a banker in Westchester. That at least is the theory . . . " Or, of the wartime prohibition on the use of distilled grain for recreational drinking: "Do you like potato juice? You'll learn to love it in the days ahead." Headlines began to take on the whimsical glow that they still have today, as with a story about the highly controversial labor boss John L. Lewis:

"He hates Roosevelt; He Hates War; He Wants a Showdown— Ready to Go Through With the Coal Strike Hell or High Water." Or, with a story that illustrated the pinch of metals shortages: "Warning to Golfers: Control Your Tempers! You May Not Be Able to Replace That Choice Club."

Most reporters clung to the notion that the only point of a *Journal* story was to measure the impact of some development on stocks. Pulling more interesting matter from them was a laborious process. Kerby explains that he tried making each man summarize his story orally before putting it down on paper. He wanted something approaching good dinner-table conversation rather than traditional news copy. But once the man sat down at his typewriter, the message seemed forgotten and reporters reverted to the newspaper's arcane, old style.

Gradually there emerged a small cadre of younger men who caught on to what Kilgore wanted. They formed the nucleus of the rewrite bank, and they gave so much attention to polishing the *Journal*'s prose that the paper soon acquired a luster that larger metropolitan papers could not match. The rewrite team made sentences shorter and more precise. Kerby says he declared war on what he called "lazy words," posting a notice that thenceforth there would be "virtually no *virtuallys*" used in the paper. The editors either simplified or eliminated financial jargon. They created an index file of lay translations for certain unavoidable terms like "prime rate" or "short-selling," which never again appeared in the paper unless accompanied by a brief, simple explanation.

Kilgore was determined to rid the *Journal* of typographical errors, a task somewhat akin to expelling all the ants from Yellowstone Park. "If a reader keeps stumbling over 'typos' in our paper, he'll begin to wonder what else he can't believe in it," the managing editor insisted. And so the *Journal* became the most heavily proofread daily newspaper in the country.

Slowly Kilgore's program began to generate enthusiasm. One day Kilgore put a notice on the board saying he wanted reporters to spend more time outside the office and less with their feet on their desks. He invited each man to leave town for a week. The reporters were free to go anywhere and to interview whomever they chose. The only catch was that each man had to produce at least a story a day while he was gone. Among the first to volunteer was Joe Guilfoyle, a young New Yorker who had started at Dow Jones as a fourteen-year-old messenger boy. Guilfoyle recalls taking the train to Buffalo, Pittsburgh, and northern Ohio, interviewing executives by day and pounding out stories by night in his hotel room. Three of his stories, all company profiles, landed on page one, and Guilfoyle became an instant convert. Others, including some of the older men who could scarcely write a simple sentence, discovered that it was much more fun to land a story on Kilgore's front page than to spend their time feeding dull tidbits to the Dow Jones ticker. Kilgore was constantly urging them to take on more ambitious stories, never mind the routine chores.

It was obvious that the new managing editor was on a collision course with Eddie Costenbader, the ticker czar. More than a few men put their money on Costenbader. While Kilgore was the managing editor of Hogate's choice, Eddie Costenbader had the ear of Joseph Ackell, the Dow Jones business manager and Hogate's true right-hand man.

A clash between Kilgore and Costenbader was perhaps inevitable, for the newspaper and the news ticker had always created conflicts. In 1937, for instance, Sydney Self, the dapper chemicals industry reporter, happened onto the story of DuPont's "Product X." Whether by design or by accident, Kerby recalls in his memoirs, Self did not tell his editors about the story until late in the afternoon, well after the stock exchanges had closed. The story, as it appeared in the next morning's paper, was about the invention of a new synthetic fiber, later called "nylon." The news quickly punctured the price of raw silk futures and made the price of DuPont stock soar. Eddie Costenbader saw the story for the first time when he read the paper, and he went into a rage. Costenbader found it highly unlikely that such important news had broken after the close of the exchanges the previous day. But had the ticker put the story out, it would have done more than affect trading; it would have given the *Journal*'s exclusive story to every newspaper in the country. Dow Jones & Company would have undermined its own scoop.

This sort of friction between the news ticker and the newspaper would never really vanish. They would remain two separate entities, each vying for the reporters' time and energy. *The Wall Street Journal* offered reporters more fun and more glory, but the ticker had to be fed all the same. To this day a reporter who ignores the ticker's insatiable needs will soon get a bone-rattling lecture from above.

But in 1941 and 1942, the conflict between the newspaper and the ticker was acute. The problem was not simply that the ticker made demands on reporters' time. It was threatening to wreck Kilgore's plans for remaking the *Journal*. Dow Jones & Company was itself torn between the two. On one side Costenbader, presumably backed by the business manager, Joe Ackell, wanted to uphold the primacy of the ticker—and for sound financial reasons. On the other side, Kilgore and his small band of allies wanted to make Dow Jones, first and foremost, a newspaper company. And Casey Hogate wanted to have it both ways.

It was the world war that finally put wind into the sails of Barney Kilgore's newspaper, just as it breathed life into America's Depression-sapped economy. *The Wall Street Journal* had been in search of a purpose ever since the end of the clubby Wall Street era of the twenties. Now the nation's attention was riveted on war-preparedness, and the *Journal* suddenly had a new mission of compelling importance. No one else was so well qualified to brief the American businessman on the problems he would face at home—the manpower shortages; the raw materials allocations;

the rationing of everything consumers held dear, from gasoline to shoes and cigarettes. Suddenly the country's fate was in the hands of its government, and news of the government's war needs became indispensable. The government was issuing raw materials restrictions, inviting bids, letting contracts by the hundreds each day. Most newspapers marched overseas to cover the shooting war; the *Journal* wisely stayed home to cover the economic one. It was the newspaper with all of the important war news that happened away from the battlefield.

By what could only have been divine intuition, Kilgore made a decision in the first week of December 1941 that the staff could no longer write Monday's newspaper on Saturday and enjoy a day of leisure on Sunday. No one could remember a Sunday when more than a few printers had been on hand to make corrections, finish up the typesetting, and roll the next morning's *Journal* through the presses. Kilgore thought the practice unprofessional and ordered that a full team of editors and printers be present.

The new policy took effect on Sunday, December 7. Shortly after 3 p.m. that day, the wire service bells began clanging, alerting the country to the astounding story of Japan's sneak attack on Pearl Harbor. The United States was at war, and, for once, *The Wall Street Journal* would handle a major story in the manner of a real newspaper. Reporters and rewrite men poured into the office to put together the details of the Pearl Harbor wreckage, to get reaction from Washington, and to assess the current state of U.S. military preparedness. Kerby, who several months earlier had written a series of stories about the industrial implications of war, had just finished editing front-page copy, with half an hour to press time. Kilgore asked him to write a new story to lead the next day's paper. The result was a breakthrough; for the first time ever, the *Journal*'s front page was actually ahead of the news. It began:

War with Japan means industrial revolution in the United States.

. . . It implies intense, almost fantastic stimulation for some

industries; strict rationing for others; inevitable, complete liq-
uidation for a few.

. . . American industry now divides itself automatically into
war-useful and war-useless categories.

This was to be the daily reality of the war for tens of millions
of Americans not in uniform, and it was a side of the war that
badly needed covering. The *Journal* invented the round-up story
one day soon after the Federal Office of Price Administration
instituted price controls for food. Through its bureaus around
the country, the *Journal* had some fifty reporters and their
spouses checking supermarkets to determine if a specified basket
of groceries cost what the OPA said it should cost. That afternoon
the reporters and their wives found wide disparity in prices
throughout the country. It was an unscientific survey if ever there
was one, but it was sufficient to show that the nation's supermarkets were ignoring the OPA. It was a story with great impact.
Hours after the paper appeared, the president of A&P, the
country's largest supermarket chain, reportedly phoned the news
desk at the *Journal*. For God's sake, he pleaded, was the *Journal*
talking about A&P?

Just before Pearl Harbor, Casey Hogate was attending a dinner
at the Waldorf-Astoria when he slumped over with a stroke. Hogate, still just forty-four, would never fully recover. As Kilgore
continued to make changes, Hogate withdrew more and more.
Before his illness the publisher had often descended to the newsroom to cross-examine the young managing editor on his latest
moves. Hogate would want to know why there was a story about
the renewed popularity of cranberries on page one when an important story about Western Union's quarterly earnings lay hidden inside the newspaper. Any survey of *Journal* readers then
would have shown a greater interest in the Western Union earnings than in light feature material, so Kilgore would patiently
explain his plan for broadening the newspaper's audience all over
again, reassuring Hogate that the paper was on the right course,
and Hogate would go away satisfied.

But now Hogate was rarely in the newsroom. When he did

appear there, his purpose was vague and his humor halfhearted. Though Casey Hogate would live for another six years, it would be as an invalid. And by the end of 1942, Hogate knew that he had to designate a successor.

Hogate evidently approved of the changes that Barney Kilgore was making in the newspaper and encouraged the managing editor to carry on with them. But for all Kilgore's talents, Hogate had no intention of giving him control of the entire company. For that he wanted Joseph J. Ackell, a man just a few years older than Kilgore but with vastly more preparation for running Dow Jones & Company. Ackell knew the nuts and bolts of the business, and he could be trusted to keep them screwed down tightly.

Joe Ackell reportedly was something of a school superintendent in appearance. Stiff in bearing and stern in countenance, he favored dark clothing that accentuated his sallow complexion. He had thinning hair and silver-rimmed spectacles, and if you came on him abruptly, some said, he could seem almost sinister. Ackell spoke in a low, rigidly controlled monotone, and he often seemed to have something cynical to say. Nor did it help that many on the news side felt Ackell distrusted them.

Despite his disposition, though, Ackell was a skilled and thoroughly self-taught administrator. He had joined Dow Jones in 1925 as a secretary in the advertising department. He displayed a knack for tinkering, and soon he was put in charge of the mechanical department, which maintained presses and office equipment. Next Ackell took over the purchasing department, then the news ticker manufacturing and maintenance department. He evidently was one of those from whom neither machines nor office systems could long withhold their secrets. And he was a first-rate office manager, capable and reliable to the core.

Since Hugh Bancroft's death in 1933, Casey Hogate had considered himself a trustee for Bancroft's widow and three children. Now, nine years later, he had to confess to himself that the company really was not much better off. Hogate had steered the firm through the Depression—no small accomplishment—but he had hardly turned Dow Jones into a money machine. Perhaps Hogate would have liked to put Kilgore in charge, for he might have been the most promising young journalist in the United States. But in the end Dow Jones & Company really came down to the news ticker, not *The Wall Street Journal*. The most responsible thing Hogate could do was to leave the company in Joe Ackell's hands, for Ackell understood problems that Kilgore had never even considered. He knew things like cash flow and taxes, meeting payrolls, and keeping the ticker business humming. Ackell had run all of the important divisions of the company except the newsroom and had done so with precious few resources. Though Joe Ackell had little visibility in the company and apparently less popularity, he was the man who always delivered. And he was the man whom Hogate felt bound to leave in charge.

But Hogate had underestimated Barney Kilgore. Though just thirty-three and managing editor for less than twenty-four months, Kilgore sensed that this was the time to make a stand. Deep down, Kilgore believed that the *Journal,* and to a lesser extent perhaps, the struggling papers in Boston and Philadelphia were the heart and soul of Dow Jones. The ticker made money, but it was a mechanical thing, devoid of spirit. The printed word was what gave Dow Jones its editorial voice, its prestige, and its purpose. If *The Wall Street Journal* was to become a great newspaper—and Kilgore fervently believed that it could—then it had to be Dow Jones & Company's utmost concern. It could no longer stand in the ticker's shadow. And to that end the company needed a leader whose clear commitment was to producing a fine newspaper, not just to balancing the books.

There are no surviving witnesses to what happened next. On a frosty December night in 1942, Kilgore called on William Henry Grimes, his neighbor in Brooklyn Heights, and the two apparently had a long and difficult talk. Kilgore would never repeat their conversation that evening—not even to his wife—but he decided to stake his career on the general manager's job—the title Hogate's successor would assume. Many years later, in a note to managing editor Ed Cony, Kilgore alluded to the episode and asserted that he would have happily remained in the managing editor's post ("an honorable title," he called it) had circumstances been different. "I took this job [general manager] mostly because I was sure that if somebody else got it, it would quite likely upset what we were trying to do with the paper." The "somebody else," of course, was apparently Ackell, whose close ties to the intractable news ticker staff still grated on Kilgore.

Grimes must have listened to Kilgore with swirling emotions— resentment and envy, affection and admiration. Here was an ambitious young man who had already surpassed him. Now he was ready to gamble for control of the company. Listening to Kilgore's reasons, Grimes had to agree that there was principle at stake. The two of them could not possibly stand by idly while Casey Hogate handed the company to a non-newsman.

Grimes went to the telephone and called his other neighbor, Bill Kerby. He told his young protégé that Hogate was planning to name Joe Ackell general manager of Dow Jones, in effect, the chief executive of the company. Grimes said to Kerby that he and Kilgore planned to resign if Hogate went ahead with Ackell's promotion.

"I'll quit, too," said Kerby.

Then Grimes reportedly called Jack Richardson, a Bancroft family attorney in Boston. Evidently he wanted to avoid direct dealings with the ailing Hogate. This was, quite possibly, the hardest moment in Grimes' career, for he himself was the logical candidate for general manager after Ackell. Kilgore might well have agreed to work under Grimes, and Kerby certainly would have. But for reasons Grimes never discussed, the former managing editor decided not to push for the job himself. He told the attorney that Barney Kilgore was the man to run Dow Jones, not Joe Ackell. He went on to say that should the family go ahead with plans to appoint Ackell general manager, it would lose its three top men in the news department and undoubtedly others as well. The Bancrofts would have their money-making news ticker operation, but *The Wall Street Journal* might well be dead. Was that what Jane Bancroft wanted?

Hours later Grimes phoned Bill Kerby again and asked him to come over. Kerby said he arrived within minutes to find Grimes and Kilgore sitting opposite one another. Grimes reportedly told Kerby that Kilgore was "in" as general manager, that he, Grimes, would stay on as editor and that Kerby was to be the new managing editor. Then Grimes began to weep.

CHAPTER 5

"Grandfather's Company Is Not for Sale"

THE FORTIES WERE the *Journal's* hothouse years. The paper began the decade as a bland stock and bond sheet and ended it as fundamentally the newspaper it is today. Where its front page had been a mishmash of turgid news stories, brokerage ads, and, every now and then, a photograph, by the end of the decade, it had evolved its present-day look: six clean columns of type, each distinct in purpose from top to bottom. And for the first time, the front page was stripped clean of advertisements and photographs.

Kilgore got rid of front-page advertisements because they branded the paper as a second-rate industry trade sheet. He got rid of photographs for more subtle reasons. In large part he saw pictures as an obstacle to making the New York and Pacific Coast editions of the *Journal* identical, one of his first dictates for the new "national newspaper." Words could be telegraphed from New York to San Francisco, or vice versa, to be set in lead by Linotype operators in each location. But photographic transmission was crude in those days. To run a picture the same day in both editions, *The Wall Street Journal* would have to fly the photo across the country a day or two in advance.

Besides, as every newspaper editor knows, no genre of photograph is duller than that which routinely graces business and finance pages. No matter how absorbing the news story, the accompanying picture invariably depicts either the balding visage of some middle-aged executive or some all too ordinary-looking industrial assemblage. Kilgore decided to dispense with pictures and hope the readers would not miss them. His sole concession to graphic decoration: a small chart atop the front page each day, usually a graph of some economic indicator, like copper consumption or bond yields.

One of Kilgore's first moves had been to launch a new kind of news story for the two outer columns of the front page—column one, on the left, and column six, on the right. These stories about serious topics of broad interest were dubbed "leaders," because traditionally the most important story in any newspaper, the "lead story," is positioned in the upper right-hand corner of the front page and the second most important, the "second lead," goes in the upper left.

The summary of major news events called "What's News"— Casey Hogate's innovation—already occupied twin columns on the front page, but their contents were limited to dry financial matters. Kilgore revamped the "What's News" section, making each column distinct. One was labeled "Business and Finance"; the other, "World-Wide," carried bulletins of general news events drawn from wire services. For the first time major news about war, politics, and calamity had a proper place on the *Journal*'s front page.

When Kilgore was Washington bureau chief, he had managed to sell Casey Hogate on the idea of the regular Friday "Washington Wire," a lively column of Washington insights and inside information similar in style to the proliferating newsletter publications of the day. As managing editor, Kilgore made column five, the one next to the right-hand leader, into a different newsletter each day. On Mondays it was called "Progress of the Week," a lengthy commentary on some topical issue; on Tuesdays it was the "Commodities Letter," about the effects of wartime rationing and shortages; on Wednesdays, the "Tax Report"; on Thursdays, the "Business Bulletin"; on Fridays, the "Washington Wire"; and on Saturdays—the *Journal* still published a Saturday edition as late as 1954—the "London Cable," with news about Great Britain under siege. Like most of the changes Kilgore made in his early years, these columns became permanent fixtures in the paper, with only a few modest changes. The "London Cable" was dropped a few years after the war ended. The "Commodities Letter" was stopped once material shortages had ceased to be of concern, and a "Labor Letter" was substituted in its place. The "Progress of the Week" column was rechristened "The Outlook" and was given over to problems that were mainly economic, much in the style of Kilgore's old "Dear George" column.

The last part of the page that Kilgore brought under rein was column four, the one to the right of center. Kilgore wanted the column to contain stories that were distinctive without detracting from the two leader stories in columns one and six. These he wanted to remain paramount. All through the early forties, Kilgore, Kerby, and McCormack wondered what to do with column four. Often they filled it with short, dry news briefs reminiscent of the pre-Kilgore era. Gradually they found that by plugging the column with amusing, offbeat stories or stories that appealed to consumer interests rather than business, they could attract attention without upstaging the two more weighty leaders. Thus was born the "A-head" story, so named because of the copydesk's designation for the different headline style it demanded. Probably the first such story had to do with Wells Fargo & Company getting back into transit work after decades of nothing but banking. It began: "Buffalo Bill's old boss is back in business again." Another had to do with a sudden demand for ostrich feathers attributable to Sally Rand and her imitators. A typical A-head of April 1945 began this way:

> The Foreign Economic Administration is persuading Pacific Island natives, including retired head hunters, to grow about two million dollars' worth of vegetables a month for troops in exchange for harmonicas, jews harps, brass rings and calico after they refused to work for U.S. currency.

The fourth column of the *Journal* took on a delightful quality. It dealt with amusing topics of little or no consequence with a mock seriousness that amounted to a parody of the dry, conventional news story. The joke was all the better because of its environment, the front page of *The Wall Street Journal*, without question the grayest, most serious-looking newspaper of all.

Newsprint, like all other useful commodities, was in short supply throughout the war. All papers had to cut back their size. The *Journal*, which contained as many as eighteen or twenty pages just before Pearl Harbor, could no longer exceed sixteen pages, and even that was exceptional. More often it shrank to twelve pages or so.

The newsprint shortage brought the reader's interests into conflict with those of the advertiser, for there was not enough paper to satisfy both. While readers had never been more eager for news, advertisers were just as anxious to get their messages into print.

Business advertising budgets surged despite the shift from a consumer-based economy to one oriented toward war production. The reason was the federal "excess profits tax" on companies that did business with the military, a measure imposed to inhibit war profiteering. Pentagon contracts were helping almost everybody's business to swell, and most businessmen were looking for ways to use the extra revenues to avoid giving the money back to the government in the form of excess profits tax. By spending their extra revenues on advertising campaigns with public-spirited themes, businessmen could show smaller profits while building up goodwill with the public. And while most businesses had only limited quantities of goods to offer consumers during the war, every business looked forward to peacetime, when the ration-weary public would go on a spending spree unequaled in history.

The news-versus-advertising dilemma proved to be a turning point for many newspapers. The mighty *New York Herald Tribune* cut back on news content to make space for more advertising, and the decision was ultimately fatal. The readers defected in droves for the *Times*, which spurned vast amounts of advertising in order to print more news. Kilgore made the same decision at the *Journal*, even though his paper had never been far from financial worry. Kilgore reportedly told Bill Kerby to figure out how much space the *Journal* really needed to print its news. Kerby reviewed some thirty back issues, re-editing the lengthy stories to see if they could be compressed without loss of substance. By squeezing out the excess verbiage, Kerby said he determined that the *Journal*'s news content typically required the equivalent of nine full pages, including space for editorial page columns and stock and bond market listings. That might leave only three pages of space for advertisements, but Kilgore was adamant about printing all the essential news. "Now is the time to build," Kerby recalls him saying. "There'll be lots of time later to get advertising."

Accordingly, advertisers were asked to limit their submissions to the *Journal* and to provide optional dates on which advertisements could run. It was a difficult sacrifice for the financially strapped paper, one that could only have been made by men with delusions of grandeur. But seldom has an investment in journalistic principle paid off so handsomely. The *Journal* emerged from the war not a great deal richer, but with a reputation for integrity and quality that it could not have earned otherwise. From that point on the profits would grow geometrically.

The other great shortage plaguing the *Journal* was one of talent. Kilgore had the same problem Hogate had faced: Not many top people wanted to work for a newspaper called *The Wall Street Journal*. Moreover, the war kept taking away good young men as fast as Kilgore could recruit them. The *Journal*, led by Kilgore and two other men in their early thirties, was especially vulnerable to the draft. Quickly Kilgore went outside Dow Jones to hire some older men who seemed capable of running the paper if necessary. His top recruit was George Grimes, a former editor of *The Omaha World-Herald*. He also got Sam Lesch, city editor of *The New York Post*, a pugnacious, no-nonsense newsman.

To the *Journal*'s good fortune, Kilgore himself got a 4-F draft deferment because of childhood tuberculosis; Kerby was deferred because of a slight limp from polio. Both might well have passed their Army physicals later in the war, when standards were lowered, but by then their civilian jobs were deemed essential to the war effort. George Grimes was then sent to shape up Dow Jones' midwestern bureaus. Sam Lesch, meanwhile, would almost single-handedly impose order on Kilgore's chaotic newsroom.

Kilgore and his young assistants had diffident natures. They tended to ask the staff for cooperation, and when it was not forthcoming, they took on the extra work themselves. Lesch ranted about the room throwing tantrums instead. He was a stocky, combative man of five-foot-five, a storybook city editor who barked reporters into submission. And he was obviously Jewish, an ethnic type that had been conspicuously absent at the *Journal*.

Not surprisingly, the older men who had disliked Kilgore were said to hate Sam Lesch even more, for the irascible Lesch showed no hint of patience with their obfuscatory writing or their hurt, uncomprehending looks. That was the sort of thing that made Lesch shift into high-gear hysteria. The men hated him so much, in fact, that when the strapping Bob Laffan, the daily stock market columnist, reportedly picked Lesch up one day and deposited him headfirst in a wastebasket, the entire room stood to cheer.

But then, as Lesch worked over their copy, the spite melted into awe. He was as able as he was abrasive. The saying was that Sam Lesch's pencil moved so quickly he could edit a page while it was fluttering from the reporter's hand down to his desk. Lesch would temper Kilgore's softness with hard-edged professionalism, getting real mileage out of a largely mediocre staff and ending the New York newsroom's country club atmosphere once and for all.

It was in the reporting ranks that Kilgore had to scramble hardest for talent, for this was where the draft kept punching holes. Kilgore sent out scores of letters to every journalism school he could think of, asking if they had any capable young women who might like to come to work for the *Journal*. If the answer was yes, Kilgore would often dispense with an interview and hire the women by mail, paying whatever it took to snare them.

This tactic, born of desperation, was doubly ironic, for Kilgore had little use for journalism schools and even less for women reporters. His distrust of journalism schools was perhaps understandable: They had trained generations of reporters to write in a style that Kilgore was now trying to jettison. His discomfort with women was a bit harder to fathom.

In Clarence Barron's lifetime Dow Jones, like many business establishments, had had male secretaries—"stenographers" was one euphemism for them. An executive could not travel with a female secretary then without creating talk, and besides, secretarial work was considered a starting point for men aspiring to be managers. During the Depression and the Second World War, however, male secretaries became an anachronism. Not only were there more women to do the work, but they were often the sole support of families and needed the jobs badly. Nonetheless, Kilgore always refused to have a female secretary.

Robert Feemster, retiring as Dow Jones general sales manager in the early 1960s, sensed that Kilgore would try to use his departure as an excuse to get rid of his secretary, a shapely young woman whose desk stood within eyesight of Kilgore's office door. Just before his retirement day, Feemster took the liberty of telling Kilgore that his secretary was pregnant and ought to be kept on for a few more months, after which time she was sure to leave anyway. Initially Kilgore agreed, but then the months dragged on, and Feemster's secretary somehow hid her condition remarkably well. Kilgore grew impatient and sent his own secretary, Bill McSherry, to inquire about the expected date of delivery.

McSherry reported back: "She's not pregnant and never has been."

Kilgore turned bright purple, realizing that he had been duped by Feemster. "Well," he stammered, "at least get a shield for her desk so we won't have to look at her legs!"

Kilgore was certainly no bigot. His newspaper would endorse the Supreme Court's landmark *Brown* v. *School Board* integration decision in 1954 with less hesitation than either *The New York Times* or *The Washington Post*. But Kilgore had a closed mind where women were concerned. He saw no room for them in the news business, perhaps because he liked the all-male atmosphere of it, the license he felt there to wear his tie at half-mast and to swear a little, something he never did at home.

It was another of Kilgore's personal idiosyncrasies that would mark the company for years to come. At most major newspapers the Second World War did much to lower the sex barrier, at least at the reporter level. Washington, D.C., was full of these war-vintage "news hens." But the *Journal* had an unwritten rule against hiring women. For almost thirty years more, it argued that business executives would not take a female reporter seriously. Not until the early 1970s, when the feminist movement became too forceful to ignore, were women allowed a real chance at the *Journal*.

None of this prevented Kilgore from hiring several women in wartime, when he was really desperate. Some of this so-called "beauty chorus" would prove talented, some indispensable. But all soon realized that they had little future at Dow Jones. By 1949 every last one of them reportedly had gone.

Women aside, the staff of *The Wall Street Journal* was transformed during the war years, as Kilgore's wonderful enthusiasm and preposterous goals gradually infused everyone. In New York, Kilgore had his close band of young men, most of whom idolized him. And he had Sam Lesch using the whip when the carrot did not suffice. Kilgore was winning converts in the distant bureaus as well, though it took a little longer outside New York. He had marvelous skill at communicating, not just in person but with little notes that he would bat out on his typewriter or over the Teletype. He could keep people laughing and working at the same time. Behind it all was a very quiet brand of arrogance: Though *The Wall Street Journal* was nothing at all in the national consciousness, by God, it was going to be important. The *Journal* had a destiny to fulfill, even if no one outside the paper knew about it. Kilgore was convinced of this, and, as people were discovering, Kilgore was a man to be believed.

In the summer of 1942, the *Journal*'s Washington bureau was literally a sweatshop, six or seven men stripped to their undershirts pounding out stories in the withering Washington heat. They sat in three tiny, airless rooms of the National Press Building, where they worked like demons. *The Wall Street Journal* was, by any measurement, a feeble little newspaper, and yet this was a fairly large bureau for an out-of-town paper. More than that, the bureau had arrogance, for the *Journal* Washington office was the place where Kilgore had won his earliest converts for the national newspaper concept, and it was still a place where the conviction was strong. Despite the puniness of their paper, these men wrote about Washington from Mount Olympus, as though the superiority of their publication somehow placed them above the fray in which more ordinary members of the press corps scrambled.

Henry Gemmill, a young Yale graduate, came to work in the bureau then and went on endless rounds of interviews with the "dollar-a-year men," wealthy businessmen and patricians who volunteered their services to the government. Gemmill found, to his dismay, that many of them had confused *The Wall Street Journal* with *The New York Journal of Commerce*, the newspaper that specialized in shipping, insurance, and commodities. In fact, the two newspapers probably were read by much the same crowd of New York financial men, but they were growing more different all the time. "The *Journal of Commerce* seemed to know its place," remarked Gemmill. "At *The Wall Street Journal*, we had our heads in the clouds."

The *Journal*'s grand pretensions were what first attracted Gemmill, a promising writer whom bureau chief Eugene Duffield had pirated from the Washington *Evening Star*. The *Evening Star* had much more prestige than *The Washington Post* in those days; it was the best-read newspaper in Washington and probably the wealthiest paper in the country, but it was also stuffy and pedestrian, hidebound by its own success and influence. The *Journal* was just the opposite. It had few rules, no territorial jealousy among reporters, no rigid pecking order, and hardly any office decorum, and it was giddy with Barney Kilgore's ideas. Moreover, the *Journal*'s Washington bureau was remarkably good. Besides Duffield it had Ken Kramer, who would later edit *Business Week;* George Bryant, Jr.; Vermont C. Royster, soon to depart for Naval duty; and Alfred "Mike" Flynn, a bureau veteran who seemed to have more news sources than anyone in town. One of Flynn's biggest scoops was a story that sounded so absurd that the New York editors had trouble swallowing it. Flynn reportedly learned that during a 1943 Cabinet meeting, Secretary of the Treasury Henry Morgenthau had proposed stripping post-war Germany of all industry and manufacturing and returning it to a purely agricultural economy, as in medieval days. The Morgenthau Plan sank quickly once it was made public, for wiser heads soon pointed out that whatever the Germans' sins, they would still have to live in the modern world after they were defeated. Another of Flynn's great coups: He was evidently the first to learn that several major American oil companies were planning to set up an Arab-American consortium, Aramco, to exploit Middle Eastern oil reserves after the war.

Henry Gemmill could not match these men in experience or contacts, but he had something that Kilgore had been looking for—a well-honed sense of irony and the ability to put it down on paper with grace and wit. Among his first efforts for the paper was a story about two men he found in the Office of War Administration who were charged with censoring newspaper comic strips. One of them was trying to kill the "Krazy Kat" strip because he felt it contributed nothing to the war effort; the other was taking a more positive tack, trying to dream up themes for cartoonists that he deemed "useful." After a few such tongue-in-cheek stories, Kilgore sent a note to Duffield, the bureau chief, saying: "Hadn't we better give Henry a raise before the wolves get him?" Gemmill got an extra $15 a week as a result, but it was Kilgore's note, he says, that had captured his heart.

Kilgore could not only spot great writing talent—and Henry Gemmill would turn out to be one of the greatest—he could also hold on to it. Considering the paper's paltry reputation, its low pay, and the long hours it demanded, this was no small achievement. The newspaper was so short of funds that when the Chicago bureau received its new paperbound editions of the annual Moody and Standard & Poor stock market guides, the outdated volumes would be shipped off to the Ottawa bureau, which could then discard its two-year-old editions. Even the best reporters rarely got raises without first having an outside job offer as leverage. Jack Cooper, for instance, a reporter in Chicago, solicited employment offers from friends at *Newsweek,* U. S. Steel, and the Santa Fe Railroad on various occasions, all for the sake of getting a few dollars extra per week out of Dow Jones. Each time, he would report his new job offer to his boss, Chicago bureau chief John McWethy, telling McWethy that he would gladly stay on for just a small increase in pay. Cooper recalled that McWethy would scratch his chin and say: "Well, you're making progress here all right, but you're already making $60 a week. That's getting into an awfully high bracket."

Kilgore made no bones when he hired people. He told them that they would never get rich at the *Journal* but that they could expect to have fun. Somehow they went for it, even though the prestige of the place was still no more than a figment of Kilgore's imagination. Not only did they come to work for Kilgore, but many of them soon became thoroughly dedicated, both to the man and to the institution. Among Kilgore's men *The Wall Street Journal* was a religion well before it was much of a newspaper.

Kilgore's innovations started getting results almost immediately, even though the *Journal* remained too small to attract much notice. At the start of 1941, when Kilgore became managing editor, the combined circulation of the New York and Pacific Coast Editions was 31,895, of which the New York edition represented about 28,000. By the end of the year, circulation had climbed 8.5 percent, to 34,611. The growth over the next few years was more dramatic: In 1942 it rose 11.4 percent; in 1943, 29.2 percent; in 1944, 11.8 percent; and in 1945, 27.4 percent. By then total circulation stood at 70,982, hardly enough to qualify the *Journal* as a best-selling newspaper, but still more than double the number of copies it had been selling when Kilgore took over.

During 1945 Casey Hogate finally admitted to himself that he would never return to Dow Jones in any active capacity. Though Hogate was still president of Dow Jones, he had rarely been in the office since his stroke four years earlier, and his health was getting worse. But Hogate's nominal grip of the company had been useful. He had held on to the presidency long enough for Kilgore to succeed beyond anyone's expectations. The *Journal's* circulation now was some 20,000 more than its peak in the 1920s, and its future seemed brightly promising. Accordingly, with the consent of Clarence Barron's descendants, Hogate now named Kilgore president of Dow Jones, taking for himself the largely honorary title of chairman.

Kilgore reacted to his new status unceremoniously. "We did not want to announce that Casey had given up hope of coming back to work," he wrote years later in a letter quoted in the company's authorized history. "I cannot personally remember anything about this particular promotion except feeling awfully sorry for Casey." Hogate would spend most of his remaining days in Palm Springs struggling to recover. He died there on February 11, 1947, six months before his fiftieth birthday.

Hogate's death was followed two years later by that of the newspaper's principal owner, Jane Waldron Bancroft, on December 21, 1949. Together they had brought the *Journal* and Dow Jones through the Depression to the brink of renaissance. Nearly all great newspapers have been owned by people of sufficient wealth to assure their independence, but such beneficence usually exacts a toll. Most newspaper families also insist on taking charge personally, as though the mere inheritance of the newspaper property also implies great gifts of publishing acumen. Though some publishing scions do indeed distinguish themselves, even the best newspaper family must sooner or later produce mediocrity, and then the fate of the newspaper becomes a hostage to family pride.

The Wall Street Journal, however, was singularly blessed with matriarchal ownership. The family had no great interest in running the newspaper—only in assuring its survival. The legacy began when Jane Bancroft inherited the *Journal* from her father. She not only urged Casey Hogate to keep the newspaper going at all costs, but also forwent dividends during the worst years of the Depression in order that the company might keep a bit more working capital.

In the three years before her death, Mrs. Bancroft retained a Boston lawyer named Laurence Lombard to tidy up her affairs, along with those of her companies. As Lombard advised, virtually everything was consolidated into a streamlined corporation, with a board of directors replacing the old board of trustees. Clarence Barron's old money-losing *Boston News Bureau* was folded, with the more robust *Wall Street Journal* taking over its subscription lists. Mrs. Bancroft's interest in Dow Jones—about eighty percent of the stock—was willed to her family, chiefly to her two daughters, Jessie Bancroft Cox and Jane Bancroft Cook. Like their mother before them, they would have ample representation on the company's board of directors but would otherwise keep their distance from its daily affairs. Before her death Bill Kerby remembers Mrs. Bancroft once telling him: "You know, I have a very important job. I have a say in naming the president of Dow Jones, and then I leave him alone. And that's a big part of my job, too."

Her daughters and heiresses would pursue much the same line of action. They would tie up their controlling stock in an assortment of legal trusts designed to protect Dow Jones from merger-hungry outsiders as well as from future family divisiveness. When Joseph Kennedy tried to buy Dow Jones shortly after Jane Bancroft's death, Jessie Cox, her elder daughter, is said to have curtly replied: "Grandfather's company is not for sale to anybody—at any time, at any price."

With the end of the European war in sight, Kilgore began laying plans as early as 1945 to expand the *Journal* aggressively once newsprint became freely available. He commissioned an outside marketing company to make a survey of *Journal* readers to determine how many would stick with the paper after the war and, if possible, to determine the size of the paper's potential readership. The survey disclosed that the *Journal* already had a higher readership than Kilgore thought, for the average copy was being read by more than one person. Furthermore, the survey predicted that the paper might eventually achieve a circulation of perhaps half a million copies, an estimate that so flabbergasted Kilgore that he told Kerby, now executive editor, "We've hired crazy men."

Kilgore was wrong for once. He had created a publication of immeasurable appeal. But it would take much more than the new front page to make the *Journal* the national newspaper that Kilgore had envisioned. It would take one of the greatest sales jobs in publishing history, for the notion of rounding up readers and advertisers across the United States for a paper called *The Wall Street Journal* made about as much sense as hawking copies of *The Farmer's Almanac* in downtown Manhattan.

CHAPTER 6

The Show-off

ROBERT FEEMSTER, WHO supplied the business brains for the rebirth of *The Wall Street Journal*, was a natural provocateur. A grade school teacher in Cambridge City, Indiana, wrote on his report card: "Robert talks in class and annoys the other children." People who knew Feemster as an adult would have considered that an understatement. Feemster was short and rotund, loud, pushy, and manipulative. He was a preposterous man who wore ten-gallon hats, smoked extra-length cigarettes held effetely in the tips of his fingers, and fancied himself a lady killer. A lifelong needler of people, Feemster would test a new man on his sales force by waving an unlit cigarette in his face while lecturing him on one topic or another. If the man rose to the bait and produced a cigarette lighter, Feemster dismissed him as sniveling and subservient.

It was obvious that Feemster's pomposity disguised a serious inferiority complex. His corpulent five-foot-six body had set him apart even at DePauw University, where he graduated four years behind Barney Kilgore. As general sales manager of Dow Jones, Feemster mounted his gargantuan desk on a platform and shortened the legs on other office chairs so that he might tower over visitors.

And he was capable of much worse. Hating the title of general sales manager, Feemster persuaded Kilgore to bestow on him the more prestigious-sounding sobriquet "chairman of the executive committee," though the title carried no real meaning. Outside the office Feemster would abbreviate his impressive-sounding title to simply "chairman of Dow Jones." From time to time people meeting Kilgore would tell him, "Ah, yes, I met your boss the other day." And Kilgore, to his lasting credit, would smile and change the subject.

In 1954, on the seventy-fifth anniversary of *The Wall Street Journal,* Feemster gave a speech about the company before the Newcomen Society, a New York business group. He noted that practically all the men then running *The Wall Street Journal* had been trained by Kenneth C. Hogate. "Your speaker tonight is a member of that group," he crowed. "So is another guest with us tonight, Mr. Bernard Kilgore." Without pausing to point out that Kilgore was not only his boss but the master architect of the newspaper, the "chairman" continued: "About twelve years ago . . . *we* began to talk first among ourselves and later in public about the 'new' *Wall Street Journal.*" In the back of the room, Kilgore nodded and smiled to himself.

Feemster's flamboyant boorishness had a predictable effect on the shy, conservative men working their way up in the *Journal*'s news department. He repelled them. The appeal of the place under Kilgore was its dignity, its quiet determination to become a great paper without sacrificing principle. The man the news staff worshiped was Barney Kilgore, a soft-spoken, good-humored diplomat who displayed no appetite for self-aggrandizement or fame. Though Kilgore had to have a large ego, he disguised it artfully. And Kilgore was such a sharp judge of talent that the men working for him did not need to push themselves forward. All they had to do was perform well in their jobs. That was the great attraction of working for the man: Modesty was the accepted style of office demeanor. You didn't have to play politics.

But here was this fat lout Feemster trotting all over the country asserting that he ran Dow Jones and upstaging Kilgore. Worse yet, he seemed to be Kilgore's friend; they had an understanding of some sort—Kilgore and Feemster. It nettled the newsmen who wanted to play John the Baptist to Kilgore's Jesus Christ, the men who dressed and talked like Kilgore, shrugged their shoulders like Kilgore, and aped his every word. They couldn't stand Bob Feemster, and they liked to think that Kilgore tolerated him only for his sales acumen. Bill Kerby, Kilgore's top assistant, disliked Feemster profoundly. In his memoirs Kerby would write that Feemster was "highly insensitive, abrasive" and "almost pathologically defensive." He "deeply offended large stockholders at social gatherings," Kerby continues, noting that Feemster divorced his wife, a lifelong friend of Mary Lou Kilgore, in order to marry his secretary. Feemster "repeatedly produced unrealistic budgets which enabled him to triumphantly point to his success in exceeding sales and revenue goals," observes Kerby, and toward the end of his career at Dow Jones "became completely absorbed with building his own image, taking long speechmaking trips, hobnobbing socially with celebrities."

Such criticisms may have been accurate enough, yet they hardly gave a fair picture of the man. Feemster was the *Journal*'s P. T. Barnum, the man who made the newspaper seem larger than life when it was really a paltry thing. He was a daring salesman and a promotional genius. Without him *The Wall Street Journal*, no matter how well written and edited, very likely would have foundered. Kilgore, a man incapable of braggadocio, was perhaps the only one who understood how indispensable Feemster really was.

Kerby, like most die-hard newsmen, felt that if the *Journal* was a superior newspaper, the world would beat a path to its door. The attitude said much about the news profession, for one of the field's greatest attractions has always been that it offers potential power and high status without compromising a man's ideals. Reporters can stay detached, never stating personal views or risking ridicule, keeping faith with truth and high principle. Newsmen enjoy a privileged feeling of superiority over jackals and self-promoters of all stripes—the self-serving politician, the too friendly public relations man, the would-be celebrity, and the most enduring of all American business figures, the overly persistent salesman.

Even at *The Wall Street Journal,* people in the news department would rarely give much thought to the fact that their own particular medium was itself a business. When they thought of the paper's business employees at all, they imagined slick back-slappers who devoted their energies to buttering up the advertising community. Journalists like to think of their field as a kind of public utility that stays in business because people depend on it, not because some boorish salesman goes out and hustles up paying customers. The thought that their newspaper's survival might depend upon the work of mere salesmen would strike most as thoroughly unattractive—especially when the salesman in question was someone like Bob Feemster, a loudmouth in a cowboy hat who loved throwing his weight around.

The fact remains that few enterprises succeed without promotion, least of all new publications. And the more unusual the publishing venture, the gaudier the effort required to hawk it. In the beginning Barney Kilgore's newspaper seemed highly improbable. No one had ever conceived of a national daily newspaper about business before, let alone a high-quality one. Selling readers and advertisers on the idea would take a bit more gumption than the news staff realized. Had they understood as much, they might have been grateful for Bob Feemster's egotistical excess. Someone at the *Journal* had to have it.

After graduating from DePauw in the summer of 1933, Feemster had enrolled in the University of Michigan law school, but illness forced him to drop out after a few weeks. Upon recovering, he wrote to Casey Hogate asking for a job, and Hogate, a DePauw trustee and a fellow member of Sigma Chi, sent an offer of a sales job in New York.

Though jobs of any description were scarce, it was debatable whether Hogate's offer constituted much of a favor. An ad salesman's income was based largely on commission, and in 1933 a commission on Wall Street was like loose change on the sidewalk—a rarity. The average edition of *The Wall Street Journal* was just twelve pages with only two pages' worth of advertisements. The end of Prohibition brought in a few new whiskey ads, but for the most part, the *Journal* relied on two kinds of old standbys: the "financial tombstones," formal announcements of new stock and bond offerings, and "brokerage cards," small rectangular ads that resembled brokers' calling cards. The tombstone ads were scarce, for the financial markets were in no condition to absorb many new stock and bond issues. And even when such ads abounded, the *Journal* ran a distant third in them, well behind the financial pages of *The New York Times* and the *Herald Tribune.* Brokerage cards could be more plentiful at times, but when the market dipped, they were as elusive as a summer breeze. The select brokers who survived the crash were a cautious group who kept a weather eye on expenditures. To make matters worse, *The Wall Street Journal,* with its minuscule circulation, had the highest advertising rates in town on a cost-per-reader basis. By any standard the *Journal* was a tough sell.

Feemster had the sort of contentious personality that thrives on adversity. He took on sales calls no one else wanted and managed to bring in business no one had expected. His real ascent at Dow Jones began in 1935, when Hogate shifted him from general accounts into financial ad sales, the most laggard part of the *Journal*'s business. Most of the potential lay in ads announcing recalls of various bond issues. The Depression had forced interest rates down, so companies that had outstanding bonds that paid interest of 4 percent or 6 percent could recall them and replace them with new bonds paying interest as low as 2.5 percent. In order to recall bonds, companies were required by law to run redemption advertisements in a "daily newspaper of general circulation," expensive ads that might run up to four full newspaper pages in length.

There was a hitch, however. *The Wall Street Journal* was certainly a daily newspaper, but did it have general circulation? Generations of bond lawyers had thought not. Feemster, armed with a few weeks of law school training, made the rounds of the staid old Wall Street law firms to do battle with some of the more hidebound attorneys anywhere. He argued that the *Journal* was indeed a general circulation paper where the financial community was concerned and that this was sufficient to meet the legal requirements. The argument appealed to the bond-issuing companies and their underwriters because the *Journal*'s ad rates were much lower than those of the larger papers in simple dollar terms. Gradually Feemster persuaded one lawyer after another, and soon the recall ads began to pour in. His reputation as a resourceful salesman grew accordingly. By 1938, when the *Journal*'s advertising manager had a heart attack, Feemster, twenty-seven years old, was the obvious choice to replace him.

Most of the *Journal*'s sales staff in those days suffered from the same lethargy that afflicted the newsroom. Many had come there in the twenties, when the Street seemed paved with gold; now they simply hung on to their jobs for want of something better to do. Feemster ignited them with his blustering style. He was slow-moving but had frenetic energy. His favorite reading was airline and train schedules, and his favorite pastime was seeing how many business calls he could make in out-of-the-way places while on routine business trips to one city or another. He goaded people into doing likewise, and most of the salesmen responded because, once they got to know Feemster, they found him eminently fair, a softy at heart, and an exciting man to work for.

There was no question that the man had effrontery. Feemster never took no for an answer. When chief executives' secretaries or their corporate advertising departments tried to fend him off, Feemster kept badgering, writing letters to the top man asserting that his subordinates were incompetent. Ultimately Feemster would find a way to see the head of the Chevrolet division or the president of Container Corporation of America, infuriating the middle-echelon people, who thought they already had given Dow Jones a firm turndown. After a long round of discouraging responses from Buick, Feemster brazenly placed a call to division chief Harlow Curtice while he was on the golf course. Once he had the boss's ear, Feemster frequently discovered that he was talking to an avid *Journal* reader who readily agreed to advertise. If not, Feemster kept on pushing, ignoring the man's hints that it was time to end the meeting and pounding away at the merits of the newspaper. When all else failed, Feemster blurted: "The money at stake here means nothing to *you*, but it is everything to *us*. Call your advertising department and tell them to put us on your schedule!"

These were acts of raw nerve, but Feemster had more going for him than that. He had great facility with sales patter, and he could tailor it to fit any situation. At Chrysler Corporation the vice-president in charge of sales could see no reason to advertise a working man's car like a Plymouth in a wealthy man's newspaper like *The Wall Street Journal*. Feemster won him over with the argument that most auto dealers did business on money borrowed from a local bank and that it would certainly do no harm for the local banker to see a plug for the car in his favorite paper.

Another executive trying to fend off Feemster told him: "Why should I advertise in the *Journal?* It's neither fish nor fowl; it isn't a magazine and it isn't a real newspaper." On the spot Feemster coined a phrase that *The Wall Street Journal* would use for years to come. He shot back: "We're the only national business daily," which sounded wonderful, though it was not quite true at the time.

The Wall Street Journal fell far short of being "national" until the 1950s. It was readily available in the Northeast and in California, but elsewhere distribution was spotty. In South Carolina or Pine Bluff, Arkansas, a businessman might have to wait a day or two for the paper to come in the mail, and even then the *Journal* was hardly the essential reading that it later became. But Feemster developed a chart that measured industrial employment in each of the forty-eight states. By laying a map of the *Journal's* distribution next to it, he could make an argument that the newspaper's readership roughly followed the ratio of each state's manufacturing base. His use of statistics was highly inventive, but in the end enough advertisers bought his arguments to make them come true.

There is a half-cynical saying among marketing professionals that good promotion generally improves the product in question. It was absolutely true in the case of the *Journal,* for Feemster's exaggerated claims for the newspaper were a reflection of Barney Kilgore's dreams for it. "The only national business daily" was the first slogan, and by hammering away at the theme, Feemster gave the men at the *Journal* little choice but to live up to it.

The *Journal*'s most intractable problem was its lingering image as a Wall Street trade publication. In retrospect, it is hard to conceive of *The Wall Street Journal* having a troublesome image, for it has become a badge of the American elite. Young executives carry the paper ostentatiously; it shows up as a frequent prop in magazine ads for fancy hotels, limousines, and attaché cases. A subscription is almost as sure a sign of class distinction as an Ivy League degree or membership in the University Club. But back in the 1940s, "Wall Street" was an unsavory phrase, even among businessmen. In the war years the very notion of a newspaper whose subject was making money seemed crude to nonreaders, almost incompatible with the snob appeal that the *Journal* badly wanted. Attaining that snob appeal would be Feemster's greatest achievement.

The more pedestrian job at hand was selling advertising space, but this, too, was complicated by the paper's image problem. Selling ad space in the old *Journal* had been hard enough, but at least back then the paper had been a familiar quantity. Now no one really knew what to make of it. The executive who complained that the *Journal* was "neither fish nor fowl" had been right. The *Journal* looked and smelled like a newspaper, yet it wasn't one. It had a highly selective readership and no local or regional identity other than Wall Street, and its ad rates were higher on a cost-per-reader basis than any newspaper known to man. All of which made it sound like a national magazine. But the *Journal* was not really that either. Its circulation was too small—just 55,000 by the end of 1944; its pages were too big; and it could not print in color. The newspaper-sized page and the lack of color printing meant that even if an advertiser wanted to reach the *Journal*'s readers, the big, glossy advertisements he had produced for the pages of *Time, Business Week,* or *Fortune* would not look very good in the *Journal.* A full-page magazine ad would become less than a quarter-page ad in the *Journal,* and the glorious color photography on which the ad agency had lavished so much care would be relegated to shades of gray. Designing a new ad for the *Journal* in black and white hardly seemed worth the effort.

Feemster could well have sold the *Journal* to advertisers as essentially a local newspaper for wealthy Northeasterners and Californians, which is precisely what it was. The New York edition even carried the New York City weather forecast in the upper right-hand corner of the front page. But Feemster foresaw the limitations: Prestigious local advertisers like Tiffany and Saks Fifth Avenue were few in number, and they already reached the bulk of *Journal* readers through the *Times*.

True to character, Feemster opted to push the paper forward into a class where it did not belong at all. He invented a new "field group" of rival publications. The group consisted of *Time, Newsweek, Fortune, Business Week, U.S. News & World Report*—and *The Wall Street Journal*. Thereafter, any corporation that placed an ad in one of those periodicals got a call from Feemster wanting to know why the firm was ignoring a publication in the same "field group," a publication with the added virtue of being "the only national business daily."

This "field group" business was nonsense, and Feemster knew it, but so long as the *Journal* was behaving outrageously, why not behave that way on all counts? Feemster pushed ad rates much higher than the rival magazines on a cost-per-reader basis, arguing that the *Journal* had a more desirable readership. The result: Within a decade or so, a full-page ad in the *Journal* cost approximately the same as a full page in *Fortune,* and it still does. The difference now, however, is that Feemster's "field group" is taken seriously, and rather than being the runt of the group, the *Journal* is far and away the leader, the publication in which advertisers spend their money first.

Feemster thought the advertising content of the *Journal* should be consistent with the news content. He wanted it to be a forum for national business advertising, just as Kilgore was making it a paper of national business news. It was a worthy idea, but not an easy one to implement. There was enough business and financial advertising to fill magazines like *Fortune* and *Business Week,* but these were not daily publications. Getting the same advertisements that the magazines had was hard enough for the *Journal;* generating more seemed altogether fanciful.

Two kinds of advertising looked utterly hopeless. The *Journal* was too expensive a vehicle to attract ads for most consumer goods—tires or cigarettes, say. And there was only so much financial tombstone advertising to go around. The key to getting new business had to lie in industrial advertisements, corporate "image" advertisements. And fortunately no one was more qualified to discuss the subject of "image" than Bob Feemster. While most companies were used to advertising their wares, relatively few were accustomed to advertising their corporate identities. It seems perfectly obvious, for example, why a food company advertises its cake mixes or why an electric utility advertises the merits of electric heat. But what good does it do to flog a corporate name like General Foods or Commonwealth Edison? The answer is "image." People like doing business with successful firms, and advertising makes a firm look more successful. It conveys the rosy glow of prosperity to suppliers, customers, stockholders, stock brokers, employees, and, last but not least, bankers.

Feemster was such a meticulous salesman that he persuaded executives of the tangible benefits of such advertising. Once, in the late fifties, he visited Minneapolis, where a promising young salesman, Bernard Flanagan, was preparing to call on Northern States Power. Flanagan's sales pitch was going to be that the Minnesota utility should advertise in the *Journal* in order to persuade corporations elsewhere to build new plants nearby. Feemster listened to the young salesman rehearse, then suggested a different attack: "Did you ever think of saying that utilities like Northern States Power always need to borrow money and that they always wind up paying the local bank's prime interest rate? Then you could say that by advertising in *The Wall Street Journal,* they might become well known in financial circles and get a slight break on interest rates that would more than pay for their advertising."

Not only did Feemster's sales pitch persuade Northern States to advertise, said Flanagan, but, as Feemster had predicted, the utility wound up borrowing money below prime rate. When the Minneapolis banks saw the advertisement in the *Journal,* they suddenly feared that one of their best customers was flirting with the bigger banks in New York and Chicago.

The *Journal* had never attracted much classified advertising, even when the paper was essentially a local financial sheet for New York. This was unfortunate, for the classified ad pages are the single most profitable part of any newspaper and among the best read. Now that the *Journal* was becoming a national newspaper, Feemster thought that there might be a way to attract a new kind of classified—personal ads with national interest. He guessed that the same wartime experiences that had made business attitudes less parochial might also have created new personal needs for the *Journal* to exploit.

With more and more young executives hopping from one city to another every few years, Feemster reasoned that they must be continually buying and selling houses that were too expensive for almost anyone except another executive. When a man was transferred from Chicago to Denver, he probably had to sell his Chicago house to someone being transferred there from Cleveland or Atlanta. In 1948 Feemster put his right-hand man, Ted Callis, in charge of the new "Real Estate Corner," the paper's first concerted effort to crack the classified ad market. Callis, yet another DePauw alumnus, started drumming up business through real estate agents around the country, quickly drawing a quarter-page worth of classifieds. The ads began to multiply, for there was no other advertising vehicle quite like it. Then Callis decided that the paper could attract similar interest in resorts and vacation rentals, so he started a classified ad column called "Florida Beckons," another instant success.

The paper had considerably more difficulty attracting executive employment advertising, though the *Journal* was a natural place for it. The problem in the 1940s seemed to be that not enough middle-level executives were reading the paper to get such advertising off the ground. In 1951 Callis made another stab at employment classifieds, with a column he called "The Mart," a name inspired by the Chicago Merchandise Mart. Rather than just inviting readers to place job-seeking ads this time, Callis made the rounds of employment agencies in major cities, convincing them of the advantages of advertising in a national business paper. If an assistant corporate treasurer in Harrisburg wanted to advance, Callis argued, there probably were only four or five other companies in town who would be interested in him. Moreover, the executives in those companies undoubtedly played golf with the president of the firm he already worked for, so that it was almost certain that if the man went job hunting around town, word of his discontent would soon get back to his boss. An anonymous advertisement in *The Wall Street Journal,* however, could work wonders for him, even if his real desire was to stay in Harrisburg. As Feemster and Callis kept telling people, the *Journal* was really no different from a community paper, except that the community it served happened to be national.

Wartime paper shortages had begun to ease as early as 1945. Promises of a peacetime economy made business blossom. By the end of 1946, the circulation of *The Wall Street Journal* had risen to 96,000, and the newspaper took a major step toward becoming truly national. Thanks in no small part to Feemster's promotional efforts, Clarence Barron's descendants were persuaded of the need for a new Southwest edition, which began publication in May 1947 out of Dallas. The new edition was not an instant hit; it took years to become successful. Though the paper carried almost all of the news that was in the New York edition, plus a bit more regional coverage, it remained starved for regional advertising. Some longtime subscribers in the area could not be convinced that the thin paper they were getting in Texas was equal to the one they had previously gotten by mail from New York. Then Feemster hit upon the concept of regional advertising rates, later copied by *Time* and *Newsweek.* An advertiser could place his ad in any regional edition of *The Wall Street Journal* or in all three of them, thus enhancing the paper's appeal for advertisers that were essentially regional businesses. Still the Dallas edition continued to languish.

The time had come, Feemster concluded, to launch a major public relations blitz for the paper, even though his promotional budget remained meager. In early 1949 he called Charles Robbins, Kilgore's old DePauw roommate, who had just taken a position in New York with the public relations firm of Bozell &

Jacobs. Would Robbins' new firm be interested in having Dow Jones as a client? asked Feemster. "Well, I'm not sure," Robbins reportedly stammered, probably knowing full well that Feemster's budget was small. But Martin Speckter, a more seasoned PR man who shared Robbins' office, had been eavesdropping. He recalled nodding his head briskly and signaling that Robbins should break off gracefully. "Look, these people are my friends," Robbins reportedly told Speckter after hanging up. "We couldn't take on their account and then fail to get results for them." Speckter, however, saw the account in terms of prestige, not profit. *The Wall Street Journal* had great cachet in a limited circle, and the farsighted Speckter guessed that the circle might grow.

From the beginning Speckter found life with Bob Feemster exhilarating. The *Journal* had a serious image problem. Even in 1949, with circulation edging over 140,000, *The Wall Street Journal* was poorly understood. Few people knew that it had made a conscious change in editorial content. Virtually no one understood the concept of a national business community, which sounded like a contradiction in terms.

Before the war most businesses had been local in character. They manufactured goods close to the place where the goods would be sold. The average manufacturer did not produce a nationally known brand but rather a Chicago brand or a Cincinnati brand. It still made sense to speak of a local economy as opposed to a national one. The war changed all that, though just how much it changed things would not become clear for many years. The war plucked GIs out of their hometowns and showed them that the world was a larger place. The enormous demand for war matériel brought local companies around the country into contact with one another, so that afterward geographic ties meant less and less to business. Meanwhile, the great national corporations were gobbling up the smaller local ones. One city became like another, and business became so homogenized that one executive's dilemma was apt to constitute a nationwide trend.

In the late forties very few people saw all this happening. The notion that a West Coast businessman might need the same news as an East Coast businessman seemed farfetched, though to Kilgore and Feemster, nothing could have been plainer.

Feemster wrote a memorable slogan for his public relations assault: "Everywhere, Men Who Get Ahead in Business Read *The Wall Street Journal.*" It was a masterpiece of copywriting, for in twelve short words Feemster had captured the essence of Barney Kilgore's newspaper concept: "Everywhere [the newspaper was ubiquitous], Men [clearly it was a virile publication] Who Get Ahead [aggressive types, not fat cats with their feet propped on their desks] in Business [the new subject matter of the paper] Read [they don't just use it as a coffee table ornament] The [a unique product] *Wall Street Journal.*" The *Journal* would stick with the slogan for more than twenty years—until the advent of the women's movement.

The irony was that when Feemster carried his slogan to the *Journal's* high-powered advertising agency, BBD&O, the account executive reportedly tried to change it. He was John Caples, author of the legendary "Everyone laughed when I sat down to play the piano." Caples took one look at Feemster's line and, recalls Speckter, declared it vulgar. "Let's try this," he told Feemster. " 'Everywhere, Men Who Achieve Greater Success in Business . . .' "

Feemster exploded. "Damn it, people don't talk that way, John. They don't say, 'Men who achieve greater success.' They say, 'Men who get ahead,' and that's what we're going to say."

Feemster and Speckter went ahead with the *Journal's* first full-scale promotional campaign, all centered on the new slogan, "Everywhere, Men Who Get Ahead in Business Read *The Wall Street Journal.*" Despite the paper's tiny promotional budget, the advertising community was convinced that the *Journal* was spending lavishly to promote itself. The secret was that Feemster combined a few very large advertisements in conspicuous publications with hundreds of small ones, giving the impression that the *Journal* was suddenly flush with cash. While the *Journal* was spending just $140,000 to $150,000 a year on its promotion campaign, most of Speckter's colleagues apparently had the impression that it was a multi-million-dollar account, and advertising agencies that had previously considered the *Journal* small potatoes began to take notice. Capitalizing on the agencies' newly aroused interest, Feemster introduced a second slogan, a corollary to the

"Men Who Get Ahead" theme: "No One Is More Responsive to Advertising Than the Men Who Get Ahead in Business." To lend credence the *Journal* soon began running ads that featured newly promoted executives who were loyal readers of the paper.

Other slogans followed, all of them emphasizing one or another of the ideas put forth in Feemster's original slogan. Speckter wrote: "The Same News, The Same Day, All Over the U.S.A.," which was meant to prick the interest of the advertising community in the technological problems of printing a national daily. A Dow Jones promotion manager, Francis X. Timmons, came up with "The News That Changes Business Changes Every Business Day," suggesting that a reader could not afford to wait for a weekly or monthly magazine. Speckter designed a promotion campaign around the slogan *"The Wall Street Journal* Reader Gets More Because He Pays More," to stress the paper's high-priced appeal, but the campaign was killed at the last moment, he recalls, when someone on Feemster's staff divined a double entendre.

Another of Feemster's ideas was to reproduce the entire front page of that morning's *Wall Street Journal* in other newspapers across the country, usually with an advertising slogan scribbled across the top of the page saying that this very page was being read that morning by many thousands of America's top businessmen. Not only did these ads give non-*Journal* readers a sampling of the newspaper, they also gave the advertising agencies a spectacular display of the *Journal's* technological virtuosity, for no other paper was capable of disseminating the printed page so quickly in so many parts of the nation.

For the news department, however, these ads had serious drawbacks. One of the *Journal's* Boston correspondents, Lester Smith, had painstakingly pieced together a nearly complete financial dossier on the Ford Motor Company, still a family-owned company whose finances were a deep secret. To the *Journal's* dismay, the very morning that Smith's story ran on page one, *The New York Times* had an abbreviated version with the same figures. Obviously a *Times* deskman had spotted the story in the *Journal's* promotional advertisement and had ordered a hasty rewrite for the *Times'* late edition, a bit of piracy to which the *Times* later confessed.

There are really only three ways to promote an advertising medium, be it a newspaper or a magazine, a radio or television station. The salesman can harp on the sheer size of the audience and how little it costs the advertiser to get his product before each individual reader or listener; he can talk about the demographics—the wealth, age, and sex of the average subscriber or how much disposable income he has; or the salesman can ignore the audience and boast about the magnificence of the medium itself. By and large that was Feemster's strategy—to extoll the *Journal's* excellence at every opportunity. Often his ads would point out that the *Journal* was such an excellent product that it naturally attracted an excellent readership, but never did he make very much of the *Journal's* burgeoning circulation, even after it became possible to do so.

The theme was always the quality of the paper and the exclusiveness of the readership. In 1966, when the *Journal's* circulation topped one million, Speckter wrote an ad that said: "It Isn't How Big You Become, But How You Become Big." *The Wall Street Journal's* circulation had just topped the million mark, the ad noted, but it had done so "one subscriber at a time . . . because eagles don't flock."

Like Kilgore, Feemster had a missionary zeal about the newspaper. He bore a conviction that the *Journal* had a distinct purpose, even a moral purpose. He saw the *Journal* as a new kind of publication for a new kind of reader—the positive-thinking, upward-striving American businessman, whose destiny was to lead the country into unprecedented prosperity. It was the right paper for the right people at the right time.

What finally made Feemster so effective was not merely his enthusiasm, but his extraordinary respect for the product he was selling and his determination to improve it. He was such a fervent believer in the righteous cause of *The Wall Street Journal* that he could sound evangelistic. Before a Houston audience in the 1950s, he made the preposterous boast that had the *Journal* existed in its modern form thirty years earlier, it would have prevented the stock market crash through its powers of enlightenment.

This was nonsense, but nonsense of a sort that set Feemster apart from other sales executives in his field, for the vast majority are blinded by the bottom line, their publication's salability to advertisers. Feemster's chief concern was never for the paper's marketability but for the success of its overall mission. He was transparently envious of the men who edited the paper—Kerby, McCormack *et al.*—and let them know that he thought he personally could do a better job of it. Yet Feemster understood the importance of editorial independence and never interfered. Indeed, Feemster built his sales strategy for the *Journal* on the twin pillars of quality and integrity. Though Feemster was certainly capable of doing almost anything to win over an advertiser, he quickly gave up groveling in favor of arrogance. In the early forties, soon after Kilgore was made managing editor, Feemster started to cut back on the number of front-page advertisements, and by 1946 he persuaded Kilgore to abandon them completely, letting customers know that henceforth the ads would take a back seat to the news.

Soon after the war technological improvements in the Dow Jones news ticker precipitated a business crisis for the company. Previously the news ticker had been aimed primarily at New York banks and brokerages. Out-of-town subscribers got their ticker service via telephone relay, which entailed delays that were unacceptable for heavy market players. But now the ticker was made more compatible with telephone lines, and for the first time brokerage offices all over the country could get ticker news simultaneously with New York. Once the ticker became a truly national network, brokerage offices around the country demanded service as never before. The difficulty for Dow Jones & Company lay in meeting the new demand for service without going broke in the process. Previously each subscribing firm had paid the same rate for ticker service, no matter what its size or how many offices it had. Merrill Lynch Pierce Fenner & Smith, with thousands of offices all over the country, paid no more for its ticker service than a one-office firm confined to lower Manhattan. Now Merrill Lynch and others wanted tickers installed hither and yon at no extra cost.

Feemster approached the crisis with his usual self-assuredness.

He marched into a meeting of top brokerage officials and, as he later described it to Kerby, "told them that the way things had been going, we could wind up with one machine in one office and everybody else in the United States getting their news free from that single service. Then I told them, maybe that's a good idea for all of us. We'll deliver the news to the Stock Exchange, and the Exchange can relay it all over. The price, subject to later increases, will be two million a year."

The major brokers agreed on the spot to large price increases. Feemster sold them on a new pricing formula for the ticker service based on "opportunity for use." The price would depend on how many offices a brokerage firm had, so that Merrill Lynch would end up paying far more than before. But having stared down the big brokerage houses and forced large price increases upon them, Feemster promised that in return they could expect to get the finest financial information imaginable. From then on the smallest mistake or delay on the ticker brought angry complaints from Feemster and his sales assistants, who were adamant that the news department live up to their billing for it.

Feemster's early claims about the *Journal* being a "national" business newspaper had been exaggerated, but nearly everything he said on the subject was calculated to build the image of a newspaper whose ethics and news service were unimpeachable— both in news and in business. He seemed to make every business decision on the basis of its effect on the reader, on the assumption that a top-notch readership would ultimately bring in the best advertisers.

During the late forties, when the *Journal* was preparing for its great leap from obscurity, Feemster began talking contemptuously about a promotional campaign used by *The Saturday Evening Post*. It claimed that the magazine was the favored reading of a class of people it called "The Influential." The promotion was close enough to the one Feemster was planning to invite comparison. Feemster groused that the *Post* was not entitled to claim an "influential" readership while simultaneously offering discount subscriptions to bolster circulation. In his view the cut-rate subscriptions were an act of pure flimflam. If people were being induced to subscribe with discounts, then there was no reason to think that they were an especially exclusive group. He decided that *The Wall Street Journal* would never resort to discounts, trial subscription rates, or any other circulation-building gimmicks. Rather, it would deliberately keep subscription and newsstand prices thirty to forty percent higher than those of other newspapers so that it could stoutly maintain that its readership was a class apart.

In the long run subscription discounting would prove to be a major factor in the demise of magazines like the *Post, Life,* and *Look.* They would build up huge circulations by practically giving copies away. Then mounting postage rates would devastate them, and advertisers would begin to realize the extraordinary extent to which they had been subsidizing the readers. It was inescapable that when people got a magazine like *Life* for about eight cents a copy they might not attach much importance to it. Interestingly, in the late 1970s and early 1980s, when the *Journal* was boosting its newsstand price almost annually to stay ten cents or so ahead of the *Times,* it found that hardly any readers objected to paying more for it. If anything, the more expensive the *Journal* became, the more readers seemed to prize it.

Feemster sometimes seemed to push the standards of quality and integrity to extremes that made even Kilgore uncomfortable. After seeing the direction in which Kilgore was taking the front page of the *Journal,* Feemster hit on a revolutionary idea: He would make the advertising in *The Wall Street Journal* every bit as classy as the editorial content. To anyone who had ridden out the storms of the Depression, such talk sounded crazy. The *Journal* had skated over very thin ice during the 1930s, and now, when there was finally a little extra money coming in, Feemster was talking about turning much of it away.

Feemster wanted to make any advertisement appearing in the *Journal* conform to certain standards of taste and truthfulness, just like the news columns. Ad content would have to be accurate and consistent with the paper's dignity. Moreover, the advertisers themselves would have to be reputable, especially when an advertisement involved some sort of open solicitation, a stock offering or investment opportunity. It sounded very noble, but a good proportion of the ads that kept the *Journal* presses turning were what the ad staff called "sucker ads," touting highly speculative stock offerings and land deals. Their main purpose was to entice the unsophisticated into investments that they had no business making. Both Kilgore and Hogate objected to Feemster's new policy. They said that the paper could not possibly afford to forgo such an important source of revenues, even if some of the advertisements bordered on fraud. Feemster was more farsighted. He had the quintessential Hoosier's instinct for piling up seed corn, forgoing profits one year to ensure big harvests later on. "We'll just do it my way," he told Kilgore airily. "I will be responsible for making up the lost revenue—and more."

The *Journal* had become a mecca for mail-order advertisers. A small Manhattan tobacco store, John Surrey, had placed an ad that included a clip-out coupon. Word got around that the store had been flooded with orders, and other, less familiar advertisers placed similar ads. Actually they were placing mail-order ads at a discount, for the *Journal* and other publications often allowed retailers to advertise at reduced rates on the theory that readers liked to read such ads. Soon the *Journal* was getting so many mail-order ads that it could not possibly investigate the people who were placing them. Sure enough, readers began to complain about being burned by slow mail-order deliveries and fly-by-night operators. Many firms were placing ads in the *Journal* on credit—to sell desk calendars, for example—then waiting for the orders to come in before buying any inventory. Feemster settled the problem decisively: no more mail-order advertising unless the advertiser was thoroughly well known. And, he ruled, there would be absolutely no advertising on credit. If a firm did not have the financial wherewithal to pay in advance, it did not belong in *The Wall Street Journal*.

He also ruled out ads for body-contact products, anything from hair tonic and razor blades to deodorant and hemorrhoid cures. Anonymous job opportunity ads had to be checked out thoroughly and the names of the advertisers kept on file to ensure that they did not come from headhunting firms that were merely fishing for the names of restless executives. These and other standards would remain in force at the *Journal* for the next four decades, though some policies would prove unnecessary. As the

Journal's ad rates climbed ever higher, the paper became far too expensive an advertising medium for a mass consumer product like Preparation H or Ban deodorant. Still, the *Journal* would reserve the right to turn down any ad it considered distasteful. In the 1970s it turned down an ad placed by one of the major menswear manufacturers for a man's business suit that sold for a vulgar $6,500. The *Journal*'s reasoning: The ad would offend certain favored retail advertisers like Brooks Brothers for whom it wanted to maintain a dignified advertising environment.

The *Journal* also turned down tombstone advertisements for new stock issues that seemed either too flimsy or too speculative for its general readership. In 1969, a bumper year for such offerings, the *Journal* turned down so many tombstones that several angry investment bankers whose ads had been rejected filed a formal complaint with the Federal Trade Commission. They made an interesting point: *The Wall Street Journal* had become so predominant a means of communication for Wall Street that to be denied access to its advertising space was tantamount to being shut out of the marketplace.

Attorneys for the Commission trooped over to the *Journal* offices to confront one of Feemster's protégés, Donald A. Macdonald, a trim, bespectacled man who speaks bluntly and does not suffer fools graciously. Macdonald said he laid out all the stock prospectuses that his advertising department had screened during the year, and sure enough, they showed that the *Journal* had rejected more than it had accepted. Macdonald pointed out to the FTC lawyers that the paper had not only given up substantial revenue by rejecting the advertisements, it had also gone to great expense in order to do so. Screening the prospectuses and checking references and legal claims was, after all, a time-consuming process that required a fair-sized staff of auditors.

The government attorneys were far from satisfied, says Macdonald. By rejecting certain stock offering advertisements, they contended, the *Journal* was practicing restraint of trade. The job of determining which offerings were honest and which were not belonged to the government, not the newspaper. Macdonald stared at the men incredulously. "Okay," he recalls telling them at last. "Here's what I'll do. I'll run any ad in *The Wall Street*

Journal you want, but before I do, I'm going to run a full-page ad in the paper that says that the Federal Trade Commission— created for the protection of consumers—forbids this newspaper to evaluate new stock issue advertisements on behalf of our readers and that henceforth our readers should not believe *anything* they read in *The Wall Street Journal.*"

The lawyers departed in a fury, never to be heard from again.

Feemster retired from Dow Jones in December 1962, when he was only fifty-one. Like Kilgore, success had made him restless. There was not much challenge in hawking *The Wall Street Journal* when all that it required was polished manners and high-minded sermonizing. Feemster's talent had been more along the lines of screaming from a soapbox. He died only a few weeks later in a private airplane accident, and the *Journal* editorial page accorded the coolest of tributes, saying: "His was no small contribution." Only those who had worked directly under Feemster seemed to harbor much fondness for the man, and that was because only they understood how necessary his abrasiveness and raw hucksterism had been. Don Macdonald would say that success had destroyed Bob Feemster. "Success has its own momentum, you know, and it removes the necessity for certain kinds of people," said Macdonald. "And the people who are left no longer know how the company got there. They think the company has just been around forever, and they think that all the money and the success that come rolling in are their just due.

"The truth is that those people who aren't around anymore, the people whom success removed, are the ones who had the fun. It's more fun to build from the bottom than to sit on top of everything protecting your success. As Royster says, 'The times will make the men.'"

CHAPTER 7
_____

Avoiding Sabotage

UNLIKE OTHER NEWSPAPERS *The Wall Street Journal* never experienced much pro-union sentiment in its newsroom. The Newspaper Guild's most important gains came in the 1930s, when the newly hatched National Labor Relations Board was urging unionization in all sorts of trades so as to rectify the past abuses of big business. The Newspaper Guild president was Heywood C. Broun, a Harvard-educated Socialist who wrote a somewhat dilettantish column in the *World-Telegram*. Said Broun: "If you belong to a union without any reds in it, for God's sake go out and recruit a few!" That sort of rhetoric might appeal to newsmen at other papers, but *The Wall Street Journal* did not collect many Marxists, not even many Democrats. By and large the men who worked there still identified with Wall Street financiers. Heywood Broun's protestations that a man could not be well informed unless he regularly read *The Daily Worker* left them cold.

Broun's Newspaper Guild began an earnest campaign to organize the *Journal* in 1937, starting with a few left-leaning news clerks. But most reporters quickly rallied to defend the management. To help their employer fend off both the Guild and

Charles H. Dow (left) and Edward D. Jones, founders of Dow Jones & Co. and *The Wall Street Journal.* (DOW JONES)

Dow Jones & Co.'s first headquarters in 1882 was in the basement of 15 Wall Street, the middle of the three buildings in the foreground. The entire block is now occupied by the New York Stock Exchange. (NEW YORK STOCK EXCHANGE)

Clarence W. Barron (left), publisher of the *Journal* from 1912 to 1928, with his step-daughter Jane Waldron Bancroft; a visiting Belgian dignitary, Kamiel Léfebre; and the ill-fated Hugh Bancroft, who briefly succeeded his father-in-law as publisher. The time is August 1925. (UPI/BETTMANN)

Kenneth C. Hogate, in a photo from the 1918 DePauw University yearbook. (DEPAUW UNIVERSITY)

William Henry Grimes in 1951, during his heyday as an editorialist. (WIDE WORLD)

Bernard Kilgore's graduation picture in the 1929 DePauw University yearbook. (DE PAUW UNIVERSITY)

Eddie Costenbader, czar of the Dow Jones news ticker, at his command post. (DOW JONES)

The Dow Jones news ticker, circa 1935. (DOW JONES)

Bernard Kilgore in the mid-1960s. (DOW JONES)

William F. Kerby, Kilgore's right-hand man and his successor as *Journal* publisher. (DOW JONES)

Vermont C. Royster (WIDE WORLD)

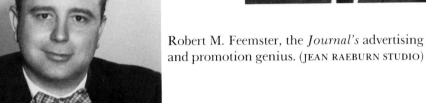

Robert M. Feemster, the *Journal's* advertising
and promotion genius. (JEAN RAEBURN STUDIO)

Dan Dorfman, as he appeared on
the June 1973 cover of *Institutional Investor*, at the height of
his power.

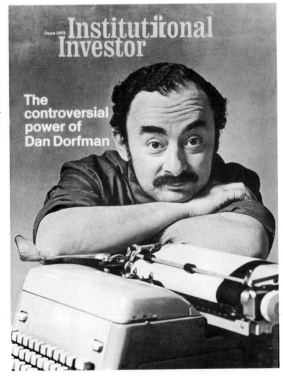

Warren H. Phillips (left), Ray Shaw and Peter R. Kann in early 1980. (VIC DE LUCIA/
THE NEW YORK TIMES)

Edward Cony (DOW JONES)

Laurence G. O'Donnell (DOW JONES)

Robert L. Bartley (DOW JONES)

Jude Wanniski (POLYCONOMICS INC.)

R. Foster Winans after his sentencing in 1985. (WIDE WORLD)

the NLRB they formed a house union, and Buren McCormack and Bill Kerby would always boast of having been charter members. The employees' association would negotiate with management over salaries and benefits, but it would never view its members' interests as being radically at odds with those of the management. The right to strike was not even part of its charter.

Blessed with such pliant employees in the newsroom, Kilgore and his aides would learn to approach labor relations with unusual fearlessness. Early in the 1950s he quit the New York Publishers Association, which negotiated labor contracts for all of the city's newspapers. It was a brazen declaration of independence, but the other publishers barely noticed. They ought to have paid more attention, for it was one of the shrewdest moves Kilgore ever made.

Even within the *Journal* people misread Kilgore's motives. Some had an almost diabolical fear of the powerful *New York Times,* believing that its publisher, Orville Dryfoos, wanted to effect an unnecessarily expensive labor settlement in order to hasten the demise of his rival, the *Herald Tribune.* As the *Journal* grew, Kilgore's men also wondered when the *Times* would finally wake up, strengthen its own business and financial coverage, and thus crumple *The Wall Street Journal* like a piece of old newsprint.

Kilgore was indeed wary of Orville Dryfoos, but not necessarily for these reasons. He suspected that the *Times'* publisher would make almost any compromise in order to avoid the indignity of missing a day's publication. More important, he suspected that the New York Publishers Association, under Dryfoos' leadership, would attempt to buy labor peace for the smallest possible wage increases, a drastic mistake in Kilgore's view. Labor peace was important, he thought, but it was not worth what other publishers were willing to sacrifice. From Kilgore's conservative Middlewestern perspective, the trade-offs that the Publishers Association was contemplating were shortsighted. He saw it bargaining away the right to decide what kinds of new machinery could be introduced and how quickly. And he saw the association accepting all sorts of featherbedding, keeping men on the job long after there was useful work for them to do. Such practices struck Kilgore as debilitating for both the men and their newspapers. Better to give fifty percent pay raises to ten hard workers than to let fifteen loll about on the payroll without purpose or commitment. He would not compromise on such matters.

Not one major newspaper in the United States had then achieved a significant degree of automation in its pressroom, and the New York chapter of the International Typographers Union was not about to let the *Journal* become the first. Kilgore's paper was still small potatoes by New York standards—its combined national circulation stood around 250,000—but it was growing faster than any paper in the country. Dow Jones slyly asked the New York office of the International Typographers Union to consider a one-year experiment: The *Journal* wanted to set stock market tables—and stock tables alone—by automation. No jobs would be lost. The union local refused even to discuss the idea.

In the end it was not really Kilgore who tamed the ITU; it was Joe Ackell, the man whom Kilgore had shouldered aside for the general manager's job in 1942. Aloof and seemingly unapproachable, Ackell had apparently lost status within the company until he found sanctuary in the little machine shop on lower Sixth Avenue where Dow Jones manufactured and repaired its news tickers. Ackell spent more and more of his time inside a workroom about twenty feet square. He had always been an inveterate tinkerer. Ackell liked to take apart someone else's invention, study it, then put it back together again in ways that made it a bit faster or more reliable.

Ackell's crowning achievement probably came in 1952, when he invented a device he called the Electro-Typesetter. Essentially it was a package of simple electrical switches which, when fed with the punched paper tape being introduced by the major news services, would operate typesetting machinery automatically. Such a device had long existed for the Linotype machines in use at the *Journal*, but Ackell's version was different. The more delicate part of the system—the part that translated the punched paper tape into electrical signals—could be operated at a distance from the typesetting machines. That made sabotage far more difficult. No printer would ever come near the detested paper tape that threatened to make his trade obsolete. Ackell's Electro-Typesetter was designed to do its work within the safe confines of the newsroom.

The only real obstacle that remained to automation was the stubborn ITU, the printers' union. To the surprise of Kilgore's men, Ackell decided to go over the heads of the union's New York leadership, and, amazingly enough, the ITU's national leaders agreed to talk. The *Journal* was, after all, a burgeoning national publication, not just another New York City newspaper. At first, negotiations with the ITU went nowhere. Ackell explained his new Electro-Typesetter to them and flatly declared that the future of his company depended upon it. Dow Jones would use the invention with or without the cooperation of the Typographical Union, Ackell is said to have insisted. The union officials wanted a guarantee that Dow Jones would always employ at least the same number of printers as were then employed in its New York printing shop. The company would do no such thing. All it offered was hope for the future: If the newspaper grew according to plan, opening new printing plants across the United States, there might be a decline in the number of printers in any one plant but a net gain in printers' jobs nationwide. Finally the company did promise that no printer then employed would lose his job, though he would not necessarily be replaced upon retirement. And during a one-year trial period, whenever the Electro-Typesetter was in use, the dislodged printer would be assigned to hover around the typesetting equipment as a "machine tender."

By the time the year's experiment was over, the ITU evidently realized that the *Journal* had the technology to break a printers' strike. There was no question that it had the will to do so. From then on unions would regard *The Wall Street Journal* with respect and trepidation. A decade later the ITU would shut down all of New York's other papers for 114 days—over many of the same issues. The prolonged strike of 1962–1963 was blamed by many for hastening the demise of four newspapers, the *Mirror*, the *Journal-American*, the *World-Telegram and Sun*, and the *Herald Tribune*. But in 1953 the ITU succumbed to *The Wall Street Journal*'s arguments without incident.

The union obligingly renegotiated its contract, allowing the paper to set all its type with the Electro-Typesetter. The company agreed to retrain many of the printers to work the far less demanding keypunch machines. Successive contracts allowed the *Journal* to use fewer and fewer machine tenders, and within a few years the newspaper employed only as many printers as it actually needed. Other papers, meanwhile, found themselves devising more and more preposterous forms of make-work for obsolete craftsmen, and all the while their relations with the ITU and other unions continued to deteriorate. The *Journal* would not escape labor strife completely in the years ahead, but it would come close. There was obviously something to be said for Barney Kilgore's simple Hoosier instincts. Under no circumstances would the paper give the unions an iota of control over production questions. As the *Journal* opened more and more printing plants around the country, union resistance to automation weakened to the point of irrelevance.

When the three-month newspaper strike hit New York in late 1962, the *Journal* was the only regular paper that continued publication in the city. Immediately afterward, however, Kilgore announced that the *Journal* would cease publication in New York that summer. After July 1, 1963, the *Journal* began trucking newspapers to the city from its new printing plant in Chicopee, Massachusetts, almost two hundred miles distant. The true reason, though Kilgore did not articulate it at the time, was that Dow Jones was fed up with the intransigence of the New York printers' local and no longer wanted to deal with it. Dow Jones' contempt for the New York printers soon broadened into an aversion to all large metropolitan locals. As the *Journal* opened more and more regional printing plants—seventeen of them linked together by satellite at the end of 1985, with plans for five more—it was careful to place them on the extreme periphery of metropolitan areas, well beyond the reach of most entrenched union locals.

Only twice in its history has the *Journal* ever suffered serious strikes. The first was in 1967, when stereotypers struck the paper's Silver Spring, Maryland, plant outside Washington, and other blue-collar workers honored their pickets. But by then the company was awash with mechanically competent executives. Most of the Dow Jones national production managers descended on the Silver Spring plant the next day, rolled up their sleeves, and resumed printing the paper. After three days the strikers gave up and went back to work.

The second walkout came in 1970, just after the paper opened its South Brunswick, New Jersey, plant near New York City. The New York truck drivers boldly attempted to assert union jurisdiction over the New Jersey plant's entire operation—from presses to mailroom. The strike lasted a little over a week before the truck drivers gave up. The company simply delivered the newspaper via the U.S. Post Office, as it had long been accustomed to doing in other parts of the country.

Dow Jones' ability to behave rationally toward unions was enhanced by the leverage it gained from being a national newspaper. By the mid-sixties the company had so many printing plants so widely dispersed that it was impossible for a local union to do much damage by shutting down any one of them because the extra burden could easily be shifted to another plant. But even without this leverage, the company had always taken a fairly straightforward approach toward labor that was far more enlightened than the rest of the industry. Labor talks at other large papers usually involved so many theatrics, such bombastic threats and accusations, that neither side really had much idea where the other stood. The Dow Jones management tried to state a position and stick to it. The company generally aimed to pay decent wages, but it would not be played for a sucker. In the *Journal's* suburban Washington plant, vice-president William Dunn's management team once began negotiations with printers by announcing that the company would pay them $50 a week less than printers were making at *The Washington Post.* "We thought the *Post's* salaries were insane," Dunn recalled, "and our printers finally admitted that they didn't understand why the *Post* paid so much either."

There was another, more tangible difference between working conditions at a newspaper like the *Post* and *The Wall Street Journal.* During the 1970s, if one walked through the composing room of almost any large, unionized newspaper, it was impossible to ignore the tension in the air, the increasingly sullen attitude of the blue-collar men that would climax, in October 1975, with several workers sabotaging and setting fire to the *Post*'s presses and beating the night foreman. If someone from the news department inadvertently touched a piece of type instead of pointing at it, shouting would break out, perhaps even an exchange of blows. The blue-collar printers had become jealously defensive of their turf, and they viewed nearly everyone else—the management, the editors, the reporters—as a threat to their security. Most of them had ceased to care about the larger enterprise in which they were involved—the publication of a daily newspaper— and it was probably just as true that their newspaper's management had ceased to care about them.

Such tension was conspicuously absent at the *Journal,* where, for the most part, even low-level employees took pride in the enterprise. It helped, of course, that Dow Jones & Company was growing at a frantic pace, creating new job opportunities in one part of the company as quickly as they were foreclosed elsewhere. It also helped that Dow Jones' printing plants were cleaner and more pleasant places than most, and in a curious way it may also have helped that these printing plants—located far outside the cities they were intended to serve—paid reasonably well but not as much as most big-city dailies. It was not a place where one worked to get rich. Most people seemed to work there because they liked it, and in the decades of newspaper automation, that kind of employee loyalty was all but extinct.

CHAPTER **8**

Innocents Abroad

THE NEWSPAPER'S FIRST major investigative story grew out of a press release delivered to the Chicago news bureau in October 1952. The reclusive Howard Hughes was announcing the sale of his controlling interest in RKO Pictures to a retailing concern called the Empire Mail Order Company. The news was briefly noted in the *Journal,* as elsewhere, then forgotten by all but the newly installed managing editor, Henry Gemmill, the editor who, next to Kilgore, would leave perhaps the greatest mark on the newspaper.

Gemmill was the first managing editor who really understood how much the *Journal* needed to break big, attention-getting stories in order to gain respect and prestige. He wanted the Chicago bureau to find out more about Empire Mail Order. At first the bureau turned up nothing, so Gemmill tossed the story to Tom Wise, who covered retailing in New York. But Wise's sources had never heard of Empire Mail either. Exasperated, Gemmill sent orders back to Chicago to forget about trying to locate the company and concentrate instead on tracking down the executives named in the Hughes press release.

A year earlier Dow Jones had bought the *Chicago Journal of Commerce* from Ridder Publishing for $1.5 million, renaming it *The Chicago Journal of Commerce Edition of The Wall Street Journal* and firing most of the reporters there. Ames Smithers, a rare survivor from the *Journal of Commerce,* placed a desperation call to the Chicago Crime Commission, which yielded a small lead: One of the Empire Mail Order principals had been linked to some petty mail-order frauds.

With that slight bit of information, Gemmill organized the newspaper's first investigative team. A few weeks later the *Journal* published a series of articles linking nearly all of the men at Empire Mail Order to gangster activities. Hughes had to cancel the RKO sale, which so deeply upset him that for weeks afterward he persisted in calling various *Journal* executives in the wee hours to complain. The RKO-Empire Mail stories won the *Journal* a Sigma Delta Chi public service award, its first major reporting prize. But the Pulitzer Prize Committee, guardians of daily journalism's holy grail, only sneered. They dismissed the *Journal's* stories as "special interest" and proceeded to bestow their big public service prize upon the *St. Louis Post-Dispatch* again.

Gemmill was, at least in Kilgore's view, the finest writer the newspaper had ever had. He had been front-page editor for the previous four years and before that the star of the *Journal's* critically important rewrite desk. A droll, literary sort of man, Gemmill was virtually unknown, even to regular readers of the *Journal.* His by-line almost never appeared, but his prose sparkled throughout the newspaper. When Gemmill finally did fulfill an old fantasy and become London correspondent in 1955, one of his first by-lined pieces in years would begin:

> Britain's scheme of socialized medicine has a little brother you should know—socialized law. He's four and a half years old, and growing like crazy.
> Instead of offering free false teeth, Legal Aid puts the public purse behind those who have the urge to litigate but not enough money to pay the lawyers. . . . Amy Edith Gwendoline Greenwood was taken to divorce court by her husband, Herbert, who had the socialized suing system backing his claim

that she refused to let him bathe more than once a week. But
the judge granted the decree to the wife instead, noting Mr.
Greenwood had once written her: "The best Christmas present
you could give me would be to jump in the river."

As front-page editor, Gemmill had elevated the fourth-column
A-head story to something of an art form, applying his characteristic dry wit, but as managing editor Gemmill knew that no
amount of literary polish would be sufficient to catapult the paper
into the front ranks of journalism. The *Journal* was still regarded
as a narrow business publication—a neat piece of packaging perhaps, but no *tour de force*. Gemmill was the man who would change
that.

Howard Hughes intrigued Gemmill. Tom Wise and Dick
Cooke dug further into the reclusive financier's affairs and picked
up a rumor that a syndicate composed of financier Spyros
Skouras, real estate developer William Zeckendorf and various
members of the Rockefeller clan was preparing to pay half a
billion dollars for Hughes' entire empire, including Hughes Tool,
Hughes Aircraft, and Trans World Airlines. Naturally the rumor
was hard to nail down. After discussing the problem with Cooke
on a sweltering day in the airless newsroom, Gemmill pounded
his desk and declared: "I'm going to call Skouras as managing
editor of *The Wall Street Journal* and demand to know whether
or not he's going to buy out Howard Hughes." Gemmill dialed
Skouras' office, got the tycoon on the phone, and asked his question. Gemmill recalled Skouras hesitating, then saying nervously:
"Mr. Gemmill, I am perspiring."

"We are all perspiring, Mr. Skouras," Gemmill said impatiently.

"Yes, Mr. Gemmill, we are all perspiring," Skouras continued,
"but *my* office has a new air conditioner."

Skouras' grudging confirmation of the rumor unfortunately
did not make it altogether true. As it happened, Howard Hughes
had no intention of selling his beloved companies. Like many a
rich man, he simply enjoyed counting his money, and who better
to assess his holdings for him than a clique of the smartest financiers in New York, who thought they were being asked to buy
them?

Such classic Hughes tales made good reading, even if their importance was open to question. But Gemmill also produced stories of considerable weight. He had Joe Guilfoyle spend months researching the housing industry to find out why new homes had become so expensive. Guilfoyle turned in a series of articles explaining that the two main reasons for escalating housing costs were the proliferation of inefficient building ordinances at the local level and labor insufficiencies—matters of common knowledge now perhaps, but real revelations in 1951. Gemmill also had the newspaper buy a transcript of Estes Kefauver's landmark Senate hearings on underworld crime. The editor picked out a minor footnote in the transcript that linked Mafia members to some commercial laundries and launched an investigation that ended in a spate of stories about gangsters penetrating legitimate business. Later, after the Watergate scandal spawned a generation of "investigative reporters," Gemmill would find the term pretentious. "I never drew a distinct line between exposé and ordinary reporting," he would say. "The essence of what we did was allowing reporters great time when a story seemed interesting."

The story that finally put the *Journal* on the map, at least so far as other newspapers were concerned, came about in the least expected way. The subject was not a big-time crook, a mysterious tycoon, or a shady politician, but General Motors Corporation, which would stun the newspaper into recognizing that writing tough-minded business stories was as difficult as any job in journalism.

The reporter was named John Williams, a square-built, swarthy man with a reputation at the *Journal* for tenacity. Another DePauw scholarship student, Williams had been hired by Buren McCormack in 1947. He started in the *Journal's* bond section, went to Washington as a junior reporter, and then returned to New York to cover the textile industry, in the throes of upheaval because of newly introduced synthetic fibers. In October 1951 Gemmill asked Williams to move to Detroit to run what the managing editor considered the newspaper's weakest bureau.

After Washington and New York, Detroit was also the *Journal's* most important bureau. The auto industry was exploding, as car-crazed consumers rushed to put money down on whatever tail-finned extravaganza Detroit wanted to sell them. The difficulty lay in getting any real news from Detroit. The reporters there had been successfully co-opted by the auto industry, which was said to have at least one public relations man on salary for every reporter in town.

The ethics of business reporting in that era were none too strict anywhere. In New York even the lowliest *Journal* reporter could expect to cart home a load of Christmas gifts that included, say, a case or two of whiskey, a dozen highball glasses, and a couple of turkeys—all from people in the PR trade. In Detroit the Yuletide largess exceeded the wildest extremes. Reporters might get golf clubs, cars, almost anything they were not too timid to request—including, some believed, a little female companionship. Henry Gemmill was troubled not so much by the ethics of the situation as by the Detroit bureau's meager news output. The bureau chief, William Black, was an old hand who reportedly did not take kindly to New York's suggestions. Soon after Williams' arrival he would leave to work for Chrysler. Gemmill surmised that the reason the *Journal* got so little news from Detroit—though it got no less than other publications—was that before a reporter had thought to ask a question, the industry had already told him the answer—"off-the-record."

There is an important code of honor among news people. If a source begins a conversation by specifying that it is "not for attribution," then the reporter can print everything he hears, so long as he does not identify the source. But if the source specifies "off-the-record," then the information is for background use only. The reporter cannot print it unless he can verify it elsewhere or talk the source into altering the terms of the conversation. The auto companies wielded this gentlemanly code like a garrote, choking off any kind of news that the industry did not want printed: not just news of industry intrigue, but almost anything that did not square with the auto manufacturers' carefully choreographed plans for self-promotion. The Detroit news corps had become a captive to the auto companies' public relations departments. From the typewriters of Motor City correspondents flowed a steady stream of stories glorifying the automakers and their products, which, to be sure, were already the apple of every consumer's eye. Detroit reciprocated in kind, entertaining the reporters royally, elevating them to a social status in opulent Grosse Pointe that made them feel on a par with the up-and-coming auto executives. It was sheer flattery, of course.

Into this Circean den of wood-paneled club life and lavish cocktail parties wandered John Williams, a shy, newly married *Journal* reporter in his mid-twenties, who worked Monday through Saturday for less than $100 a week. Gemmill says his brief instructions to him were: "Don't take *anything* off-the-record."

From his first day in Detroit, Williams began to feel the social pressures of the place close in on him. He was admitted to the Presbyterian church in Grosse Pointe, where the minister kept invoking names of the high and mighty parishioners who ran the auto companies. The senior Associated Press man invited Williams to join a fraternity called the Off-the-Record Club, a correspondents' group that huddled regularly with industry executives to discuss business—for background only. Williams thanked the AP man but had to decline on Gemmill's instructions. They got to talking about the reporter's life in Detroit. "One thing you should never do," the veteran reporter counseled, "is write about new car models before they are announced." His reasoning was that the auto companies spent millions designing promotional campaigns for the new models each year, planning their unveiling as if the event were of earthshaking significance. Reporters had an unspoken agreement not to interfere.

Eager to break new ground, Williams quickly set about writing such a story about forthcoming changes on 1953 models, but when it appeared that summer, nobody paid any attention, possibly because there were no major design changes in the '53 models. Williams soon turned to more pressing developments: the razzle-dazzle of auto sales, the dramatic wage increases won by a newly independent United Auto Workers, and the merger of Nash and Hudson into American Motors. There was plenty to report without making waves.

Williams did not attempt another scoop on new model changes until two years later, in the spring of 1954, when Detroit was abuzz with rumors that the 1955 models would introduce a sleek, powerful new generation of cars, a radical departure from the tanklike vehicles of the Korean War era. He spent several weeks talking to people in Detroit's tool and die shops, which were already at work on the '55 models, and he talked to auto company executives about what their competition was up to. In the end he was able to assemble a fairly comprehensive view of the entire field. Better yet, he obtained blueprints of several new models.

Williams' front-page story of May 28, 1954, began:

> Forecast for 1955 auto models: More makes will be thoroughly restyled than ever before in the half century of automotive history. Under many of the hoods will be new, more muscular engines.
>
> Ford, Chevy, Mercury and Pontiac, Lincoln and Packard will get that greenhouse look by joining the wrap-around windshield trend.
>
> Dodge and Plymouth, which two years ago were shortened enough to fit into tighter parking spaces, will be stretched back out—because it seems the populace loves the long, sleek look.

Williams' real coups, however, were the drawings of the '55 Ford, Chevy, and Dodge that appeared on page ten of the *Journal*. Because of the newspaper's infrequent use of pictures, they looked more than a little like an advertisement.

The resulting furor did not surface until more than a week later, when *Advertising Age* reported that General Motors had canceled all of its advertising in *The Wall Street Journal*—a quarter-million dollars' worth a year, big money for the newspaper. Harlow Curtice, the president of GM, fumed that the *Journal* was guilty not just of a breach of confidence, but of illegal copyright infringements as well. Letters poured in from auto dealers around the United States, complaining that Williams' story would stifle sales of current car models and throw thousands of men out of work. The country's most important industry seemed to have its hands around the *Journal*'s throat.

In New York, Kilgore and his men brooded over the problem. There may have been something to what Curtice said: blueprints probably *were* protected by copyright, and yet the *Journal* could not be seen bending under pressure. Hence, Kilgore staked out a bold position for the paper on the editorial page:

> A newspaper exists only to provide information for its readers; it has no other reason for being. It provides that service only so long as it diligently seeks out what is happening and reports it as accurately and clearly as it can. . . . When a newspaper begins to suppress the news, whether at the behest of its advertisers or pleas from special segments of business, it will soon cease to be of any service, either to its advertisers or to business, because it will soon cease to have readers.

Williams was an instant outcast in Detroit. *Ward's Automotive Reports,* the industry bible, canceled his subscription, he recalled. All the auto companies stopped giving him information, and GM's public relations department, representing fifty percent of the auto industry, would not even return his calls. Much of the press corps ostracized him, too. *Time's* correspondent filed a dispatch questioning the worth of Williams' reporting. "Those who have seen the new models thought that the *Journal* had picked up some old blueprints," *Time* noted. *Newsweek* was downright catty: "Detroit newsmen view the fracas with mixed emotions," it said. "Some felt that Williams was a bit too aggressive . . . for example, by opening his notebook at trade cocktail parties. And it is an old Detroit truism that any reporter can get at the news of future car plans—if he wants to break the story."

But the reaction in other quarters was quite different. While Williams may have been a villain to some of his Detroit peers, he was a hero everywhere else. Gemmill had stringers all over the country contributing piecemeal items about the auto industry to help compensate for the Detroit news blockout. The managing editor would not pull Williams out of Detroit, though there was no doubt that the industry wanted his head on a platter. Other newspapers as well as members of the advertising community noted the *Journal's* gallant stand against its most important single advertiser, and the paper suddenly found itself lionized as a symbol of courage and integrity. General Motors, on the other hand, looked like a bully trying to intimidate a young reporter who had only done his job. "For years," Kilgore told reporters from other papers, "almost everything in Detroit has been 'off-the-record.' We just decided not to play it that way. It isn't journalism."

GM called off its advertising boycott after two months, following a round of meetings with Kilgore. Both sides agreed to let the other save face. Kilgore issued a statement saying: "We have no desire to injure or transgress property rights." And Curtice apologized: "It was never our intention to interfere in any way with [the *Journal*'s] publication of news." But the *Journal* had won. It recovered its advertising without compromising its important new status as a business newspaper that did not cower or cater to the interests of advertisers. In the long run its new-won reputation was worth inestimably more than the General Motors advertising account.

Williams, unfortunately, could not take immediate pleasure in his new role as hero. The auto industry, he recalled, continued to make life miserable for him during the two remaining years that Gemmill felt compelled to keep him in Detroit. To move Williams to some other bureau might have looked like an act of contrition, and the *Journal* could not risk that. In 1956 the newspaper did finally transfer Williams, naming him assistant managing editor of the Chicago edition to emphasize that his transfer was a promotion. His replacement as Detroit bureau chief was Dan Cordtz, an affable young reporter whom the industry mistakenly expected to be far more malleable than John Williams. General Motors threw a lavish welcoming party for Cordtz at its glistening Recess Club on the top floor of the Fisher Building. The company wanted the new *Journal* bureau chief to know that, as far as GM was concerned, the era of bad feelings was past. Cordtz said that one of the first to greet him was a General Motors public relations man. "Call on us anytime, Dan," the P.R. man told him with a smile. "We'll give you anything but information."

"He wasn't kidding," Cordtz would later recollect.

Gemmill wanted to improve the *Journal*'s foreign coverage, which had always been embarrassingly scant. Partly because he personally harbored an ambition to be a foreign correspondent,

Gemmill says he knew how difficult it was to persuade Kilgore to send anyone of talent overseas. The paper had groped its way through World War II with just two men abroad—George Ormsby in London and Charles Hargrove in Paris—both holdovers from the Clarence Barron era. Afterward, it had signed on a capable London stringer named Joseph Evans. Coverage, however, remained spotty. Lack of international reporting perhaps had been forgivable during the war, when the *Journal* was still fighting for survival. But by the late forties, the newspaper was thriving. Larger papers and wire services were now recalling their correspondents from abroad, leaving the European recovery—the biggest economic story of the fifties—almost wholly uncovered.

Part of the problem at the *Journal* was that Barney Kilgore and his fellow Midwesterners were isolationists at heart. Almost none of them had ever traveled outside the United States, not even in wartime. Apart from their somewhat provincial worries over the spread of world Communism, they saw little of real interest beyond the American shores.

William Henry Grimes, editor of the editorial page, was perhaps the major influence on the newspaper's intellectual character, for Kilgore preferred publishing to politics. Grimes' editorial page reflected his stolid Middlewestern convictions. Often it sounded oafishly narrow-minded. As late as the spring of 1941, for example, Grimes had written:

> . . . Four-fifths of us don't want war. One-fifth does. Pretty soon the one-fifth plans to say to the four-fifths something like this: "Well, whether you like it or not, you are in a war. So get about the business of fighting it."
> It won't work. It never has. France tried it. Mussolini tried it. They drove luke-warm people to war. They met disaster.

After Pearl Harbor, of course, the *Journal* swung around foursquare behind the war effort, supporting such necessary evils as price controls and rationing that it would have abhorred in normal times. But five years of war would not end the newspaper's parochialism. Once there was peace again, the *Journal* lost most of its interest in Europe, apart from worrying about the Soviets. The Marshall Plan, for example, President Truman's program to forestall the spread of Communism by speeding European recovery, got only lukewarm support from the *Journal*.

Grimes' influence went well beyond the editorial page. Ever since he had helped Kilgore to topple Joe Ackell from the Dow Jones leadership in 1942, Grimes had been the paper's elder statesman. Grimes' shadow extended even further after 1947, the year he won the Pulitzer Prize for editorial writing, the first Pulitzer in the paper's history. Though self-educated, he was a forceful essayist whose earthy imagery lent an air of Mid-American common sense. He would describe the elusive effects of inflation—always his pet demon—as "eating the paint off the roof," and he would compare some of the farfetched claims made by liberal dogmatists to the sort of yarn an Ohio farmer could take in stride:

> Like the two-headed calf which always is born in the next county, the success of the managed economy always seems to be taking place at some distance; the greater the distance, the larger the claims for success.

In October 1946, when former Vice-President Henry A. Wallace, one of Grimes' particular *bêtes noires,* was named editor of the liberal *New Republic,* the crusty editorialist penned a two-sentence riposte with the headline "Justice":

> Henry Wallace has become editor of the *New Republic.* We suggest that it serves them both right.

In the news department Grimes' role was that of editor emeritus. Kilgore, Kerby, and McCormack often deferred to his judgment, especially in political matters. In the late 1950s, for example, *Journal* reporters still were forbidden to use the word "liberal," except in quotation marks, to describe someone's political views. Both Grimes and Kilgore thought the adjective sounded unseemly. Hence, people to the left of center were usually called "New Dealers," even if they had still been in knee pants during the early years of the Roosevelt Presidency.

Fortunately Kilgore and his men ignored Grimes' stubborn conservatism where the future of the newspaper was involved. In 1951, when Kilgore persuaded Laurence Lombard and the Dow Jones heiresses to pay $1.5 million for the *Chicago Journal of Commerce*, Grimes was vehemently opposed, believing that the purchase would bankrupt the company. In his mind the launching of the *Pacific Coast Edition* in 1929 was forever linked to the stock market crash and the Depression. He seemed convinced that the Chicago venture would bring on some similar debacle. On the day that negotiations for the purchase were completed, Grimes' lurked in the corridor outside the office of his protégé, Bill Kerby. When Kerby finally emerged, he recalls that Grimes grabbed his sleeve and said hoarsely, "Bill, I want you to stop by the newsroom on your way out. Those people are all your friends. Many you hired. You know their wives and their children. Then think to yourself, 'I'm on my way to ruin Dow Jones and put all these people out of work.' "

The sale went through, of course, but Grimes' sentiments were not completely lost. For decades to come the company would proceed with extraordinary caution, as if on tiptoe, gaining in size and influence almost despite itself.

Early in 1949 a gangling young man appeared in Bill Kerby's office to say that he had been offered an opportunity in Germany with *Stars and Stripes*, the U.S. armed forces newspaper, and that he was going to take it unless there might be some chance of his going overseas for the *Journal.* "Oh, there's no future in that, Warren," Kerby assured him, not really believing that the fellow would be so foolish as to leave.

Warren Henry Phillips was a sober youth of twenty-two, the son of a garment industry man. He had grown up and gone to college in Queens, and if he did not see something of the world now, he feared that he probably never would. He had been with the *Journal* for less than two years, first as a proofreader, then on the copydesk rim, and finally in the tricky job of writing front-page news capsules. Phillips was plainly very smart, and he was not a man who made a great many mistakes. Quitting the *Journal* to work in Europe would turn out to be a pretty smart move.

While the resignation of a twenty-two-year-old might not cause much stir in most offices, the *Journal* was desperately short of talent, and Phillips had clearly been on the rise. Most of the top men in the newsroom viewed him as a bit of a turncoat. They were all working twelve- and fourteen-hour days, and here this promising young deskman on his way up was quitting on what seemed to be a whim. But Henry Gemmill secretly envied him. He confessed regret at not having done something similar at Phillips' age. The front-page editor—who was soon to become managing editor—took Phillips aside and assured him that he was making a wise move. And he told Phillips that the *Journal* would welcome any stories that he felt like sending from Europe as a freelance. Gemmill made the offer sound casual, but in fact he had had to twist Buren McCormack's arm to get approval for it, for McCormack was among those who resented Phillips. Still, Gemmill never expected Warren Phillips to write much. After all, Phillips had never even been a reporter.

Phillips arrived in Frankfurt that February feeling "footloose and itchy." The job on the *Stars and Stripes* copydesk from 3 p.m. to 11 p.m. was not terribly stimulating, he recalled, so he began using his morning hours to report for the *Journal*, writing story after story about the situation in West Germany: the refugees, the economy, the emerging political state. At first his work amounted to well-researched memos, usually three times too long. He sent them to New York by regular mail because the *Journal* would not pay telegraph costs. Gemmill gave his work to Betty Donnelly, one of the few female holdovers from the war and one of the best hands on the rewrite bank. Occasionally, Gemmill remembers, Miss Donnelly sent Phillips a note explaining why she had made certain changes in his writing, but for the most part, Phillips seemed to figure it out for himself. At any rate, his stories came closer and closer to the mark until they were nearly perfect, and Warren Phillips' by-line was among the most frequent in the newspaper. He was devoting mornings, weekends, and vacations to reporting for the paper, and by late summer Gemmill was able to persuade his superiors that they could save money by hiring Phillips back as their regular Bonn correspondent, rather than paying freelance rates for his voluminous output.

Phillips was back on the *Journal* staff by September. That winter he was dispatched to London to help cover a big election in which Britain's Labour Party under Clement Attlee narrowly averted defeat by Winston Churchill's Tories. Phillips was working under George Ormsby and Joe Evans, now foreign editor, who had flown in from New York for the campaign. Ormsby died of a sudden heart attack, and when Evans returned to New York, Phillips, twenty-three, became the *Journal's* top man in London.

Warren Phillips was not the sort of London correspondent one might have expected to represent the *Journal*. He struck others as a skinny, self-contained fellow, neither slick nor outgoing, and he was certainly not the type who made a big first impression; otherwise, he might never have come to work for the *Journal* in the first place. Though Phillips had been editor of the school newspaper at Queens College and worked as a part-time copyboy for *The New York Times* and the *Herald Tribune,* both papers had turned him down for a permanent job, he said. So had the *Journal-American,* the *World-Telegram,* the *Sun,* the *Post,* and the *Daily News.* He was even turned down by the glossy Columbia School of Journalism, the news profession's top employment agency. Phillips applied at *The Wall Street Journal* as a last resort. Having been a Socialist as a student, he confesses he was not much intrigued by the thought of becoming a financial journalist. On the other hand, his next stop probably would have been at some trade publication or some paper in New Jersey, a place of perdition for a born New Yorker. And so when Kerby and McCormack offered work as a proofreader, Phillips took it. At least the job was inside a newsroom.

Phillips was quiet and unassuming. Nothing stood out about him except his ability. He never seemed ruffled or hard-pressed, but his output was double anyone else's. Besides shrewdness and intelligence, he possessed immense discipline, a mind that never dwelled on anything without purpose. Phillips had a quick sense of humor that surfaced infrequently, though he was always more or less pleasant. But the thing about Phillips that really struck everyone sooner or later was his efficiency. Warren Phillips got things done.

In London he turned out stories at a blistering pace, stories about the rise of Socialism, about the titanic clashes between the Labour and Tory Parties, about U.S. Secretary of State John Foster Dulles' efforts to frighten the Europeans into shouldering some of the defense burden against Russia. Though not the most colorful of writers, he was a thorough reporter, and he had a grasp of what was wanted. Phillips sent back lively coverage of the 1951 election, when Churchill finally barged back into power; then he chronicled the Churchill government's futile efforts at "denationalizing" industry and pushing back the welfare state. Inevitably Phillips was acquiring an internationalist viewpoint that was worlds apart from his bosses' perspective in New York. He was beginning to understand, for example, that while the word "capitalism" implied all the fruits of free enterprise in the United States, Europeans associated it with the uncompetitive nature of their own large corporations.

What surprised everyone was how adept the reticent Phillips could be in his formal role as the newspaper's London envoy. Touring the continent to view the post-war rubble was becoming fashionable for Americans, and gradually the brass at *The Wall Street Journal* began shucking their xenophobia. First came Oliver Gingold, the British-born stock market columnist who had been with the paper since 1900, then William Henry Chamberlain, one of Grimes' editorial page writers. Jessie Bancroft Cox, one of the newspaper's principal owners, came through with her husband, Bill. While Mr. Cox liked to retire early, his wife often wanted to dance the night away, so Phillips would make sure that a bachelor reporter was available to take her out on the town.

At last William Henry Grimes himself appeared. The flinty editorialist had never been outside the United States before, but someone, apparently Laurence Lombard, the Bancroft family attorney, persuaded him that he ought to go. They made an odd contrast—Grimes, the crusty small-towner, and Phillips, the skinny young New Yorker. Phillips was acquiring a cosmopolitan air, a quality that normally made Grimes suspicious. Phillips, according to lore, greeted the older man and showed him to his room at the Savoy Hotel. "What's this thing?" Grimes demanded, eyeing the bidet. With a perfectly straight face, Phillips told him that the fixture was a European device for chilling champagne. "By golly," Grimes said with a nod, "they do have a few things over here that we haven't thought of at home."

Grimes appeared in the *Journal* offices around the corner on

The Strand brandishing copies of his favorite tract, Andrew Dickson White's 1876 essay, "Paper-Money Inflation in France," to which Grimes frequently alluded in his editorials and which he had had reprinted. Doubtless he bestowed the pamphlets upon *Journal* reporters as a kind of prophylactic against the libertine ideas that he thought were infecting Europe. For his part Phillips was careful to treat Grimes as a visiting dignitary, arranging private interviews with cabinet members, leaders of the opposition, and important industrialists. Grimes' visit concluded with a banquet to which Phillips invited the *Journal*'s most impressive sources. Grimes was bowled over. Not only were these Londoners alert and intelligent, but, contrary to expectation, they actually admired the United States; they knew of *The Wall Street Journal;* and, wonder of wonders, they were eager to court its chief editorialist.

William Henry Grimes reportedly returned to New York brimming with new interest in Europe and singing the praises of the young London bureau chief. Thereafter, he was a regular visitor to Britain and the Continent, interviewing ministers and heads of state, much as Clarence Barron once had. By the end of 1951, Grimes is said to have persuaded Kilgore and everyone else who counted that Warren Phillips was a whiz kid. In late 1951 they recalled him to New York to take over as foreign editor at the age of twenty-five. A few months later Grimes was at the Savoy again, dining with Phillips' London replacement, Edward Hughes. When Phillips' name came up, says Hughes, Grimes remarked: "Warren's going to be editor one of these days."

Foreign reporting became increasingly important to the *Journal* once Phillips was installed as foreign editor. In addition, the veteran Paris correspondent Charles Hargrove retired in 1952, opening the way for a young replacement, Al Jeffcoat, who had been fully schooled in the *Journal*'s front-page feature-writing techniques. The New York editors were beginning to realize that international coverage could be more than dry analysis of foreign finance. It could, in fact, help broaden the newspaper in precisely the way that Kilgore wanted, giving an intelligent, entertaining picture of the world unavailable in other newspapers.

From London and Paris *Journal* reporters covered Europe, Africa, and Asia. They could afford to spend a few weeks on each story because the appetite for foreign stories remained limited. Thus *Journal* readers began learning about such far-flung subjects as the Mau Maus in Kenya, the DeBeers diamond monopoly in South Africa, copper mining in Rhodesia, and the young colonels who had overthrown King Faruk in Egypt, in addition to the substance of European politics and economics.

For the most part the editors were content to leave foreign reporting to youngsters. Most of the major foreign stories went to the more senior men in Washington, like W. C. Bryant and Al Clark. But now and then the London and Paris bureaus had to handle stories of real consequence. Ed Hughes, for instance, interviewed a pajama-clad Premier Mossadegh of Iran shortly before the U.S. Central Intelligence Agency contrived to overthrow him.

In January 1952 Hughes and Jeffcoat were on a ski trip in Davos, Switzerland, when a cable arrived from William Henry Grimes. Through his contacts in the Republican party, Grimes had prevailed upon a press-shy General Eisenhower to grant the *Journal* an exclusive interview. The only real reason for interest in such an interview was Ike's personal political plans. Moderate Republicans were attempting to push the war hero into running for President, but Eisenhower steadfastly refused to indicate his intentions. The telegram ordered one of the men to break off the ski trip and proceed to Eisenhower's military outpost in Paris. Hughes and Jeffcoat considered the assignment a long shot, so they flipped a coin to decide who would go. Hughes lost and had to hurry to Paris to negotiate with Eisenhower's press aide. With his minimal knowledge of U.S. politics, the young London correspondent says he was "filled with horror at the whole project. Horror turned to shivering panic when I contacted the press aide, who warned me, of course *NOT* to bring up politics during the interview. 'But . . . but . . .' I burbled. 'No buts about it,' said the aide. 'No politics!' "

The agonized Hughes debated whether to phone New York and beg off the story. He reached for the telephone several times but caught himself short. Mr. Grimes doesn't like that kind of failure, he thought, and before he could think further he was whisked into General Eisenhower's massive office.

"He was reading some document," recalled Hughes, "and left me standing there for minutes until he curtly waved me to a seat. Then he stood up, grabbed a stick and turned toward a huge map as if to say, 'Well, here are the Russians, and here we are . . .' Indeed, he was off on a fifteen-minute military briefing and it was only with great difficulty that I could stop and get in a quavering question on American politics and his plans.

"This made him apoplectic, and he reminded me sternly that he had always refused to talk about this to the press. At which point, he did indeed proceed to talk about exactly that. I didn't want to take notes, for that might turn him off, so I tried to memorize. Anyway, he made it abundantly clear that he wanted nothing of politics and would not campaign.

"His tirade on the subject lasted a good twenty minutes, at the end of which I fled. And I fled straight to the nearest men's room and locked myself into a cubicle, sat down and scribbled notes for a good half an hour. Outside my booth I noticed highly polished boots and shoes pacing back and forth, visible through the slit under the door. Finally, I realized I was in the generals' can. I hastily wound up and stepped outside to finish scribbling in the corridor. Who did I find waiting but General Montgomery!"

Hughes' big scoop ran the next day, January 14, under the first two-column headline in the *Journal* since Pearl Harbor. The headline: "The Really Reluctant 'Candidate'; Eisenhower Is Hoping He Won't Be Nominated." This was not to be the *Journal*'s most prophetic moment, for less than two months later Eisenhower was campaigning for the White House with demonstrable enthusiasm.

Vermont Connecticut Royster was the only one of Kilgore's close disciples absent during the war. He had spent five years as a reporter in Kilgore's Washington bureau before accepting an ensign's commission in 1941. Upon Royster's return from the Navy in 1945, Kilgore immediately installed him as the new Washington bureau chief. Kilgore knew talent when he saw it, and Vermont Royster—"Roy" to his colleagues—was among his best.

Royster was the great exception to all the rules of office behavior at *The Wall Street Journal.* Where others made a great show of submerging their egos for the good of the newspaper, Royster never hid his ambition to make a name for himself. Where others hung around the office for ten, twelve, or fourteen hours a day, Royster was apparently so brilliant that he seemed to get his work done in no time at all. He purposely disdained the Hoosier affectations with which he felt Kerby and others venerated Kilgore. Royster admired the boss, too, but by his own admission he couldn't bring himself to don baggy clothes and middle-class mannerisms. Royster wore natty suits and kept his tie straightened, even on the most torrid summer days. Rather than loosen his collar and yank down his tie in the Kilgore style, he would tuck a white handkerchief around his neck to soak up perspiration. He obviously wanted people to know that he was a proper North Carolinian, an upholder of civilized customs and concerns. The outcome of the Civil War remained a deeply personal matter to him, or at least he behaved as though it did. And at dinner with other journalists, he might open the conversation by asking whom they considered the most interesting man in fourth-century Greece.

The term "Southern gentleman" did not quite befit Royster, for he was feisty and contentious. He had a cracker-barrel patter that was funny and engaging, but despite great charm, others saw him as professionally cantankerous. Colleagues say Royster loved to niggle and criticize people, but he did it so artfully that they always forgave. He could seem terribly arrogant, but as a young man he had evidently learned to adopt the privileged airs of a senior citizen. Thus equipped, he could get away with sometimes outrageous behavior. Once, wanting a new desk chair, Royster took to phoning Kilgore's personal assistant, Bill McSherry, almost every hour for two days, McSherry relates. *"McSweeny,"* he would drawl, purposely abusing the man's name, "where's the goddamned chair?"

Royster's upbringing was as old-fashioned as he wished his demeanor to seem. Descended from a long line of school teachers, his father, Wilbur, had taught Latin, Greek, and law at the University of North Carolina. Royster's great-great-grandfather had had seven children and had named all of them after states in the union, and Royster's father had revived the idea. Royster's father was a stickler for traditions of all sorts. "He never made peace with the twentieth century," Royster would say rather proudly. Wilbur Royster started drilling the classics into little Vermont before the boy could read or write English. "A six-year-old can delight in chanting *tango, tangere, tetigi, tactus,*" Royster would later explain. Formal Latin study began at eight. For prep school he was shipped to Webb School in Bellbuckle, Tennessee, which required four years of Latin and two of Greek. "They had a fellow there and he'd make you write an essay of 265 or 389 words and you had to write it just that way. You had to go and count them because you couldn't have one word more or one word less. He taught me discipline."

Disciplined or not, Royster found that he did not need to work very hard as a classics major back at Chapel Hill. It was two years before he read anything in college Latin that he hadn't mastered in high school. As a consequence he turned to *The Daily Tarheel* for excitement, having acquired a taste for sports writing at Webb because it meant that "all those giants on the football team began to treat me like I was somebody."

Graduating Phi Beta Kappa in 1935, he quickly discovered that classics scholars were in limited demand. In New York he took jobs as a busboy and a bank messenger, and made futile applications to every newspaper in town. At last he found temporary work with the City News Bureau, a wire service for local newspapers, where he covered night court, fires, and a few police precincts. He had gotten the job of an older man who'd been taken ill, but after a few months the man returned, and Royster was out on the street again. In desperation he applied to the parochial *Wall Street Journal,* and William Henry Grimes, liking him, hired him as a "temporary." (Twenty-two years later, when Royster asked Kilgore to make his job permanent, Kilgore would answer: "Let's not rush things.") Royster's first job had been in the stock exchange comparison room, scoring the Dow Jones news ticker against Tammany's. After a few months Grimes asked

Royster if he would go to Washington as a clerk. He had planned on staying at the *Journal* for only a few years, then moving on to a "good paper" like the *Sun* or the *Telegram,* but Washington sounded interesting, so Royster shrugged and agreed. The job was not much—taking dictation from reporters over the telephone, helping out on the copydesk—but the *Journal* was a loosely structured place then, especially in Kilgore's Washington bureau. Within a few months Royster had tagged along to his first Presidential press conference, then an intimate deskside affair. That summer Kilgore thought that Royster should at least witness the Democratic Convention, though he had no official business there. The *Journal* would pay expenses for only two reporters, Kilgore and Mike Flynn, so the bureau chief himself bought Royster a ticket and pushed him aboard the train to Philadelphia.

Royster soon evolved into the most graceful of writers. He had the mind of a classical logician, but his prose had no sharp edges. Royster almost never yielded to hyperbole, the common vice of journalists; rather, he used words with such precision that his writing took on a magical combination of gentleness and force. Traveling the small towns and industrial centers of the Midwest to record the 1950 political campaigns, he would write from Akron:

> The inside of the foundry was dirty and deafening. The floor was littered with shavings and fragments of flying scrap. Giant track-hoists zipped overhead daintily carrying two-ton thimbles of molten metal.
> . . . Through it all the tall, bald, bespectacled man neatly dressed in a gray suit, felt hat and light topcoat plodded from press to pit. . . . Robert A. Taft looked as much at home in this foundry as a sandhog at a tea party.

And from Vienna, Illinois:

> Under the hot sun of a southern Illinois Indian summer the crowd was mostly in shirt sleeves and galluses. They had come from all over Johnson County to eat catfish, to talk and to listen. The men had come from the fields in the early after-

noon, for many were not shaven and nearly all were in their
working clothes.

. . . The evangelist came, appropriately, in a rush and a cloud
of dust. Besides his own car, there were two carloads of fol-
lowers and the inevitable pickup truck equipped to take his
voice and spread it loud around the countryside. Everett
McKinley Dirksen had come to wrestle with a very live devil
as he has done some 1,500 times travelling 200,000 miles along
the Illinois roadways.

. . . After it was all over and the fish fry proceeded, one could
not be sure that he had licked his devils. Everywhere Mr. Dirksen goes he blows a lonesome trumpet.

. . . But when sundown came on a weary day no one could say
there had not been a battle. And if it should come to pass that
on election day his enemies surprised should have to ask, who
hath done this thing?—the answer in the book of Judges will
be that Gideon alone hath done this thing.

Much later in his career, Royster would reflect upon the passing
parade of news events, perhaps taking the essence of Kilgore's
newspaper philosophy to its logical end:

A little trick in this business, returning from a vacation, is to
read the accumulated papers backwards. Working from the
present to the past, many earlier stories can be skipped because
events have outmoded them. This leads to the rueful corollary—rueful at least for a news-gatherer—that many of the
stories could have been skipped in the first place. The suspicion
grows that "keeping informed" is not only frequently time
wasting but often futile.

Knowing that Singapore has seceded from Malaysia, and
agreeing that it's a sad business, what do you propose to do
about it?

Compulsively ambitious, Royster entered the Navy during
World War II determined that he would command his own ship.
In the end he commanded three of them—two submarine chasers
and an escort destroyer off Okinawa. The Navy offered him a
permanent commission, and the challenge of working his way
up to admiral seriously tempted him. But then he considered

that the best job in the Navy was the one he'd just had—ship's commander. He could not abide the idea of not moving up, but moving up in the Navy meant a bureaucratic desk job.

And so he'd returned to the *Journal*, confident that this was a place where he could enjoy getting ahead. Much had happened in the years Royster had been away. Royster looked at Kilgore's new paper and found it a bit baffling. "I didn't know what in the hell they were after, though I understood *why* they were after it. But, by God, whatever they wanted, that's what I would give them."

Royster found the bureau chief's job easy going, especially compared to his wartime work. He was a good, tough administrator and a past master at reporting, but Royster had outgrown the job, for all of its prestige. Never the most diffident of men, Royster felt increasingly frustrated in the role of objective observer. The years of naval command had added to his life considerable self-confidence. He had opinions about virtually everything, and like some allergic rash, they were bound to surface.

Keeping the Washington bureau up to snuff was child's play. Besides the old hands there, Al Clark and W. C. Bryant, Royster could have his pick of brainy young men like Al Otten and Phil Geyelin, who later shaped *The Washington Post*'s editorial page. The *Journal* now had about fifteen men in Washington, many of them eager young fellows who gladly worked sixty or seventy hours a week for $15 and hung around the office the rest of the time just in case they were needed. Competition was fierce because they knew that after two or three months they might find themselves either covering the White House or else out of a job. But at any other paper in town, they would more likely have spent a couple of years as a glorified clerk before getting to write so much as a murder story.

By tradition the *Journal*'s Washington bureau chief covered the top economic beats—the Department of the Treasury and the Federal Reserve. Royster dutifully took them on, but he soon found them tedious. He started looking for subjects that cut across more than one reporter's beat and writing essays about them. These he submitted to Grimes' editorial page under Thomas Woodlock's old rubric, "Thinking Things Over." Before

Royster knew it, he was working full time for the editorial page. One morning Royster had an appointment with Marriner Eccles, the Federal Reserve chairman. Grimes had published a particularly nasty attack on the central bank's liberal economics in that day's paper. Eccles reportedly began railing at Royster from the moment he entered. The chairman went on and on, and when Royster finally did get a chance to protest that he'd had nothing to do with the editorial, he said, Eccles began ranting anew: "I don't give a damn! I've known Bill Grimes for twenty years, and not once in all that time has he had a single new idea. Everybody knows that he belongs in the nineteenth century, but *this thing* just makes me so goddamned mad . . ."

Listening to Eccles, Royster says he perceived that no matter what people said about Grimes' editorial page—most Washingtonians hated it—they paid attention. The editorial page of *The Wall Street Journal* had a great deal more impact than most people would admit.

Grimes asked Royster to move to New York in 1948 as an associate editor of the editorial page. Royster confides that he balked at the idea of working beneath Grimes. Editorial writing was anonymous work, after all, and Royster loved both the bylines and the status of being Washington bureau chief. He extracted a promise from Grimes that he could continue as a part-time political correspondent, and Grimes reluctantly honored it. Royster wrote an analytical piece to run the Monday before Election Day. It began: "By all the polls and portents, Thomas E. Dewey will be the next President of the United States. But it's hard to say why." The article went on to say that the incumbent President Truman's campaigning was generating great crowd enthusiasm, much the opposite of Governor Dewey's stiff, *pro forma* engagements.

Grimes killed Royster's column, calling it a cruel slap at Tom Dewey, whom the *Journal* obviously favored. There was simply no sense in insulting a new President before he took office, Grimes told his young associate. Royster was incensed, as he often would be with Grimes. He later claimed to have heard that the next spring's Pulitzer Prize Committee had searched high and low for any reporter who had detected signs that Dewey would lose. "My story would have looked awfully good on the morning after," he groused.

In the end Royster would owe almost everything to Grimes, who had hired him as a youth, sent him to Washington, then recognized his real calling as an editorialist. Still, the two scrapped with one another all the time. Royster says he admired his boss's uneducated brilliance but thought him irascible and unpredictable. Grimes evidently thought Royster a willful young puppy who, like Kilgore, might get the paper into all sorts of trouble. There were differences in the two men's political views, though usually differences of degree, not substance. Both were believers in the *Journal*'s long-held creed: free enterprise, maximum individual liberty, minimal government interference. But Royster was both more worldly and more moderate than his editor. Grimes once killed a theater review about a play that dealt with homosexuality, contending that *The Wall Street Journal* should not discuss the subject in any regard. Royster reportedly protested: "You can't do that! For one thing, the play is open, and for another, it's four p.m. and we have a hole in our page for it." Grimes killed the column all the same, and Royster stormed out. Frequently Grimes would also kill letters from readers whose points of view he thought too liberal. When Royster objected, Grimes would shout, "The man's a fool!" and turn back to other work.

The two men fought heatedly in April 1951 when President Truman relieved General Douglas MacArthur of his Korean War command. Contrary to orders, MacArthur refused to conduct a limited war, attacking a large concentration of Chinese troops near Manchuria. When Truman protested, the General wrote to the Speaker of the House criticizing the President's war policy. Much of the country sided with the arrogant MacArthur. Republicans in particular held him in greater esteem than the President, and they, too, found the concept of a limited war both vague and frustrating. Grimes supported MacArthur, but Royster stood firmly behind the President. Nevertheless, Grimes agreed to let Royster write the editorial, provided he gave full treatment to the anti-Truman argument. Royster's essay began:

> The situation which brought about the dismissal of Gen. MacArthur ought never to have arisen.

> If the policy toward Korea had been planned and thought through instead of being makeshift and "off-the-cuff"; if it had been firm instead of wavering . . . But the policy being as it was, and Gen. MacArthur being not at all a negative or over-modest character, he went into rebellion.
>
> . . . Given the situation as it stood, it is hard to see how President Truman could have done other than what he did in dismissing Gen. MacArthur.

The editorial was an example of what Royster liked to call his "give-it-to-'em-and-take-it-away" technique. He began by mar-shaling all of the best arguments for the side he opposed, then proceeded to demolish them. Grimes was hardly mollified, though. He read Royster's MacArthur editorial and tore into it. Royster, like the President, saw MacArthur's letter to the Speaker as intolerable insubordination. The public was entitled to know MacArthur's opinion, wasn't it? Grimes shouted. Yes, agreed Royster, but the General should have resigned his command be-fore articulating it. Grimes shook his head and warned that the editorial would only enrage both sides. Here there was no ar-gument. Angry letters arrived by the sackful.

Grimes and Royster fought another big battle in 1954 when the U.S. Supreme Court handed down its landmark desegre-gation ruling in *Brown* v. *Board of Education.* The decision ter-minated the fifty-eight-year-old "separate but equal" doctrine that made racially segregated schools legal. Now the high court was saying that the very existence of separate black and white school systems had a detrimental effect on the black minority, no matter how equal the physical facilities might appear.

Grimes thought the country was unprepared for desegregation. To his astonishment his Southern associate disagreed and sug-gested that they endorse the Supreme Court decision unre-servedly. Again Royster prevailed, in part, he thought, because he was a Southerner. Grimes again warned that readers would be furious, and again he was right. The editorial ran on May 20, three days after the court had announced its decision. ("Never feel that you have to write about an event the next day," Royster would tell younger generations of editorial writers.) The editorial described the *Brown* decision as a mediocre piece of legal work but went on to call it "inevitable":

> The philosophy of racial distinction under the law could not have forever survived . . . because it does not comport with the majority view of the equity of government. . . . There is a burden upon the Southern states to accept the principle of the Court and to work diligently toward a method of living with it.

Curiously, more liberal newspapers found themselves tongue-tied over the *Brown* decision, not wishing to offend their readerships. *The New York Times,* for example, mustered lukewarm approval and lamely insisted, "This nation is often criticized for its treatment of racial minorities, and particularly of the Negro. There have been little grounds for this criticism."

Kilgore was always fastidious about preserving the independence of the *Journal*'s editorial page. He appreciated the delicate genius required to write lively opinion and the subtle forces that could easily undermine it. Once, an irate reader suggested that he do something about one of Grimes' editorial positions, and Kilgore answered: "Well, I suppose I might fire him, but how long could I keep any editor if he got fired every time a reader disagreed?" After Royster became editorial chief in 1958, he walked into Kilgore's office to show him the piece he had written on a Presidential State of the Union message. Knowing the weight that his reaction might carry—even with Royster—Kilgore declined to look. "I'll read it in the paper," he insisted.

Royster, who won his own Pulitzers for editorial writing in 1953 and again in 1983, took on more and more responsibility for the page in the mid-fifties, becoming its *de facto* editor long before Grimes' retirement. He steadily pushed the newspaper toward a more independent ideological course. Just as the editorial page had once been a Wall Street mouthpiece, Grimes had let it become something of a hobbyhorse for Taft Republicanism, with its isolationist instinct and its inherent distrust of virtually everything emanating from government. Royster did not abandon the *Journal*'s traditional conservatism. The basic themes of his editorials remained the paramount importance of individual freedom from the tyranny of the mob and the concomitant rightness of free enterprise. But Royster was less doctrinaire, less strident, more compassionate than Grimes. Royster's editorials also were a good deal more likely to offend the *Journal's* conservative readers. And despite the gentleness of his prose, Royster delighted in upsetting them. The basic function of an editorial, he felt, was to "stir up peoples' cerebella."

Once Royster became editor, more and more letters poured in from readers who were outraged over one thing or another. Often they threatened to cancel their *Journal* subscriptions. Royster invariably took these people at their word, sending a form letter:

> Dear Mr. Doe:
>   We are very sorry to lose you as a reader, but in accordance with your instructions I have asked the circulation department to cancel your subscription and refund any money that is due to you.

Usually they recanted at once and phoned to have their subscriptions reinstated, but Royster's message got through. His editorial page would brook no interference from anyone—not from readers, political groups, or other editors. Indeed, Royster seemed to relish provoking the people who least expected it. Once he complained to Jessie Cox, one of Dow Jones' principal owners, that an outside director was attempting to sway his editorial policy. "Don't you worry about those directors," he recalls her saying. "They're just hired hands." And Kilgore would kid him: "Roy, you're the only guy on this newspaper who never made us a nickel. All you do is cost us money."

CHAPTER 9
___

Can You Really *Afford* to Work Here?

FROM THE LATE forties on, *The Wall Street Journal* offered aspiring young newspaper reporters perhaps the greatest opportunity in the business. The *Journal* hired people fresh out of college as reporters, not as copyboys or clerks as most other big papers did. Dow Jones looked for bright, ambitious young people because youth was cheaper than experience. It didn't much care what colleges they had gone to. In fact, an Ivy League degree worked against you, and if there was anything that was worse than a diploma from Princeton, it was a college journalism degree. Kilgore and his men still frowned upon the conventional wisdom taught by journalism schools.

The *Journal* did have a rude apprenticeship of sorts: A new reporter usually would be assigned temporarily to the bond, stock, or commodities sections, where senior reporters would give them a few months' initiation. The new hireling would enter the long, narrow newsroom at 44 Broad Street by way of a center aisle that ran the length of the building—all the way back to New

Street. It was a world of shirt-sleeve scriveners, paste pots, pneumatic tubes, and olive-drab office machinery. In the front of the room, at the end nearest Broad Street, were the copy and news desks, the elite front-page rewrite team, and the Dow Jones News Service, still under Eddie Costenbader. The aisle ran past the reporters' desks—standard newsroom issue, knicked with age and strewn with papers—and continued back to the managing editor's office. Two old-timers sat facing one another across a battered table. They worked out the three Dow Jones stock indexes—industrials, rails, and utilities—on bulky old calculating machines. They tallied their numbers independently, then compared results. If the two had produced identical calculations, then they were finished. If not, they had to begin all over again.

Probably the luckiest young reporters were those assigned to help Oliver Gingold, the stock market sage who had been with the *Journal* since emigrating from England in 1900. Gingold was good-humored and avuncular, a throwback to the era when the *Journal* had been a more gentlemanly place to work. His longtime assistant, Woody Norton, was equally old-shoe. A new recruit— "termites," as Gingold and Norton called them—would sit down the first morning, and without warning Gingold would kick the hireling's chair so hard that it coasted out into the aisle. "You're in the hot seat now!" Gingold would cackle. Then he would introduce himself and turn mock-serious: "See here, my boy, do you have any money?" By which he meant to ask: Can you really *afford* to work here? Whether independently wealthy or not— and most young *Journal* reporters in the fifties were not—the new man was in good hands. Gingold's investment advice was renowned both inside the company and out.

Gingold sat next to an old-fashioned stock ticker, a glass-domed affair whose narrow tape emptied into a large wastebasket. After the 10 a.m. market opening, Gingold and Norton would watch the tape for a few minutes, make a few telephone calls, then adjourn to Eberlin's Bar across New Street around 10:30 a.m. Eberlin's bartender greeted them each day with two large martinis that he sailed across the bar with a practiced flick of the wrist. Thus would the *Journal's* two grand old stock market men end the morning, leaving their new "termite" behind to watch the tape. After lunch Gingold would fish the stock tape out of the wastebasket with his cane, muttering observations to Norton and the newest termite. Then phone calls would begin in earnest, and by mid-afternoon the trio would be writing Gingold's famous column, "Abreast of the Market," which carried Gingold's name for almost thirty years, until his death in 1966.

Working for Gingold was only a brief respite from the intense pressure elsewhere in the room. Sam Lesch, the fiery news editor, began barking at novitiates as soon as they entered, and he never let up. A cub reporter had to *run* to the editors with his copy, no matter if his desk was only twenty feet away. *The Wall Street Journal* did not employ any copyboys for this purpose, as other papers did, for that might have given reporters an exaggerated notion of their importance. The *Journal* would also remain perhaps the only newspaper that did not run obituaries for its staff. The legendary explanation was that the paper didn't want its reporters getting swelled heads in heaven either.

Lesch was expert at keeping people off balance, making them wonder if they would still have a job the next day. Even the tiniest mistake would prompt Lesch or Costenbader to read a man the riot act, for, in truth, the *Journal* could not afford to let reporters make mistakes, even the minor sorts of mistakes considered unavoidable at other papers. No number of clever page-one stories could ease peoples' anger over a simple numerical error in a two-paragraph stock dividend story, because that small numerical error would probably have cost some investor dearly. John Tompkins, a young reporter who came to work there in the early fifties, recalled making a fairly typical error in his second week. He omitted the "vice" from "vice-president" in his haste to get a story on the news ticker. After the inevitable bawling out, Tompkins was sure his days were limited. The storm passed, however, and Tompkins survived. But few people ever breathed easily in the *Journal* newsroom, regardless of how long they had been there. Working at the *Journal* meant constant pressure—pressure to cover routine business disclosures, pressure to feed the ticker quickly, pressure not to make mistakes, and pressure to churn out front-page stories. Writing the front-page leaders was really the only way to get ahead, for the editors kept careful count of how many each reporter had chalked up. But usually reporters had to write their big stories during off-hours. If they missed out on any routine developments from nine to five they might be sacked quickly. The *Journal* was not a union shop, except in Chicago, and the editors fired people all the time.

At the end of 1954, Henry Gemmill stepped down as managing editor to become the *Journal*'s chief European correspondent in London. The new managing editor, Bob Bottorff, had previously been Chicago bureau chief. In the office he was sometimes called the "fourth horseman," not only because he was the last and the least of the DePauw clique, but also because he preferred to manage by fear. He was a hard man—earthy, profane, and abrupt, qualities that Kilgore liked in him.

If Bottorff's ascendance symbolized anything, it was the *Journal*'s concern that success might go to men's heads. Bottorff's forte was crushing egos, reminding men that they could not bask in the newly resplendent glory of *The Wall Street Journal*. When Dow Jones bought out the *Chicago Journal of Commerce* in 1951, the *Journal of Commerce*'s travel editor was off on a whirlwind junket and did not know of the change in ownership. He sent a postcard to his office chums of the wish-you-were-here variety. Bottorff reportedly answered it with a cable that said: "Glad you are having good time but you no longer have job."

Bottorff was quick to anger. He swore loudly and chased around the Chicago newsroom with his shirttail flying, though, in fairness, he could also be generous with compliments. As managing editor in New York, Bottorff became less communicative, sitting in his office and turning thumbs up or down on stories, leaving most of the ranting to Sam Lesch, the news editor. But reporters' dealings with Bottorff were often unpleasant. Men who had started at the *Journal* and made their professional reputations there would get tempting offers from the *Times* or *Fortune* magazine. They would go to see Bottorff, hoping he would ask them to stay, but instead Bottorff might snap: "We don't meet other peoples' offers. Clean out your desk!" And off would go one of the newspaper's premier performers, soon to be replaced by another eager young college graduate working at rock-bottom salary.

More than anything else, Bottorff seemed to behave as a tightfisted guardian of the corporate honor, ever alert to snotty young reporters who wanted to borrow a little of its glitter and who, given a chance, would soon be asking for more money and more freedom.

The *Journal* also was notoriously tightfisted. When Fred Taylor left *The Portland Oregonian* to join the *Journal* in 1955, he took a $30-a-week pay cut—from $120 to $90. He told Executive Editor Buren McCormack that he would work for the *Journal* for six months at the reduced pay scale but that he would resign at the end of that time if the *Journal* did not think he was worth the full $120 he had been making in Portland. When the six months were up, Taylor recalls gingerly approaching McCormack to remind him of their agreement. McCormack muttered that he couldn't remember any such discussion. "In that case, I'm giving notice," said Taylor. McCormack grudgingly gave him the raise. Still, Taylor did not quite understand the true depths of the man's miserliness. Years later, when Taylor had become managing editor and McCormack an executive vice-president, Taylor found himself going back to McCormack four times just to get a $15-a-week raise for a newsroom secretary.

Young reporters put up with such humiliation for two reasons. First, most reporters, while professionally assertive, are personally shy. They choose newspaper work because the prestige of writing for a powerful publication helps compensate for their lack of gumption. Second, more than any newspaper around, the *Journal* had the bright shimmer of opportunity. It was an ambitious, fabulously successful institution that was knocking down all the old assumptions about newspapers. Writing for the front page of *The Wall Street Journal* was the headiest experience in journalism. It meant bringing perspective and flourish to issues that were outside the limited repertoire of other newspapers. Kilgore had thrown out all of the old rules as to what constituted "a story" and told his men to "just write what you think will be damned good reading." No bright young journalist could ask for more.

The Wall Street Journal was growing at breakneck speed now. At the end of 1949, it had less than 150,000 daily circulation; at the close of 1951, it had grown thirty-six percent, to 205,000. By 1955 circulation was nearly 400,000, and less than two years later, it crossed the half-million mark. The growth was unparalleled; no one at Dow Jones expected it to continue. People were always asking Bernard Kilgore how high the circulation would go. The Dow Jones president would name a figure 100,000 or so beyond whatever it happened to be at the moment. But after a time it became apparent that the *Journal's* potential was far beyond what even the optimistic might guess, so Kilgore began answering: "Oh, I don't know. The sky's the limit."

By the mid-fifties Kilgore had transcended the role of ordinary executive, becoming a kind of corporate saint, "a great eye in the sky," one of the reporters would call him. All of Dow Jones & Company—from the Bancroft sisters, who owned it, to the lowliest janitors who swept the floors at night—basked in the shadow of Kilgore's genius. Few people who work for a company as successful as Dow Jones can help feeling intoxicated. The growth of the business expands opportunities for people at all levels.

Kilgore's apotheosis stemmed from more than his business acumen; it came from his wonderful human touch. Throughout the burgeoning company he was known as "Barney." The pressmen felt he was as genuinely concerned with how their ink jets worked as they were; reporters felt, rightly, that Kilgore was reading every word they wrote. No matter how unpleasant Lesch made the men's daily existence, Kilgore remained an omniscient benefactor.

Still, the newspaper had difficulty adapting to success. Most men behind *The Wall Street Journal* were used to adversity. They hardly knew what to do with the torrents of money raining down on Dow Jones. The sudden wealth was frightening in a way, for they all sensed that easy money might somehow corrupt the newspaper as it had in the Barron era. Curiously, the richer the *Journal* grew, the more spartan the news department became. It was as if old demons still had to be held at bay.

Kilgore himself realized that the *Journal*—indeed, all of Dow Jones & Company—had to shift gears. *The Wall Street Journal* was a large business now, not some fragile experiment that they could fashion as they pleased. Kilgore no longer knew all his men by name. He could no longer hop from one reporter's desk to another's, as in the old days. There were too many new faces and too many new demands on his time.

Many men who worked in the New York newsroom in the mid- or late-1950s witnessed something similar: A somewhat disheveled man with thinning hair would come rambling through the newsroom and stop to chat with a young reporter. The reporter would shoo him away as politely as possible. As the older man slinked away, the reporter would turn to some colleague and whisper, "Who was *that?*" It was Kilgore, of course, and the young reporter would gasp, "Oh, my God, I thought it was some old crank from production." Once, there was such an incident late at night, when Lindley Clark was sitting on the copydesk. He saw Kilgore approach a new man at the other end of the desk and ask if he could take a copy of the next morning's newspaper from the thick stack that had just arrived from the pressroom. The copyeditor had answered brusquely that he couldn't spare a single newspaper, and Kilgore, who never pulled rank, simply said, "Okay," and vanished.

Kilgore still loved newspapers and newsmen, but the crowded New York newsroom was no longer his territory. For some reason he felt more relaxed visiting the bureaus. He had the company buy a private plane, a Grumman Gulfstream, and in it he began traveling the country, popping in on the *Journal* bureaus whenever he was near one, inviting the reporters to one of the legendary drinking bouts in his hotel suite. In the morning Kilgore would roll up his sleeves, sit down next to the bureau Teletype operator, and start pounding out his own messages: "Good morning. This is Kilgore from Dallas. What do we have on the agenda this morning?" It all reminded him of that Sunday morning in 1929 when he had first arrived at the San Francisco office and Deac Hendee, the managing editor, had sent him back to the pressroom to help out with some minor mechanical chore.

In New York Kilgore's only real contact with the news department was in the 10 a.m. meeting between top editors and executives, the *"kaffeeklatsch,"* they called it. Kilgore would have read the paper on his train commute from Princeton. He would casually hand his paper—marked in red ink—to the managing editor.

From his eighth-floor penthouse, Kilgore would dash off scores of notes containing compliments, criticisms, and story ideas— always typed on the ordinary newsprint that served as his stationery. He would write:

> I doubt you would be interested but how about an article someday about motorcycles (and perhaps scooters)?

Or:

> In headlines, watch verb-noun things like "U.S. MOVES" which sounds like a verb but turns out to be a noun and "MEDICAL CARE FORCES" where another noun looks like a verb.
> Unless two things are literally taking place at the same time, I suggest you avoid the word "meanwhile" because it is only a clumsy connective.

To his right-hand man, Bill Kerby, after an article had brought in a flurry of letters from angry readers:

> Please answer these and tell the bastards to go to hell. But don't lose the subscriptions.

And, in a note to Lindley Clark:

> If I see "upcoming" in the paper again, I'll be downcoming and someone will be outgoing.

Kilgore could still communicate with intelligence, wit, and warmth, even from upstairs, but in truth he was no longer much of a factor in the daily operation of the newspaper.

Kilgore's greatest strength had always been his fecund imagination. He had ideas by the minute, some terrible and some brilliant. Some of his editors, Henry Gemmill, for instance, weren't afraid to tell him when an idea was terrible, and Vermont Royster recalls sometimes declaring, "There's no point in arguing with stupidity!" and stalking out of a meeting. Increasingly, though, the *Journal* was run by men afraid to argue. They passed on Kilgore's eccentric notions to the staff along with his better ideas.

A young reporter was walking past the *Journal*'s modest library one day when he noticed that the librarian, Florence, was in tears. At her feet lay scattered most of the library's contents. Some of the older stock market tomes surely were collector's items. Kilgore had come through, rummaged the shelves, and ordered everything thrown out. "Reporters shouldn't read books," he'd told Florence. "They should be out gathering news." Never again would the *Journal* have a library of much consequence, not even the standard newspaper morgue.

Toward the end of the fifties, Kilgore began talking about moving the headquarters of *The Wall Street Journal* from New York to Chicago, believing that both editors and reporters developed an Eastern myopia in New York. Indeed, he was so serious about the move that he had the company buy an entire square block of land across the street from Chicago's main post office and had plans drawn for a Dow Jones skyscraper there. Someone asked Kilgore how he intended to persuade the paper's editors to leave New York en masse, and Kilgore remarked: "We won't have any trouble because the next managing editor we pick will already *be* in Chicago." The move never came off. While no one ever confronted Kilgore directly, the other Dow Jones executives succeeded in dragging their heels until Kilgore's enthusiasm for the idea waned.

In retrospect, some of those closest to Kilgore would deduce the true reason behind these farfetched ideas of his. All through the fifties Kilgore was growing restless, increasingly frustrated because his newspaper no longer needed him. Kilgore had given the *Journal* a potent formula, and now that the paper was hugely successful, the formula had become sacrosanct. The *Journal* needed managers who were custodians, not innovators. No one was going to get ahead there by proposing some new feature on the front page, which would remain virtually unchanged for more than forty years. And Barney Kilgore, by his nature, was uniquely unsuited for the role of custodian.

There were rumors at this point that Kilgore had tried to talk the Bancroft family into letting him acquire another publication or two, perhaps local newspapers. Nothing of the sort came to pass at Dow Jones until years later, but in 1955 Kilgore himself bought a flimsy hometown weekly, *The Princeton Packet*, whose circulation was about 1,000. Kilgore poured more and more of his creative energy into the *Packet*, lavishing attention on everything from its type style to its ambitious printing technology. After turning the *Packet* into one of the handsomest small newspapers in the country and raising circulation to 8,000, he bought up five other New Jersey weeklies. Kilgore, who was forty-seven when he bought the *Packet*, would tell people that he was buying the papers as a retirement business. The truth was, however, that Kilgore needed something new to work on long before he was ready to contemplate retirement.

By this time the *Journal*'s news staff had undergone a great transformation. After the chronic shortage of talent that had afflicted the paper in the late forties, it had now gathered a superabundance of ambitious, gifted young reporters. Instead of waiting for applications, the *Journal* had learned to swoop down on campuses all over the country, tapping the campus newspaper editor, who might otherwise have gone to work on some obscure small-town daily. The *Journal* not only wrote for Mid-America, it was *written by* Mid-Americans. The *Journal* had learned to reach out beyond Wall Street, beyond New York, beyond the Alleghenies for news and for talent.

One of the *Journal*'s premier talent scouts was an assistant bureau chief named John McWethy, who himself had had trouble finding a newspaper job after college. In the early fifties he first talked Kilgore into letting him make recruiting expeditions to Midwestern college campuses on the theory that the paper should search out the best men, rather than hoping that their résumés would somehow fall through the transom. When McWethy located a good prospect, he went to extraordinary lengths to hook him.

In 1953, for example, McWethy visited the University of Iowa and noticed that the campus newspaper editor, Bill Clabby, had neglected to sign up for an interview. He approached Clabby in his student newspaper office one evening and personally invited him to an interview, but Clabby still did not show up. Undeterred, McWethy called Clabby a week later and begged him to come to Chicago for an interview. "Look," said McWethy, "if it's money you're worried about . . ." McWethy had hit upon the problem, said Clabby, who was working his way through school with a part-time job at a packing company a hundred miles from campus. Moreover, he had two newspaper job offers closer to home, neither of which would have entailed an expensive relocation. McWethy paid Clabby's way to Chicago, gave him a job there, and started him on his rise to an eventual Dow Jones vice-presidency. Few newspapers anywhere would bother stalking a promising young college student. McWethy and other *Journal* managers did so routinely, and the men they recruited turned out to be both loyal and superb. The emphasis on recruiting from the heartland, begun by Hogate in the late 1920s, had profound influence on the *Journal's* character. Its staff tended to be more politically and personally conservative than at other large Eastern publications. Most *Journal* reporters were "squares"—solid, middle-class men of conventional habit who saw no personal conflict in putting the company's interests first and accepting its values as their own.

One of the most important aspects of Dow Jones' corporate value system lay in the relative pecking order of bureau assignments. Washington would always be considered the most prestigious and desirable assignment, for the *Journal* had been among the first to recognize the government's growing role in business during the New Deal. But after Washington the most desirable bureaus for an ambitious young reporter were not in staid Eastern financial centers like Boston or Philadelphia but in gritty smokestack cities like Pittsburgh and Chicago. And next to Washington, in the wake of John Williams' 1954 General Motors triumph, no bureau assignment was considered more prestigious than Detroit. The auto industry was the very essence of big business in America. By twitting the automobile manufacturers, as Williams had, a *Journal* reporter could make his mark at the newspaper as nowhere else.

The quality of the *Journal* reporters who drifted through De-

troit in the ten years after John Williams was remarkable. They
included Dan Cordtz, later perhaps television's premier business
correspondent; Fred Taylor, who became executive editor of the
Journal; Al Karr; and Jerry Flint, later with *The New York Times*
and *Forbes* magazine. They also included two Pulitzer Prize win-
ners, Stanley Penn and Norman C. Miller. In fact, the Detroit
bureau was considered so prestigious an assignment that Miller
was assigned there *after* he had won his 1964 Pulitzer.

The road to glory in Detroit was perfectly clear to these men.
It was an assignment in irreverence; their job was to publish
whatever it was that the carmakers did not want published. Dan
Cordtz, Williams' immediate successor, played the game with
consummate skill. He wrote a story about GM president Harlow
Curtice, showing that while Curtice had made his reputation by
sprucing up sales in GM's Buick division, he had actually hurt
Buick badly by cheapening its cherished image as a quasi-luxury
car. Cordtz wrote another big story on how Detroit priced its
autos for sale, showing for the first time how closely price increases were geared to the outcome of labor negotiations. No
one ever knew how Cordtz managed it, but he also began publishing the closely guarded ten-day sales figures of the major auto
manufacturers. He published them so regularly, in fact, that the
companies ultimately stopped fighting him and began distributing the figures voluntarily. And he wrote of Volkswagen's invasion of the American marketplace, describing the arrogant indifference with which Detroit executives viewed the foreign
Beetle and their smugly held conviction that only a New York
City Communist of questionable sexual persuasion might consider owning one.

Williams' 1954 story on new models had come from weeks of
careful research in Detroit's tool and die shops. The arguments
over copyright infringement notwithstanding, his methods had
been above reproach. But after Williams, getting the advance
poop on new car models became a kind of virility test for *Journal*
reporters, and their methods might sometimes have been open
to question. Fred Taylor recalled hiding for hours in a snowdrift
taking pictures of models on faraway test tracks with a telephoto
lens. Jerry Flint said he snuck into the auto factories at night to

photograph new car models with a pocket camera. He admits to then hiring an artist to make sketches from his photos so as to conceal how they had been obtained.

Once, there were rumors that Ford Motor Company was about to start building a formidable new compact model called the Cardinal. It was the talk of Detroit, though no one outside Ford had yet seen the car. Flint says he got word that a prototype was about to be tested at a track in Minnesota. The Ford engineers who took the car there naturally assumed that they were safe from prying eyes and left the prototype outside at night under a heavy cover of masking tape. Flint, who says he was waiting in a nearby motel, swooped in, unmasked the car, and took photographs from every angle, taping it up again before dawn. His story contained a full description of the mystery car, replete with the usual sketches. But there was one omission. In his enthusiasm for the story, Fred Taylor, Flint's bureau chief, apparently deleted a sentence noting that no one knew if Ford would ever put the Cardinal into full production. A month after Flint's story ran, Henry Ford decided to scrap the project.

Ironically, the greater the lengths to which *Journal* reporters went to get such stories, the less the auto companies seemed to care. They took the reporters' prying into account in planning new car promotions. The auto companies began "leaking" photographs of new models to reporters, encouraging them to think that the photos were forbidden fruit. In fact, some had spent hours discussing which new models they wanted the *Journal* to write about and how they would plant the photographs.

Ultimately, Taylor's successor, Larry O'Donnell, put an end to the sneak preview nonsense, but in the meantime the Detroit bureau had become so caught up in following the news agenda as the automakers saw it that the paper nearly missed the most important story of the era. Dave Jones, who had bolted from the *Journal* in 1963, then began writing extensively about automobile safety and pollution issues for his new employer, *The New York Times*. Though Ralph Nader's seminal book, *Unsafe at Any Speed,* had yet to rivet public attention on such matters, Jones had arrived in Detroit from Pittsburgh and had been horrified when he saw the results of automobile crash tests. He went to a press conference at which Chevrolet announced the introduction of fancy new disk brakes in its $5,000 Corvette, he says, and rose to ask division president Semon E. Knudsen why, if disk brakes were safer than conventional ones, Chevrolet did not install them in all of its cars. Knudsen responded with a joke, Jones recalls, and the entire roomful of reporters, including the competition from the *Journal*, snickered along with him.

The *Journal*, like most other Detroit news bureaus, remained convinced that Jones' obsession with public health was misguided. The big story in Detroit, the *Journal* felt, was the robust health of America's leading industry. Only in retrospect would it become clear that Jones had been recording early cracks in the industry's underbody.

Back when Dave Jones was still at the *Journal*, he belonged to a brief generation of hugely talented young men who arrived after one of Barney Kilgore's fluky pronouncements. A former college newspaper editor at Penn State, Jones was finishing his term as a U.S. Air Force information officer in 1956, secure in the knowledge that he had a job awaiting him at the *Washington Evening Star* that would pay a respectable $50 a week. His wife, flipping through a copy of *Editor & Publisher*, the newspaper trade magazine, came to a speech by Kilgore declaring that the cream of American youth was somehow overlooking the newspaper field and that, to help remedy the situation, *The Wall Street Journal* was ready to pay its beginning reporters a full $100 a week.

The Joneses were not the only ones whose mouths fell open. Some eight hundred men applied for twenty jobs. Many veterans in the *Journal*'s New York newsroom were not making that much, and they were livid. So was the Independent Association of Publisher's Employees, the house union that rarely got stirred up over anything, and so was most of Dow Jones' management, which foresaw chaos. A beginning salary of $100 a week was more than double the industry average in 1956, and newspaper editors everywhere were appalled. Still, the company would not make a liar out of Barney Kilgore.

To help soothe the older reporters' ire, Bottorff came up with a fictitious "training program" for the new bonus babies, as if the whole thing were really experimental. The "training program," not surprisingly, had no curriculum. As the hundred-dollar men arrived that fall, they were dumped unceremoniously into reporting assignments, where they could sink or swim in the usual *Journal* manner. If there was any touch of humanity about the process, it was that Dave Jones, in deference to his name, was assigned to cover shipping news, and his first by-line read: "By Davy Jones."

"The geniuses," as the new hirelings were called, got icy treatment from much of the older staff. When one of them walked down the center aisle of the newsroom, he felt hateful stares coming from every corner. "Doesn't it make you feel good to know that when you walk through the room, everyone hates your guts?" one "genius" reportedly asked another. But the new men who arrived in the next couple of years—before the rest of the newspaper industry raised salaries accordingly—were an extraordinary bunch. Besides Jones, there was Norman Miller, the future Pulitzer Prize winner and Washington bureau chief; John Lawrence, later a power at the *Los Angeles Times;* Richard Madden, John Noble Wilford, Jerry Flint, and R. W. Apple, Jr., all future stars at *The New York Times;* Thomas O'Toole, chief science writer at *The Washington Post;* and Louis Kraar of *Fortune*—to name a few.

Ironically, the *Journal* would groom these men and then, with the exception of Miller, watch all of them move on to other publications where they could attain greater fame, fulfillment, and remuneration. Most tellingly, many of the deserters felt they were leaving because of professional frustration. Once you mastered the technique of writing page-one leaders, there was very little more to accomplish at the *Journal.* They sensed a degree of smugness overcoming the *Journal,* an arrogance that seemed to say the *Journal* and the *Journal* alone possessed the magic front-page formula, the key to its resplendent success. Other newspapers could never equal it. And so while other newspapers— *The Washington Post, The New York Times,* the *Los Angeles Times—* all were striving to be better, the *Journal* in a sense was striving to remain the same. This was hardly the most appealing of prospects for an ambitious young journalist. Kilgore had succeeded in attracting the cream of American youth, all right, but once the *Journal* got them, it had no idea how to use them.

No one in Chicago knew what to expect. Bob Bottorff, the bureau manager with the extravagant temper, vanished to New York to become managing editor in late 1954. Bottorff's replacement, Warren Phillips, was an unknown. They were told that Phillips had been the *Journal*'s foreign editor for a while, which did not sound like much of a job. Then he had held some vague position on the New York news desk, apparently without leaving much of an impression on anyone. In a personal sense they were quite right, for Warren Phillips apparently did not make much of an impression on people, and almost no one could ever say with assurance that they really knew him. As Vermont Royster later described Phillips, "He's a very business-like chap, not the kind around whom anecdotes collect." In terms of ability, however, Warren Phillips had made a very good impression indeed.

In any case, Phillips' appearance in Chicago aroused great resentment. Before taking over in Chicago, Bottorff had been a senior bureau chief in San Francisco. In addition he had been a close friend of Barney Kilgore's and an obvious comer in the organization. But Warren Phillips, now twenty-eight, still looked like a gangling teenager. Moreover, his new job was a very important one. Chicago was one of four places where the *Journal* was printed. Phillips' actual title was not just bureau chief, but managing editor of the Midwest edition. Phillips did little to dispel their anxiety. He was stiff, tight-lipped, and formal. Bottorff spent several days explaining office procedure to him, and Phillips just nodded at everything, making copious notes in a little black notebook.

Had Kilgore really appreciated the mess the Chicago operation was in, he might not have tapped Bottorff for managing editor. For all the housecleaning after Dow Jones bought the *Journal of Commerce,* Chicago reportedly remained a collection of malcontents, men doing their work with minimum effort and spending their time grousing about the Dow Jones' management. The Midwest edition was far sloppier than the New York paper. It was awash with typographical errors, flaccid writing, and weak headlines, much as the *Chicago Journal of Commerce* itself had been. Bottorff had known these things, of course, but the earlier deadlines in the Midwest had offered some excuse.

Phillips, they soon learned, did not pay much attention to excuses. He wrote down what needed to be done in his little black book, then turned the screws until people complied. He was a good deal quieter than Bottorff but hardly more endearing. Phillips' approach was grinding and determined; he did not tolerate mistakes. And though Phillips virtually never raised his voice, he, too, inspired fear.

Phillips saw that much of the copy coming from Chicago reporters, while perhaps acceptable, was not really very good. A man had made a single phone call, perhaps two, then filed a story that was accurate but not terribly revealing. Phillips demanded more, throwing people out of the office and ordering them to hit the road, to plow through dusty farm towns, for instance, instead of getting agricultural reports by telephone.

He was all business all the time. If you went to lunch with Phillips, you talked about the newspaper and nothing else. You might talk about little details for improving the over-the-counter stock listings or some such thing. He would drive people crazy with details. John Williams, who became Phillips' assistant after leaving Detroit, says he was given the job of answering letters from discontented subscribers. Williams would try to write notes with a touch of warmth and humor, and Phillips would veto them. "Answer in such a way that you don't open a dialogue," he ordered. "You want to make them happy, but you don't want to get another letter back." It was all right to argue with him—all right in the sense that Phillips did not seem to take offense. But then again the young bureau manager seldom changed his mind either, so in the end arguing with him was usually a waste of time.

Williams was bowled over by the man's capacity for detail. Phillips had Williams running around the plant with a stopwatch and a clipboard, timing exactly how long it took to produce copy and get it onto the press. He was tremendously concerned with meeting deadlines, but equally so with producing a clean newspaper. Phillips was exact, dedicated, mechanistic, and—what struck everyone—he *never* seemed to make mistakes.

To those beneath him it seemed that Warren Phillips could not comprehend why other people sometimes erred. It wasn't anything he ever said—for Phillips seldom said much of anything. It was the pained look on his face, a tautness around the mouth. He never gave anyone hell; in fact, he seemed incapable of anger. But if you saw that agonized frown on Phillips' face, you knew that you had done something wrong; your stomach would knot, and then, when you tried to explain, you could not be sure he had accepted the explanation because he would nod curtly and walk away.

Though not apparent to the staff in Chicago, the fact was that Warren Phillips' star had been rapidly ascending ever since William Henry Grimes' return from London in 1951. Senior men in New York had begun to realize around 1954 that Phillips was the anointed heir to the paper. In New York and Chicago, Phillips clearly lived up to expectations; he had administrative abilities that no one in Kilgore's circle could match. In March 1957 Bob Bottorff was promoted from managing editor to executive editor, an ill-defined post. The purpose was to make room for Warren Phillips—the new managing editor and the real day-to-day power behind the *Journal*. At the age of thirty, Phillips moved back to New York, taking up residence next door to Kerby in Brooklyn Heights. Few people really knew yet what to make of him.

CHAPTER 10

His Private Pain

IN 1957, WHEN Warren Phillips became managing editor of *The Wall Street Journal*, Dow Jones & Company did not employ any blacks in conspicuous positions, nor did it hire a great many Jews. Many suspected Phillips of having camouflaged his Jewish origins in order to succeed there, but they were wrong. Being Jewish had never been a handicap for Warren Phillips at the *Journal*, except when he applied for visas to certain Arab countries as a foreign correspondent.

It was true that when Phillips first arrived at the *Journal* ten years earlier, the management had consisted almost entirely of men graduated from the same Methodist college in Indiana. And it was also true that there were virtually no other Jews there except for Sam Lesch, the news editor. It did not follow, however, that Barney Kilgore and his clique were anti-Semites. The paucity of Jews was more the result of their tendency to distrust Easterners of all sorts and their preference for hiring from the largely Protestant Middlewest.

This Midwestern bias had nothing to do with the kind of class distinctions for which Wall Street was then renowned. If anything, it grew out of Kilgore's distaste for such things. Kilgore could sound almost mystical on the subject of Mid-America. He thought that growing up there gave a man a superior sense of reality, a feel for the changing seasons and the rhythms of na- ture—matters on which he thought Easterners more or less ig- norant. Kilgore considered himself so firmly rooted in the Mid- west—he never ceased identifying himself as a Hoosier—that when he and his wife, Mary Lou, built their house on a country road in Princeton, New Jersey, Kilgore insisted on having pink brick from his native Indiana trucked in. The intense hue of the bricks, hauled from nearly a thousand miles away, made the co- lonial house look as starkly out of place in the New Jersey coun- tryside as Kilgore himself looked on Wall Street.

There was yet another reason that not many Jews worked at the *Journal*. Not many applied. The very name of the newspaper seemed to hint at Wall Street clubbiness, an atmosphere that did not encourage men from the lower middle class who tended to seek newspaper work in the forties. Warren Phillips said he never sensed an iota of anti-Jewish feeling at the *Journal*. Ironically, had he begun his career at the Jewish-owned *New York Times* in- stead of the *Journal*, being Jewish might have been a hindrance to his career, for reportedly the *Times* then bent over backward not to appear too Jewish, using by-lines with initials to keep a conspicuously ethnic name like "Abraham" out of the paper. But *The Wall Street Journal* never concerned itself with such matters. Its struggle for survival had been too acute.

It is impossible to say how much Phillips' Jewishness influenced the *Journal's* sensitive coverage of the civil rights movement in the late fifties and early sixties, but the civil rights story would mark an important turning point for the paper. Phillips says he did not feel particularly Jewish, but growing up in a Jewish family in Queens, he could hardly have escaped developing liberal po- litical instincts. He had cast his first Presidential vote in 1948, he says, not for Truman or Dewey, but for Socialist candidate Nor- man Thomas. Phillips' Socialist ideals had crumbled in the early fifties as he had watched the tragicomic spectacle of British so- cialism in action. He had begun a political conversion that would make him as conservative as the *Journal's* editorial page—on economic matters, that is. On social issues apparently Phillips would always remain instinctively liberal. In the 1980s, as a member of New York's starchy University Club, Phillips reportedly would perorate against his colleague Vermont Royster in an effort to open the way for female members, a fight he was destined to lose. In 1981 it would emerge that Warren Phillips had been the moving force behind a Pulitzer Prize that went to a young black reporter, Janet Cooke of *The Washington Post*. Miss Cooke's story about an eight-year-old heroin addict named "Jimmy" in the Washington slums had been submitted for a prize in the local-reporting category, where it had lost out to another entry. Phillips, a member of the governing advisory board, had suggested moving her story into the feature-writing category so that the Pulitzer for the first time could go to a black female reporter. Phillips apparently had not wanted his role in the Cooke award to be known, especially not after Miss Cooke had won the prize and it emerged that her story had been an utter fabrication. But there was no denying that Warren Phillips was more of a closet social activist than he let on.

Publicly Phillips would always maintain that his interest in civil rights had arisen from news instincts, rather than social conscience. While still bureau manager in Chicago, he had been struck by the 1955 bus boycott in Montgomery, Alabama, where a small band of civil rights advocates had focused attention on the segregated public buses with notable effect. It made for great moral drama, naturally, but Phillips would later say that he had been more impressed by the fact that the civil rights story was fundamentally about economics. The insight was certainly valid, for the Montgomery bus boycott had shown the potential economic might of a disenfranchised black minority. And the civil rights struggle, in a larger sense, could always be viewed as a contest between black and white groups for political and economic spoils, a push by lower- and middle-class blacks to seize their just share. In any event, Phillips would never admit that the *Journal*'s coverage of civil rights had had anything to do with his personal political beliefs. He would explain it with the bland assertion that the issue was something that the average businessman needed to know about.

Montgomery aside, the civil rights movement had been largely quiescent since the 1954 Supreme Court decision in *Brown* v. *School Board of Topeka*. Through most of 1957 it was still in the process of gathering steam. When the race issue finally exploded in Little Rock, Arkansas, on September 3, Phillips decided that the *Journal* would pursue it as no other story in the paper's history. Little Rock was inescapably a big, breaking news event. Governor Orval Faubus had called out the National Guard to prevent black children from entering the all-white Central High School; the President of the United States had sent Army infantry to clear the way. Always in the past the *Journal* had shied away from spot news developments of great magnitude, for it felt ill-equipped to compete with the larger news organizations. Kilgore had decreed that the *Journal* would always be a "second newspaper," that its readers looked to their hometown papers first for the general news and that, therefore, the *Journal* had to give them something different. The Kilgore solution was to stick primarily with business and economics, fields in which other papers did not often graze. The *Journal* would cover more general news, too, but with no great sense of urgency. *Journal* subscribers could expect to read about such things as Red China's latest anti-rightest crusade or the travails of Vice-President Richard Nixon whenever the newspaper got around to them.

Little Rock was a totally new kind of story for the *Journal*. It meant that the paper was now writing about the process of social change, a topic hitherto reserved primarily for historians. The Southern civil rights movement wasn't something like fluctuating corn prices or an election in Ottawa. There was simply no precedent for writing about it in the *Journal*'s front-page style. Other papers, of course, could follow the rhetoric, the bullets, the freedom rides, and the brutal police tactics. For them it was the paradigmatic newspaper story: a stark confrontation set in an exotic, faraway land against a clear-cut moral backdrop. The good guys were easy to tell from the bad.

But the *Journal* would not cover the story that way. It had to assume that readers would already know about the latest schoolyard incident and the red-neck ranting from television and local newspapers. The solution was to treat the story in the same detached manner that the *Journal* customarily applied to news of economics or foreign wars. The paper would not hover around the schoolyard with other papers. It would instead look elsewhere for underlying causes and hidden ramifications of the conflict, and it would learn to treat all stories about social change with a distinctively broad perspective.

The approach worked brilliantly in Little Rock, partly because Phillips dispatched two of the *Journal*'s best—Henry Gemmill, back from London, and Joe Guilfoyle. Arriving in Arkansas, the two men were taken aback by the contrast between the Little Rock they had witnessed on nightly television news and the Little Rock they saw before their eyes. The networks were portraying the Arkansas capital as a brutal, militantly anti-Negro community. The sight of U.S. soldiers patrolling Central High School appeared all the more shocking through the selective lens of television. And most of the newspapers were milking the story for every possible drop of drama, zeroing in on the police dogs and water hoses. An Associated Press photographer got a soldier to pose sticking his bayonet in the back of a young girl, and his picture showed up on front pages around the world.

But away from Central High, Little Rock was a fairly representative American community. Gemmill and Guilfoyle found most whites favorably disposed toward blacks and ready, if not eager, to comply with court-ordered desegregation. The root of the conflict, they found, was not community intransigence so much as Governor Faubus himself, running for a third term and demonically trying to inject his waning popularity with the adrenaline of lower-class race hatred. On October 1 they wrote:

> Talk to people of all kinds around town and you'll soon realize that most of them are much less provoked at the soldiers ("very nice boys," observes a leather-faced man who lives across the street from Central High) than at the reporters and photographers.

Two days later they described how Little Rock's power structure was attempting to deal with the crisis.

Very quietly—at first entirely behind the scenes, and then more
and more openly—many men were organizing to apply the
brakes. Their tactic: Do not attack the Governor. Do not force
him into a position where he will be suddenly deflated and
discredited. Instead, surround him with evidence that segre-
gationist sentiment will in the long run pack less political punch
. . . than devotion to law and order, preservation of the public
school system, and restoration of the state's good name.

Gemmill and Guilfoyle's Little Rock stories would become the
prototype for covering a generation of startling social change—
from riots and war protests to bra-burnings and gay liberation.
The *Journal* had learned that it could treat the same front-page
news as other papers but in a more circumspect manner, without
having to indulge in the same "who-what-why-where-when" style
as its competition.

By coincidence, the day after Gemmill and Guilfoyle had filed
their behind-the-scenes look at Little Rock politics, there was another event that would redirect American energies for much of
the next decade, and that, too, would have a major effect on *The
Wall Street Journal.* The Soviet Union launched Sputnik. Over
the weekend Phillips supervised the roundup story that would
lead the paper on Monday, October 7. It began:

As Russia's satellite circles the globe the Eisenhower administration faces increasing pressure from Congress, some sci-
entists and even from the government itself to speed perfection
of military missiles.

The story went on to outline the implications of the new space
race—military, diplomatic, and scientific.

Most of the country was reacting to Sputnik with the kind of
panic and anger echoed by the *Journal* editorial page, which took
the satellite launching as further evidence that the totalitarian
Soviet regime had both the will and the power to subordinate
its peoples' needs to "massive concentration on military and
propaganda objectives." Phillips, however, reacted with characteristically cool logic. He saw the space race as the start of a new
era in science, education, medicine, and defense. None of these

fields was new, but the dawning space age had suddenly given them extra propulsion. In the past the invention of nylon or radar might have had importance for specific industries or defense problems. But now technological innovation had a different, more open-ended aspect. The emphasis was now on pure research, and Phillips wisely foresaw that the *Journal* would have to deal with its implications.

It was a time when everything seemed to jell for the *Journal*. There were wonderfully talented newsmen throughout the bureaus, and Phillips could harness their efforts as no other managing editor had. He had great self-discipline and a wholly rational ability to plan. Phillips could read the first typewritten page of a story at noon and the fifth page at 4 p.m. and pick out the logical inconsistencies between the two. "Phillips trained you like one of Pavlov's dogs," said one of the men who wrote front-page news capsules under him. "He'd give you a lecture about the importance of the job and what kind of reading you had to do— all the competing papers and the news magazines. Then you'd have to leave carbons of each item you wrote on the right corner of your desk. Just before deadline Phillips would stroll over and read them, usually criticizing something about the clarity or the play you had given them. But you knew he was vitally interested."

Some of the senior men in New York were critical of Warren Phillips. They had thought him a mediocre writer in years gone by, and now they saw him as a heavy-handed editor. "Warren will dull it up," they predicted whenever a colleague was about to hand in an especially juicy story, and Phillips would. Phillips evidently tended to do the safe thing with most stories, and that usually meant toning things down to minimize the chances of offending people, his subordinates felt. On the other hand, if Phillips was cautious with his pencil, he made up for it with some ambitious story ventures.

One of his greatest triumphs was a four-part series in December 1958 that dissected the "hermit kingdom" of the Great Atlantic and Pacific Tea Company, a masterpiece of business reportage. The hulking A&P empire, by far the country's largest grocery chain, was on the verge of selling stock to the public for the first time in its ninety-nine years. Still the company declined to supply more than the most rudimentary facts about itself. Phillips assigned Gemmill and a team of twenty-six reporters all over the United States to look into the company. They laid bare a retailing giant that had been built by flouting of the anti-trust laws, one that was ruthlessly run by a high-handed autocrat named Ralph Burger, and one that, despite its elephantine size, was losing ground to smaller, more agile chains in many areas of the country.

The *Journal* now was entering upon a golden era. It was not just the leading business paper, but increasingly the subject of awe and admiration from other quarters as well. "The intellectual's pet down-towner," said John Brooks in *Harper's* magazine, and he was right. *The Wall Street Journal* had acquired genuine cachet. Even Teamsters officials and United Auto Workers negotiators liked to confide in *Journal* reporters because they were known for integrity. The paper was respected by black civil rights workers on one hand and Ku Klux Klan members on the other. By now the general reading public had overcome the notion that *The Wall Street Journal* was a newspaper about stocks and bonds—so much so that Kilgore had long since given up the idea of changing the newspaper's quaint old name to something less parochial sounding. "We keep it because it works," he declared.

But as the *Journal* was coming into its full glory, many were becoming aware that complacency was setting in, an institutional arrogance that was resistant to the smallest degree of change. The feeling may have stemmed in part from Kilgore's quirky ultimatums, but mostly it came from the inherent conservatism of the men to whom Kilgore had delegated authority. "Our approach," said Fred Taylor, then the Detroit bureau chief, "was that Kilgore had given us a *perfect* thing. Every time you looked the paper had registered another hundred thousand gain in circulation, so we thought, don't tamper with it. . . . Don't screw around with the formula."

The man who had invented "the formula," meanwhile, was increasingly bored and restless. Though he still seemed warm and good-humored with friends, Barney Kilgore could sound a bit morose when talking about the *Journal*. At one of the annual resort conclaves between bureau chiefs, editors, and top executives, somebody asked Kilgore the usual question—how much higher did he think the *Journal*'s circulation would go. Kilgore gave the usual answer: "Oh, I don't know, maybe another hundred thousand or two." But then he turned suddenly gloomy, adding: "You know, newspapers have a life-cycle of their own. They are born, they grow up, and they die." And a pall went over the room. Kilgore began to say things like that frequently. "The shores of the publishing world are littered with the remains of once-great publications," he would say. To his wife, Mary Lou, he mused: "It takes a long time for a newspaper to die." Once, reflecting upon the *Journal*'s arrival at the pinnacle of American journalism, he said to her: "You never want to get to be the best at something; it's much better to be second-best and still struggling."

Kilgore's ennui was apparent in other ways as well. Peter Vanderwicken, a Princeton undergraduate who was president of the college radio station, WPRB, recalls looking up from his desk one day and seeing that the chairman of Dow Jones & Company had come to visit him in the dank radio station office in the basement of Holder Hall. Vanderwicken had encountered Kilgore once before, at a news colloquy sponsored by *The Daily Princetonian*, of which Kilgore was a trustee. Now the master had sought out the student on a point of interest. Kilgore wanted to know if Vanderwicken thought that the little Princeton community could support a second radio station in addition to the student-run one. Kilgore, who lived barely a mile from campus, wanted to start his own station, as though he had nothing else to fill his time. Vanderwicken asserted that, no, he did not see room for another radio station, for he did not want to encourage professional competition. Kilgore never did start his station. He discovered that owning a local newspaper, *The Princeton Packet*, all but disqualified him for a local radio frequency in the eyes of the Federal Communications Commission.

By the next year, though, Kilgore had come up with another pet project—something much grander than a radio station. He decided to start a weekly newspaper. Not unlike his little *Princeton Packet*, it would be a paper full of literate general news articles about everything from armaments to arias. But this newspaper would not be so small. He would use the *Journal's* idle printing presses each weekend to print the new paper, and he would send it all over the United States.

Barney Kilgore was plainly smitten with the idea of a national weekly newspaper. The basement of his house in Princeton was strewn with his burgeoning collection of old typefaces, and he fiddled with them late into the night looking for the right combination of type styles for Dow Jones' new venture. When Kilgore found a combination he liked, he tried it out in *The Princeton Packet*, then took it to the small team of men he had working in secret on the sixth floor of Dow Jones in New York.

Kilgore almost never discussed *Journal* business with his family, but the new weekly newspaper was different. He could hardly contain himself on the subject. His daughter Kathryn, a precocious fifteen-year-old, was pressed into service as a consultant. Spreading mock-ups of the new paper on the dining room table, Kilgore would make her comment and criticize as he had never done with anything concerning *The Wall Street Journal*. No one had seen Barney Kilgore so enthused about a project in years.

Kilgore finally announced plans for his new Sunday newspaper, *The National Observer*, at the *Journal's* 1961 editorial conference in Bermuda. What he proposed sounded peculiar indeed. To start with, Kilgore thought that the *Observer* should be written for the younger generation of television viewers who had never developed the newspaper reading habit—in other words, it was to be a newspaper for people who did not read much. For another thing, Kilgore said, it was to be a newspaper without reporters. There was already a surfeit of information in the world, the publisher contended. What was needed was more understanding. "We don't need more people telling us what has happened as much as we need people who can put events together and explain them," he insisted. What he had in mind was a newspaper produced by a *Wall Street Journal*-style rewrite bank, using information gleaned from the wire services and other publications. In fact, Kilgore mused, the *Observer* newsroom might not even need any *telephones*.

Not surprisingly, Kilgore's new project had the tacit support of most top Dow Jones executives, all of whom were beholden to Kilgore for their careers. But the *Journal's* senior reporters and editors were a less toadying lot, and they were intensely skeptical. From the outset many of them seemed to think the idea preposterous. Besides the inherent illogic of a newspaper without reporters, they wondered just why anyone needed the publication Kilgore had described. Mitch Gordon stood and remarked that, to him, *The National Observer* sounded a great deal like *Time* magazine. "Maybe so," said Bill Giles, already chosen to be the *Observer's* editor, "but we'll do a better job."

"Why take *Time* on?" Gordon continued. "It's one of the most successful publications going. Why not go after somebody softer? Besides, how are *we* going to deliver a national newspaper on Sunday?"

Such objections were utterly well founded, but in the end Kilgore would have his way. Apart from Henry Luce, there was no one in publishing who could match Kilgore's track record, and if he was gung ho for the *Observer*, who was going to stop him? Only one of Kilgore's old cronies had the temerity to tell his boss that the idea was terrible. Bob Feemster, the *Journal's* marketing genius, bluntly warned that the *Observer* would have "no defined audience" and, hence, no appeal for advertisers. Instead Feemster suggested starting a magazine for professional women. When Kilgore ignored him, Feemster told his boss that he wanted nothing to do with the *Observer*.

Just then the company was invited to purchase languishing *Newsweek* magazine, but Kilgore was dead set against any acquisition that would interfere with his plans for *The National Observer*. He spurned the offer on the grounds that *Newsweek* would divert too much talent from the *Journal*, as though starting the *Observer* from scratch was going to be any easier. Soon afterward the Washington Post Company bought *Newsweek* and within a few years made it vigorously competitive with *Time*. But Kilgore pressed ahead with the weekly newspaper that would end in agonizing failure.

Feemster's prognosis for the *Observer* had been precisely right. The newspaper, though nicely written, would never muster any sense of urgency or mission. The readers remained so ill-defined a group that advertisers habitually ignored them. Mitch Gordon had been right, too. Dow Jones would never learn how to distribute a national newspaper on Sunday, and so the paper would go out on Monday instead, a day when people generally had less time for it.

In *The National Observer* Kilgore was launching Dow Jones' first new publication since the rebirth of the *Journal* some twenty years earlier. It would prove a severe test of the company's skills and resources. At heart Dow Jones & Company was timid and unassertive, full of decent, intelligent men steeped in the old-fashioned work-ethic. Their handicap was a natural aversion to risk of any sort. Since 1941 the company had done nothing but stick with Kilgore's tried and proven front-page formula that had made *The Wall Street Journal* grow like Topsy. Kilgore's men seemed to feel that they had not just the right newspaper, but the right blend of brains, staff discipline, and—could it be?— moral outlook that others lacked. They were almost constitutionally averse to the kind of self-promotion in which other publishing companies indulged.

The weighty dignity of Dow Jones & Company was almost an affliction. Hence, the failure of *The National Observer* would leave deep psychological scars, reminding Kilgore's men all too graphically that the publishing world was a brutal place, one where virtue and hard work were not always rewarded. As Kilgore himself often said, the shores were strewn with the wreckage of once-great publications, and having run aground for the first time in memory, the company would retreat to the kind of cautious conservatism with which it had survived the Depression.

The first edition of *The National Observer* appeared on February 4, 1962. It was an attractive, thoughtful paper with a mixture of serious news analysis and light feature material. The subject of the prescient lead story—indeed the subject that would occupy the *Observer* more than any other—was Vietnam, to which the rest of the media had not yet turned its attention. The *Observer* was stylishly written, as well it ought to have been. Bill Giles, the editor, had pirated some of *The Wall Street Journal*'s best craftsmen, with Kilgore's blessing.

Giles was himself the paper's greatest asset. He had once been considered Warren Phillips' chief rival for the editorship of the *Journal,* though he was an altogether different kind of newsman. Where Phillips was rigorously self-contained and disciplined, Giles was street-wise and resourceful, a native New Jerseyan who looked the part of a lean and cynical private eye. Giles had "punched his ticket" at all the right stops within the *Journal*— first writing the page-one news capsules, as Phillips had done, next joining the esteemed front-page rewrite team, then graduating to a key bureau manager's job in Dallas, and finally taking on the pivotal position of news editor in the *Journal's* Washington bureau. Giles, thirty-three, had been in Washington just two months when Kilgore summoned him to New York and asked him to assemble a small team of people to produce a prototype of the *Observer* in secret. Kilgore and Kerby assured him that they wanted the new paper to read every bit as well as the *Journal,* so Giles set out to recruit the ablest writers he could find. He took Jack Bridge, a former page-one editor, Gene Bylinsky, Roscoe Born, and Jack Volter, among others, all men of well-established reputation, and after Kilgore announced the birth of the *Observer* at the editorial conference in Bermuda, other talented men stepped forward to ask for a spot on the new paper. Their eagerness to sign on signaled not just the allure of fresh adventure but also the fact that many were becoming a bit frustrated at the *Journal,* as the path to personal success there became ever more narrow.

True to Kilgore's wish that the *Observer* be a newspaper without reporters, Giles took mainly men he considered top writers. And though such men were really the marrow of *The Wall Street Journal,* Warren Phillips, the managing editor, acquiesced for a while in Giles' pilferage. Then, suddenly, the *Journal* managing editor would have no more of it.

The incident that apparently brought Phillips and Giles into conflict, curiously enough, had nothing to do with a superbly talented writer like Bridge. Rather, it concerned a relatively unknown man, Ray Shaw, who had been with the *Journal* less than two years. Phillips himself had hired Shaw from the Associated Press on the advice of Buren McCormack, who was friendly with Shaw's former city editor at the *Oklahoma City Times.* Shaw had gone directly to the *Journal's* vaunted front-page rewrite bank, a considerable honor that younger reporters saw as something like making the all-star team. But somehow the *Journal's* writing style had reportedly eluded Shaw. Other page-one men would spend a whole day, sometimes two or three days, polishing a single story. They would go back to reporters asking for more details, different quotes, and new perspectives, ironing out the articles with extraordinary care. Shaw, on the other hand, was said to crank out a story in less than an hour. At first other rewrite men were cowed by Shaw's machine-gun typewriter, they recall, but gradually they noticed how Lindley Clark, the front-page editor, would bury Shaw's work in a drawer. In a few months Shaw was reassigned to cover publishing and broadcasting as an ordinary reporter, and soon thereafter he took over the Thursday "Business Bulletin," one of the daily front-page newsletter columns. Apparently frustrated, Shaw reportedly had come to Giles seeking to start over on the new *Observer,* but he wouldn't get the chance.

No one knew why, but it was Shaw's threatened departure that finally provoked Phillips. Suddenly Phillips was upstairs in the executive suite, reportedly demanding that Giles stop raiding his staff, and Giles was forced to begin hiring men from outside the company. From that point on Ray Shaw's career began to skyrocket until, ultimately, he became president of the corporation, Warren Phillips' chief deputy. Shaw's great talent, as it turned out, lay in organization and administration. Shaw's ascendance would surprise people, for ever since Kilgore, Dow Jones executives had had to establish themselves first as star writers and editors. Writing ability was perhaps the only thing that really got respect in the *Journal* newsroom. Warren Phillips obviously saw things differently. He seemed intuitively drawn to men with executive ability.

Once the *Observer* started publication, Giles and Phillips hardly saw one another again for a decade. Kilgore, still deeply suspicious of New York, wanted his new paper's editorial offices elsewhere. In the end he and Giles decided to put the *Observer* in Washington on the theory that the U.S. government was the greatest single source of information. In addition, the *Journal* was to open a new printing plant the following year in nearby White Oak, Maryland, and the plant easily could be enlarged to accommodate the *Observer* staff. Thus, a year after it went into print, the *Observer* relocated from downtown Washington to serenely quiet suburbia, where most of its readers were also presumed to be.

Except for the *Observer*'s fairly consistent quality and readability, almost nothing worked out as planned. The first major casualty was the low budget that Kilgore had promised the Dow Jones directors. The notion of a high-class newspaper that did not have reporters was simply impossible. The theory behind the reporterless paper had been fine: The country really did wallow in too much information, and many readers of elephantine Sunday papers no doubt would have welcomed a smaller newspaper that was better edited and more considerate of their time.

The fallacy lay in thinking that good news copy could be written without benefit of good reporting. Kilgore, with his abiding faith in the *Journal* rewrite desk, had thought that a newspaper could be produced by rewrite men ripping patchy stories from the wire services and other sources and assembling it all into graceful journalistic tapestries. It was not true. The wire services supplied but the barest essentials—the who, what, why, when, and where. They could not give the *Observer* the gritty minor detail that good writing demands—what the man was wearing, how he talked and smoked his cigarette, what his neighborhood looked like, and what kind of dog he owned.

Giles says he knew that he was inviting trouble, but he could not help testing Kilgore in the third week of publication. There was a minor stir over a proposed nuclear power plant in Delaware, and Giles sent James Perry, hired from the rewrite bank of *The Philadelphia Bulletin*, to cover it in person. To Giles' immense relief, Perry's story attracted no notice whatever in New York. The following week Giles sent someone else to cover a meeting of minor importance in Washington, and this time the story prompted a little congratulatory note from Kilgore, who had particularly liked some comments drawn from two elderly women spectators who had been interviewed. Thereafter, Giles ignored the prohibition on reporters, and the *Observer*'s budget began to swell.

Bill Giles' newspaper was nearly always journalistically good but commercially disastrous. The paper's circulation was a respectable half-million or more, but too many of those readers had to be wooed with costly promotional campaigns. The advertising community never could be won over. Skeptical Dow Jones directors had insisted at the start that Kilgore set a deadline for making the *Observer* break even, but the paper never stopped losing money, and Kilgore ignored all financial deadlines.

The lack of instant success did not seem to faze him, but it weighed heavily on the *Observer* staff. Indeed, in the winter of 1963, when the time came for the *Observer* to hold its first annual editorial conference paralleling the *Journal*'s lavish affairs, Giles reluctantly asked Kilgore not to come, for fear that his presence might intimidate those staff members who didn't know him. Things were looking up a bit the next year, and a beaming Kilgore sat at the meeting, held in Silver Spring, Maryland. The *Observer* staff serenaded him with a song about the avian figure that graced the *Observer*'s masthead: "Glory, glory, Barney Kilgore . . . Your owl goes marching on." Then Kilgore, gracious as ever, rose to say that he understood the staff's anxieties about the paper and knew perfectly why he had not been invited to the conclave the year before. "But now is the time for you to have *fun*," Kilgore insisted. "Successful newspapers have to grow up and get serious, and they *stop* having fun." He complimented them on their work, laying the blame for the *Observer*'s continuing troubles where it belonged—on Dow Jones & Company's failure to sell it—and he left them, as he left everyone, feeling reassured and enthusiastic.

But the company would never find a way to sell the *Observer*, especially not to advertisers. Kilgore once told Giles: "We may be twenty years too late or twenty years too early with this," but the truth was that Dow Jones had no notion how to go about peddling the publication. Its vending machines were mainly conspicuous in downtown office districts, far from the suburbs that the newspaper was designed to reach. And except for Kilgore, few people at Dow Jones really cared much about the *Observer*.

It was of minor importance compared with the *Journal*. Most people soon dismissed it as Barney Kilgore's plaything. Over the next decade Giles would wear himself ragged trying to make the *Observer* succeed, and after him Henry Gemmill would take over, ending his career at Dow Jones in the bitterness of the paper's demise in 1977, when Warren Phillips, about to ascend to the chairmanship of Dow Jones, finally pulled the plug. In all, the *Observer* would linger for fifteen years, tangible proof of Kilgore's aphorism that newspapers take a long time to die.

Actually the *Observer*'s fate was bound up in Kilgore's own. Had Kilgore lived longer, Gemmill felt, he would have made it succeed through the sheer force of his imagination. But in the summer of 1965, Kilgore underwent surgery for a stomach obstruction, which turned out to be cancerous. The company might just as well have folded *The National Observer* then and there.

The doctors were optimistic that summer, and Kilgore, only fifty-seven, had no inkling that his life would end barely two years later. Still, lying in Princeton Hospital, he considered the future and concluded that Dow Jones & Company had better learn to get along without him. "I have cancer," Kilgore told an incredulous Bill Kerby soon afterward, "but I'm going to live my life as though I didn't." He told Kerby that in the spring he would step aside as chief executive, keeping the title of chairman but leaving real authority over the company in Kerby's hands. Kilgore wanted to keep working on the *Observer* and be of use to the company in other ways, but he wanted to clear out of his ninth-floor office suite in New York and move into smaller quarters in Dow Jones' new office complex near Princeton. He promised Kerby "a clear field," and he meant it.

Kilgore formally announced his decision late that year at a meeting of the company's management committee, which included his old friends Kerby, McCormack, Bottorff, Callis, and Royster. "Probably any one of you would make a good successor to me," Kerby recalls Kilgore telling the group, "but I've decided on Bill Kerby." And without a word about his real reason for stepping aside, Kilgore handed the affairs of the company to his longtime number-two man.

Barney Kilgore's last two years were as remarkable as his earlier life had been. True to his word he lived as though nothing were wrong. In fact, just weeks before his death he bought two more newspapers for his string of small New Jersey weeklies. Most remarkable of all, not once after his initial conversation with Kerby did Kilgore ever mention his cancer or his impending death, not even to his wife. It wasn't so much that Kilgore couldn't face what was happening as it was his old Midwestern stoicism, his feeling that family and friends should learn to get along without him. He did not want them dwelling upon his private pain.

Kilgore instinctively wanted people around him to be independent. He never talked down to his children, for instance, not even when they were little. He was always pushing them toward adulthood. Once, his oldest child, Kathryn, a strikingly pretty teenager, informed her parents that she was going to spend the summer hitchhiking across the country. Her mother flew into the predictable rage that such adolescent pronouncements are designed to provoke, but Kathryn says her father kept quiet. Hours later Kilgore approached his daughter with a map in hand, prepared to talk her out of the dangerous trip, she assumed. She was wrong. "I've been thinking," Kilgore began. "The best way to hitchhike across the country might be aboard private airplanes." With that he unfolded the map, and they spent hours searching for private airfields, plotting just how the expedition might proceed. Kathryn soon forgot about the trip, but not her father's reaction. She remembers that he never condemned an idea as ridiculous; instead he encouraged her to think on a grander scale.

Kilgore was like that with the men at Dow Jones, too. George Flynn, a young graduate from the University of Illinois, met Kilgore in 1956, shortly after he had joined the *Journal*'s Chicago printing plant as an assistant production manager. Kilgore wandered through the plant one day while Flynn was wrestling with some nettlesome mechanical problem. "I don't think we should do things this way at all," said Flynn, referring to the *modus operandi* that caused the problem. And Kilgore shot back: "Then why *do* you do things this way?" Flynn answered: "Because New

York does it this way," meaning the Dow Jones headquarters production department. "Well," said Kilgore, "not all of the brains are in the East." It was a subtle suggestion that Flynn experiment a little, and the message was not lost. "I worshiped him for that," recalled Flynn, later the company's general manager. "Always just the right touch . . . the knack of making you feel important."

The Wall Street Journal, Kilgore's great lifework, was a newspaper about money, but his own attitude toward wealth, deeply ambivalent, would have a lasting effect on the Journal's character. Kilgore was intellectually curious about money but had little personal craving for it. In fact, he was rather suspicious of wealth and of most people who had it. Kilgore never invested in stocks. He said privately that he distrusted the stock market and thought that most people who played the market had "memories that lasted about a week." He never bought fancy cars, only the plainest Fords and Chevys equipped with the cheapest radios. Not until he was gravely ill did he accept a corporate limousine.

It was much the same in the Journal newsroom. When Kilgore had done the hiring back in the forties, he had warned newsmen that while they could expect to have a good deal of fun there, they would never get rich. As the newspaper grew more prosperous, he would let top reporters leave rather than pay them high salaries, for he thought that big money would turn them into prima donnas and spoil the newsroom ambience.

Kilgore's own salary had not been particularly large considering his stature. Until his very last years, it did not exceed $70,000 a year, though he easily might have commanded more. Kilgore's chief financial concern, as he approached death, was leaving enough to support his wife and educate their three children. He called Robert Potter, Dow Jones' chief counsel, and said, "You know all about the company, Bob. They say I've got some kind of disease. Will you draw up my will?" That was it, says Potter.

Under the terms of Kilgore's contract, signed back in 1946, Kilgore's retirement pension was to equal the annual earnings on 150,000 shares of Dow Jones stock, with his wife receiving half that amount each year if she outlived him. That would not have amounted to much money in 1946, when the company was only marginally profitable, but in 1965 Dow Jones stock was earning over $2 a share. By then the estimated worth of Kilgore's contract was more than $6 million, still not a vast amount considering that Kilgore had lifted the newspaper's circulation from about 30,000 to 1,132,000 and boosted Dow Jones' annual earnings from $211,201 in 1945 to more than $13 million.

Potter negotiated a settlement with the Bancroft family in Boston. Dow Jones bought out of Kilgore's contract for a lump sum of about $3.5 million. Potter claimed that the agreement was advantageous for both sides. It saved Dow Jones an estimated $2.5 million while enabling Kilgore to pay a reduced capital gains tax on his pension instead of the higher ordinary income tax. But some of the company resented the settlement, sensing that the Bancroft family had taken advantage of Kilgore's illness to buy him off at a niggardly price. In truth Kilgore probably did not care to leave his children an excessive sum of money. It was not the sort of legacy in which he believed.

The closest Kilgore would ever come to discussing his illness with his wife, Mary Lou, was once near the end when he was about to come home from a series of hospital operations and he asked her to hire round-the-clock nurses for him. With his oldest child, Kathryn, he was slightly more revealing. He led her down the hall at New York's Columbia Presbyterian Hospital to meet a woman with lung cancer who was just a week away from death. Sick and agonized though she was, the woman struck Kilgore as living life joyously. She was having her portrait painted, talking, writing, and making friends, and Kilgore had wanted Kathryn to see that.

Only Kilgore's closest friends could discern anything different about him in his final months. He worked a full day, refused to take painkillers, and, for exercise, continued to chop wood in his backyard in Princeton. The nervous tick—always worse when he was under strain—was very bad now. Occasionally Kilgore would lose his temper over something trivial, as he never had done in the past, and he would grab the arm of whomever he feared he'd offended and say, "I'm sorry." Once, he complained: "My damned hands! I can't type." And his relations with the Dow Jones board, though he continued as chairman, grew needlessly testy.

Barney Kilgore was the last man in the world one could accuse of egomania, but as death neared, the planned office-research complex in South Brunswick, New Jersey, took on unusual importance to him. Too much perhaps. Not only was the center to be built on a conspicuous hundred-acre tract a few miles from Kilgore's beloved Princeton, it was to be devoted to fostering new technology, which Kilgore dearly loved. The most efficient site for the new construction had been carefully chosen by the engineers on the basis of the most economical drainage system. Kilgore was not pleased. He climbed to the top of the highest grassy knoll, turned back toward busy U.S. Route One, and commanded them: "Build it here."

Carrying out Kilgore's wish would send cost projections for the complex sky-high. Kilgore did not care, but the Dow Jones board, for once, refused to go along. Kilgore just kept at them, Kerby recalls, pestering them to approve extra money for the research complex without explaining why.

Kerby says he finally snatched the project from Kilgore's hands. "What are you going to do?" a bewildered Kilgore asked him. And Kerby replied that he would get the money by briefing the board in full. In no time Kerby had won the board's approval for the funds by explaining that the new drainage system, though costly, would add to the market value of the property. The pity was that Kerby had had to do the persuading. Once upon a time Barney Kilgore would have settled the matter with a joke and a smile.

Kilgore died at home on November 14, 1967. *The Wall Street Journal* recorded his death with a fond and colorful obituary that began on the front page with the headline: "Bernard Kilgore Dies; Made a National Daily of Wall Street Journal." It carried two pictures of him, one an uncharacteristically formal portrait and the other a more typical shot of Kilgore gazing up from his typewriter, necktie askew and shirtsleeves rolled up. There were two columns of tributes from politicians and journalists, financiers and academics, but what would surely have mattered most to Kilgore was the eulogy that Vermont Royster wrote for him on the editorial page:

Somehow among those gifts given him was the boon of self-containment, if not always self-content. There was a demon in him about what he wanted to create. . . . Yet he had not the slightest need for self-aggrandizement or personal publicity to nourish an uncertain ego.

Thus his work is more famous than himself. If you ask what he did, you need only to look at this newspaper you are reading simultaneously with more than a million others in cities and villages all across the land. . . . If you ask what manner of man he was, his friends can only tell you he had a touch of genius and was to the full measure a gentleman.

Such men are rare.

CHAPTER 11

Green Berets

SHORTLY BEFORE HIS death Barney Kilgore wrote to Warren Phillips, musing about *The Wall Street Journal.* "The most significant thing about it to me," said Kilgore, "is that it is a newspaper and not a trade paper. It has more to do with the *Pittsburgh Post-Gazette* than it does with *Iron Age.*" *The Wall Street Journal* had a split personality: It was a narrow business trade paper—many stories were of very limited interest—as well as a broadly interesting newspaper for an intelligent general readership. There was no question that Kilgore cared more for the latter. Part of his legacy was the perception that businessmen were more than walking cash registers. Kilgore merely wanted to use business news as the magnet to attract them. His goal was to publish a distinguished national newspaper, and for that he needed a distinguished national readership.

After Kilgore's death, though, the men who ran *The Wall Street Journal* would have increasing difficulty navigating between the hard, practical, sometimes boring business trade paper approach and the more ambitious journalism of broader appeal. The *Journal* would always tend to look for economic aspects of every topic—that was part of the paper's uniqueness. But whether the *Journal* chose to focus its front page broadly upon questions of politics, economics, and sociology or more narrowly upon business subjects like factory inventories or steel production would make all the difference. The men who ran the paper after Kilgore would have a hard time charting a reasonable course between the two.

The problem was that in the mid-sixties the United States was entering a tempestuous era of social change that would buffet the *Journal* as it did most other institutions. Guiding the newspaper in that era was like sailing a boat through heavy seas. An editor might see the apparent winds of change, but he could only guess where they really came from. Ed Cony, the newsroom's first Pulitzer Prize winner, had been the obvious choice to succeed Phillips as managing editor in 1966, the year Phillips became the corporation's executive editor. But Cony could hardly have been more different. Where Phillips was a man of rigid self-control and dispassionate logic, Cony was emotional, given to fits of anger and enthusiasm. Phillips seemed to suffer from lockjaw, especially in the presence of underlings; Cony was voluble with praise and with criticism.

The news staff had respected Warren Phillips, but they adored Ed Cony, a trim man with receding hair. They liked Cony because he was warm and witty and, above all, because his goals seemed to coincide with theirs. Ed Cony loved exciting newspaper stories and went to great lengths to get them. He was tolerant of eccentrics, for the best reporters and writers very often are that way. "We don't want button-down minds," Cony declared when someone complained about the long-hair generation of reporters showing up in the newsroom in the late 1960s. "Think what it would be like if we had a bunch of accountants around here."

No one ever cowed Ed Cony. If Warren Phillips wanted to change a *Journal* headline, Cony usually argued with him—loudly and repeatedly. Indeed, the New York news staff grew to expect a Cony-Phillips confrontation almost every day. Cony was a deeply competitive man, a Vince Lombardi figure in more ways than one. Many a lunch hour he would lead a squad of touch football players down to Battery Park, and if a reporter muffed a pass, Cony would dress him down as thoroughly as if he had just lost a major story to *The New York Times*. He was, many felt, a contradictory personality, always wanting to be one of the boys and yet jealously defensive of his rank. One treated Ed Cony as a colleague, but only to a point, for his affability could swiftly turn to rage. And Cony's temper was ferocious. When he got mad, his face, normally ruddy and genial, went dead white. Little red spots appeared at the center of his cheeks, and then he roared.

For all of Ed Cony's talent and toughness, there was something that made a few people wonder if he really ought to be the managing editor. Cony seemed to disdain routine business stories almost openly. He was in the newspaper business for the glory, not the grind. Warren Phillips, by contrast, had emphasized industry and finance, even as he had pushed the *Journal* into fields like sociology and medicine. One kind of story Phillips particularly seemed to like was the management story, the sort of article that tells of some chief executive who works eighty-hour weeks, eats lunch at his desk, and succeeds in transforming his company from a financial disgrace into the talk of Minneapolis. Cony hated such stories—unless they delved into the sociological aspects of life at the top. He preferred to go for the jugular. He liked stories of corporate misconduct and incompetence. He wanted the exotic and bizarre, a story about a day in the life of gangster Meyer Lansky, say. And he loved tales about life's little ironies, like one about a small band of people still pushing for Henry George's single tax or another on the rise of golf carts as social status symbols. Such stories, a hallmark of Cony's regime, were often so light, one critic remarked, that they all but floated off the page, and perhaps some of them should have. But readers loved them anyway. All of this led to frequent clashes between Phillips, the executive editor, and Cony, the managing editor—and not just over headlines, adjectives, or fine points. Cony and Phillips seemed to be at odds over the direction of the newspaper itself.

This running battle between them had many manifestations. In 1966, for example, Reuters, the British news agency, decided it would try to compete with Dow Jones' ticker monopoly in the U.S. financial news arena. The Reuters threat made Dow Jones

& Company nearly apoplectic. The news ticker not only made a tidy profit, it was also the key to Dow Jones' hammerlock on breaking financial news, the main reason a business executive simply could not do without *The Wall Street Journal*. Many at the *Journal* felt that Dow Jones overreacted badly, and Warren Phillips worst of all. But as the corporation's executive editor, he was determined to stop Reuters cold.

Phillips bore into the problem relentlessly. He went to the *Journal* bureau chiefs and sketched plans for staving off Reuters. It was a job that called for great delicacy, for the truth was that Reuters' only real prayer of denting the Dow Jones monopoly was if the government intervened on anti-trust grounds. The bureau chiefs and the reporters reportedly were told to call the major companies on their beats and deliver a message: Dow Jones demanded at least an even break with Reuters on *all* news service stories. At least, that was the part of the message that was articulated. The unspoken part, reporters felt, was that Dow Jones was prepared to punish those who gave too much cooperation to Reuters.

Because of the looming anti-trust issue, Dow Jones could not afford to hurl threats like a Mafia protection thug. Nevertheless, the pressure that Dow Jones could and did bring to bear on corporate publicity men was intense. *The Wall Street Journal* is big business' national bulletin board. The threat of having important corporate announcements frozen out of the newspaper—or even "inadvertently" held back for a day or two—was enough to scare the daylights out of the average PR man. Still, as the war between Dow Jones and Reuters got under way, there were plenty of PR men who rather enjoyed Dow Jones' new predicament. They did indeed see the Dow Jones ticker as a monopoly, and an arrogant one at that. And they did not much enjoy being the goat of Dow Jones' age-old game of humiliating public relations men—a legacy of the late William Henry Grimes. Indeed, many saw this as a rare opportunity to tweak Dow Jones, and they relished granting Reuters an exclusive interview here or a generous news break there. They soon learned, however, that Dow Jones & Company was keeping score.

Phillips had an unnatural ability to focus the energies of the entire company upon a single problem. It was his tight-lipped way of making people nervous, his attention to detail, that let them know someone was always looking over their shoulders. His deputy in the Reuters affair was Joe Guilfoyle, the veteran reporter who had started running messages up and down Wall Street in the 1920s. Though now nearing sixty, Guilfoyle retained the air of a street fighter, and he terrified those who worked for him.

Guilfoyle reportedly kept a running account of stories on the two tickers, Dow Jones and Reuters, just as in the old days against Tammany. He is said to have sent a daily report to Phillips showing all the stories on which Reuters had beaten Dow, and then they would lean on the reporters and the bureau chiefs to make sure it did not happen again. If it became evident that a company had favored Reuters with an early news break, Guilfoyle reportedly would lambaste the reporter responsible for covering the company, and then the reporter would have to make a second phone call to the company with a threat that was not quite so veiled as the first one. "You are playing ball with Reuters, and we won't stand for it," the reporter might say. And most PR men, realizing that Dow Jones meant business, apparently fell into line.

Corporate PR men were not the only ones chafing under Phillips' and Guilfoyle's tyrannical behavior. The *Journal* reporters did not enjoy it either. A dictum came down that if a reporter got any sort of exclusive news break on a company, it would have to go onto the ticker immediately. There would be no more saving and developing such stories for the next day's newspaper. Better to let every other newspaper in the country share in the *Journal*'s exclusive than to miss an opportunity to deal Reuters a small setback on the ticker.

Worse than having to give up their exclusive stories, *Journal* men found themselves back covering annual meetings and press conferences with change for the telephone clenched between their teeth. In fact, there had to be two of them covering important meetings so that they could take turns phoning in every dreary little detail. All that counted was speed, getting the dividend announcement or the quarterly earnings projection on the wire before Reuters did—precisely what most reporters hated.

Barney Kilgore had had to de-emphasize just this sort of thing in order to produce a credibly good newspaper. All of these bright young journalists had flocked to the *Journal* as a direct result. Few were really enamored of business reporting; they had come to write for a great newspaper. Now they found themselves in a time war. The ghost of Eddie Costenbader, the old ticker czar, rose up against them. "Whenever Reuters gets out some tidbit ahead of us, [Guilfoyle] comes around and asks what happened, as if we'd committed some crime," one reporter complained to an outsider. "It's pretty degrading."

No one was ever really free from ticker duties. On the day when Stan Penn's Pulitzer Prize was announced in 1967, for example, the managing editor reportedly sent Penn a note reminding him that he had to attend an annual meeting that afternoon held by a relatively minor film company on his beat. A newsroom gnome, intercepting the note, allegedly scribbled on it: *"Sic transit gloria mundi."* A *Wall Street Journal* reporter knew in his heart that the company regarded him as a field hand. He could put up with the annoying piecework for the chance to write for the illustrious front page. Now, however, Phillips was increasing the demands on him, and much of the staff was at the point of rebellion.

They were further irritated by Dow Jones' deep-seated miserliness. Kilgore's $100-a-week wage for starting reporters had long since been matched or exceeded by other major newspapers. The final straw came when Reuters signed a generous contract with its reporters that fall. *Journal* reporters began deserting in droves. Eighteen reportedly resigned in late 1968 alone. The New York bureau was so short of manpower at one point that men were discouraged from making trips to interview people in midtown, and Bill Clabby, the New York bureau chief, had to press his secretary into service as a reporter one day. Many reporters who were not quitting outright were marching into Ed Cony, the new managing editor, and demanding raises, promotions, transfers—anything to ameliorate working conditions. Lunching with Cony one day after three people had resigned, some mid-level editors raised the subject of the turnover rate. Cony reportedly exploded: "The next son of a bitch who comes into my office and tries to blackmail me is just going to pack his bags and leave!"

Cony was deeply frustrated by the situation. He seemed no more pleased with Phillips' anti-Reuters campaign than the staff was. He was a combative, no-nonsense newsman, and anyone could sense that his ambition was not to defend the turf of the Dow Jones ticker monopoly—Reuters would eventually back off—but to dethrone *The New York Times* as the country's leading newspaper. He simply wanted to be the best, and this ticker matter wasn't helping.

Soon afterward there was a dinner of editors and bureau chiefs, and Warren Phillips allegedly was haranguing the assembled group about the need to forestall Reuters. Cony reportedly sat listening with mounting disdain until, finally, he could tolerate no more. "Oh, fuck Reuters!" he is said to have declared, loudly enough to be heard by Phillips.

That was why reporters adored Ed Cony.

Cony, like most reporters, favored splashy and eye-catching features, the prize-winning investigations; Phillips preferred sticking to business. It was a question of degree, really. But it was, nonetheless, a dispute over fundamentals—business versus nonbusiness coverage; trade paper versus newspaper; warp versus woof. It was a dispute that the *Journal* could never truly resolve, for it revolved around the elemental paradox in the newspaper's character.

To see just how the entire organization rocked back and forth over this battle, it helps to understand the social pecking order of the *Journal*'s news department. The New York newsroom had the largest concentration of reporters in the late 1960s, as now, and all the top editors. A new hireling in New York was often sent to the copydesk, where his job was to look out for errors of style and substance. Alternatively, he might be assigned to help a senior reporter like Lee Silberman, who supervised banking coverage. Whether on the copydesk or in some cub reporting job, a new recruit was expected to pick up some rudimentary business knowledge within the first few months, as well as the knack of avoiding factual error. But to have any future with the *Journal*—that is, to hold on to one's job beyond the first year— a new person had to prove himself with at least one front-page by-line in his first twelve months, preferably more. Sloppy work on the copydesk or the ticker would get you fired, but diligent work there would *not* get you promoted. Real advancement depended greatly upon writing ability. All the promise and all the glory belonged to those who could turn a fine phrase.

Most men—there were still almost no women reporters—who held on to their jobs beyond the first year were shipped out to bureaus around the country. (Others had been hired directly for jobs in the bureaus and had gone through the same initial trial by fire there as the men in New York.) In the bureaus, naturally enough, men were assigned to cover one or more local industries—steel in Pittsburgh, agriculture in Chicago, shipbuilding and machine tools in Boston, and so on. A man who did well in the field, producing his quota of good front-page stories, would probably be transferred in two or three years to a more prestigious bureau, say Detroit or Washington. Some might go to London, the principal overseas bureau. Finally, when a reporter had really arrived in the eyes of Dow Jones, he became a bureau chief. Only he would not be called that. He would be called a "bureau *manager.*" At *The Wall Street Journal,* the best reporters were expected to want to move into management.

There was one other way to progress, however. If a reporter showed unusual writing talent—if the front-page desk just toyed with his punctuation instead of rewriting his copy—then he was sure to be hauled back to New York and pressed into service on the front-page desk. Good rewrite people were always at a premium, for they gave the newspaper its sparkle. And being a front-page rewrite man for *The Wall Street Journal* was an estimable position. The likes of Bill Kerby, Buren McCormack, and Henry Gemmill had gone that route, after all. From the middle of the New York newsroom, young reporters glanced enviously at the rewrite bank up front. There were the page-one men at their typewriters, crafting the stories that a million or more readers would be admiring over the next week or two. Page-one men never ran for the ticker or belted out annual report items. They earned their way as wordsmiths, masters of the trade.

The front-page desk had consisted of just two men in 1941—Kerby and McCormack. By the early 1960s it had half a dozen people spending anywhere from a single afternoon to three or four days working on each story. Their boss was the page-one editor. He had a counterpart, Sam Lesch—and later Bill Kreger—whose title was national news editor and whose province was the inside pages of the paper. But the page-one editor was the final arbiter of the three full-length stories on the front page of *The Wall Street Journal* each day. It was perhaps the best job in all of newspaperdom, and he answered to no one except the managing editor.

The front-page editor during the latter years when Warren Phillips was managing editor and the early years of Ed Cony's reign was Jim Soderlind, a virtuoso at the job. But by 1967 Soderlind was weary of the post and wanted to step aside into some less harried job, and Ed Cony agreed to let him. Two rewrite men, Paul Lancaster and George Church, were the prime contenders to replace Soderlind. Neither they nor anyone else knew that the contest between them would become a kind of proxy fight between Ed Cony and Warren Phillips.

Cony reportedly wanted Lancaster, tall, erect, and well-spoken—a man who had been stopped a couple of times on his morning train ride from Connecticut and asked to pose for a cigarette advertisement. Lancaster, the son of a Methodist minister, was a graduate of DePauw University, Kilgore's *alma mater*. Gentle-natured and self-deprecating, he had gotten his first job at the *Journal* in 1955 after searching high and low for a reporting spot on a better-known publication. Lancaster spent his first year on the *Journal* copydesk, and how he survived it he never knew. It was assuredly the best place to learn a newspaper's style, but Lancaster, a literary sort, came face to face with the inescapable dullness of much that went into the *Journal*. Ninety percent of the stories he touched were of the plodding, corporate-announcement variety—of no possible interest to anyone who did not own stock in U.S. Steel or whatever. One day Lancaster let a story slip through in which some executive's name was spelled four different ways. "Who the hell handled this?" screamed Sam Lesch, scanning the faces on the copydesk with a copy of the ill-edited story in his fist. When the capable young Lancaster bravely raised his hand, Lesch realized that the lad had suffered too long. Four days later they shipped Lancaster out to a reporting job in Pittsburgh.

Lancaster flourished as a reporter. He was such a natural writer that the *Journal* sent him from Pittsburgh to Jacksonville and then to Boston without ever recognizing his secret handicap: Lancaster loathed business stories. Of course he could hold his nose and ask the questions a *Journal* reporter had to ask: "Will there be a special dividend this year?" "How much money does this division earn?" "How much money do *you* earn?" But when executives hedged their answers, Lancaster never pressed. He really did not want to know.

In 1960 Phillips asked Lancaster to come to New York as a summer replacement on the rewrite bank. He instantly became one of the best the *Journal* had. Lancaster was the first on the staff to read *The Other America* by Michael Harrington, a book that heavily influenced the Kennedy Administration. He began agitating for stories about poverty, a subject the *Journal* had never considered in the past. Lancaster made no secret of his aversion to business. Like a dainty lady whose car won't start, Lancaster never disguised his hope that someone else would volunteer for what he considered dirty work.

That someone else was usually George Church, the man who was Warren Phillips' evident choice for page-one editor. Next to the tall, handsome Lancaster, Church was an unprepossessing figure of middling height and indifferent posture. George Church was also eccentric, fully capable of boarding the train in the morning out on Long Island without remembering to switch off his car ignition or to set the brake. Yet this man—whose speech was nasal, whose gait was awkward, whose clothes were more rumpled than Kilgore's—this man was dazzlingly brilliant. Self-taught to a large degree, George Church had mastery over an incredible range of subjects. Out of his mouth would come truly obscure passages from Shakespeare and learned discourse on highly technical matters. When Church got started, the words came out haltingly amid frequent gulps for breath. Only after he had finished could you appreciate how carefully he had chosen each word, how meticulously constructed his every sentence had been, as though he had been committing it all to paper.

The oddest thing of all about George Church—so far as the front-page desk was concerned—was that he took great interest in business affairs. At a time when anti-war protests were on every campus, when the ghetto riots, the sexual revolution, and the women's movement were roiling American society, Ed Cony let a certain feeling take hold that if a reporter specialized in business coverage he was relegating himself to the sidelines. Under Cony *The Wall Street Journal* was trying to sell itself as a general newspaper that emphasized business—not as a business paper that threw in a little general news now and then. Business stories still had to be written, of course, but anyone who actually *wanted* to write them was considered hopelessly out of touch.

As it happened, George Church was that rare combination of lucid writer, flawless technician, and business aficionado. He could make the most complex business and economics stories read compellingly, while making them simple enough for a sixth-grader to understand. Reporters whose real passion was for writing stories on race or politics would hastily throw together the business stories they absolutely could not duck, saying to themselves, "Thank God George Church knows this stuff because *I* don't understand it." And sure enough, the toughest of the tough business stories would go to George Church on the front-page desk, and Church would turn the reporters' lumpy work into perfect soufflés. "He has a love affair with inventories," people said of Church behind his back, and Cony seemed to go along—though it was grossly unfair to the man.

The senseless thing about this contest between Lancaster and Church was that the outcome seemed predetermined. Ed Cony ran the newspaper, and Cony obviously wanted Lancaster as his page-one editor. Warren Phillips was nominally Cony's boss, but Cony was a strong-willed man who would not brook interference from above. Since Phillips was enamored with George Church's ability, Cony would go through the motions of giving Church a chance but apparently never with the thought that Church would actually win the job. The two men's strengths and weaknesses already were known. Lancaster's disdain for business stories was no secret, nor was Church's social awkwardness. And so, for reasons almost no one in the room could comprehend, Cony took each of the two men aside individually and explained how the page-one editorship would be decided. First George Church would run the front page for a month, then Paul Lancaster. Whoever produced the best front page got to keep the job.

The general conditions of the arrangement were obvious to all. The air was thick with tension from the first morning of Church's trial. Much of the fight involved getting fast work out of the rewrite bank. They wrote until their tongues hung out. Worst of all, Lancaster had to break his neck to show that he was working to make George Church's pages look good and vice versa. Church ordered up one business roundup story after another, the most taxing kind of story in the *Journal*'s repertoire because of its dependence on memos from reporters all over the country. Lancaster filled his page with sensitive general news stories that were heavy on drama and wry irony. Both of the candidates produced good newspapers, as everyone had known they would. But did that justify the slug-out?

At the end of Lancaster's month-long tryout, Cony took him out to lunch at the Harbor View Club and told him he had won the page-one editorship. Lancaster, every inch a gentleman, was elated, he recalls, yet he could not help wondering if he was really the better man. Back in the office he did his best not to gloat, but there is no privacy in a newsroom. He could not help noting his rival's crestfallen look.

The whole contest between them had been so senselessly public that Church felt humiliated, and Ed Cony evidently did nothing to help him save face. Church, who had put in nearly fifteen years at the *Journal* and had narrowly missed winning the second most important job at the newspaper, wrote a memo to Cony asking if he might have some special status—the page-one man in charge of planning major industrial developments or some such thing. It was the job that Church did anyway, and all he was really seeking was some confirmation of his value to the newspaper. But Cony would not give it to him.

Nearly a year went by, and at last Church could wait no longer. He accepted a fairly low-level writing position in the business section of *Time* magazine, where his talent shone and he rose swiftly. Before Church could leave the *Journal*, however, Phillips summoned him. When Church got to Phillips' office, Cony was there, too, with a rare sheepish look. Phillips was distressed over Church's departure, and Cony for the first time seemed a bit remorseful. They offered Church the title he had sought a year earlier, and Cony surprised Church by making a little speech. As a business writer at *Time*, Church recalled Cony warning, Church would be relegating himself to a secondary position. Business news, he noted, was not *Time*'s forte. Church was taken aback. Both he and Cony knew, though Cony might not admit it, that writing about business was no longer the way to the top at *The Wall Street Journal*.

Under Ed Cony the *Journal* was becoming what is called a "writer's paper," emphasizing the artistic and the offbeat over the brass tacks of business. Cony set up a team of "Green Berets," reporters with no great interest in business but with substantial writing and reporting talent. These were the privileged few who wrote about Arnold Toynbee's reaction to the first moon landing, about life backstage at a striptease show, about the oddities of Las Vegas, and about practitioners of witchcraft in New York City.

The Green Berets—named for the U.S. shock troops in Vietnam—were fiercely proud of having been excused from business coverage. Indeed, some were fiercely hostile to business; they were products of the rampant liberalism of the era. "I have no criticism of the manner in which your reporter conducted his interview with me or the resulting article," a West Coast industrialist wrote to the newspaper. "I did object to the ensuing half-hour lecture on the evils of the free enterprise system."

It was the era of advocacy journalism. Everything from the kind of car one drove to the profession one chose had political overtones, and the *Journal*, with its long-standing practice of recruiting reporters straight from the campus, was highly vulnerable to the mad excesses of the epoch. "Some unfortunate material saw print," confessed Bill Kerby, who had become chairman of the board. "I would read *The Wall Street Journal* each morning with apprehension. . . . As Barney Kilgore used to lament: 'Oh, those god-damned adjectives!' "

Never had the *Journal*'s conservative editorial page and its liberal news department been so much at odds. The editorial page did not blindly endorse the American role in Vietnam. At the time of the 1968 Tet offensive, it turned against Lyndon Johnson, warning readers to prepare for "the bitter taste of a defeat beyond America's power to prevent." It went on: ". . . the [Johnson] Administration is duty-bound to recognize that no battle and no war is worth any price, no matter how ruinous." Still, the editorial page under Vermont Royster and his deputy, Joe Evans, stopped short of denouncing the fundamental principles the United States had tried to defend in Asia, principles that had lost meaning for most younger men in the New York newsroom, men whose peers were dying in a far-off war for reasons that seemed muddy at best.

These were days when, like everyplace else, the *Journal* newsroom produced petitions over the most trivial of issues. One of them protested a *Journal* editorial on the famous Woodstock concert that suggested that hundreds of thousands of young people had journeyed there just to wallow in the mud. Another petition went up when the editorial page asserted that New York telephone service was going downhill (there was no denying this much)—all on account of minority hiring requirements. The most controversial and perhaps the silliest petition of all went up when some of the staff demanded that Dow Jones halt the news ticker for sixty seconds in honor of Vietnam Moratorium Day, October 15, 1969. When Warren Phillips pointedly refused, the breach between young reporters and the Dow Jones management grew wider.

The worst came the following May 15, after nearly a week of Vietnam protests and counterprotests on Wall Street—students manning the pickets on one side and patriotic hardhats, most from the nearby World Trade Center construction site, on the other. The hardhats had made a point of telling reporters and television news crews that they looked forward to beating the daylights out of these pimply-faced youngsters who were ruining America. It was an orgy of self-destructiveness—earnest blue-collar flag-wavers threatening young war resisters who might have been their children or their younger brothers. New York medical students were setting up a field hospital in Trinity Church for the expected casualties. And it was all going to happen at the corner of Wall Street and Broad, right under the *Journal*'s nose.

The excitement in the *Journal* newsroom that morning was intense. Young reporters could talk of nothing else. A group of them went to bureau chief Bill Clabby to dope out plans for covering the event, but Clabby, a veteran of Southern civil rights coverage, surprised them. "I've got news for you," he reportedly said. "This is a *business* periodical. We don't cover this kind of thing." And with that he let them know that at lunchtime, when all hell might be breaking loose outside, he would be having lunch with some executives from U.S. Plywood. The reporters were outraged.

The way things happened, *Journal* reporters could have covered the demonstration without even leaving the building. That afternoon a great mob of hardhats came surging right into the *Journal* offices at 30 Broad Street and hung a large American flag from the building's theretofore naked flagpole. Many reporters left the building anyway—and not just to cover the demonstration, though the *Journal* did carry a brief account the next day. They lined up with the anti-war protesters, putting on arm-bands and holding up banners that read: "*Wall Street Journal*ists."

Cony was furious. By publicly identifying the newspaper with the anti-war movement, he screamed, the militant reporters had breached an elemental trust with management that could not be repaired. The newsroom split into factions—pro- and anti-demonstration. "A newspaper reporter has as much right to picket the White House as his publisher has to eat lunch there with the President," wrote Kent MacDougall, one of the militants, in a signed article on the editorial page. Passions would cool, but it would take time for the *Journal* to regain its balance.

CHAPTER 12

Wall Street "Down and Dirty"

THE IRREVERENCE OF the late sixties went beyond the anti-war movement. Among its targets were the flag, the church, the family, one's hometown—practically any institution that seemed to represent the status quo. Many of the *Journal*'s younger reporters were openly contemptuous of big business, too, viewing it as a societal evil that contributed to racial injustice, the Vietnam debacle, and pollution of the earth and water. The staff reserved some of its venom for that great central marketplace of capitalism, Wall Street itself.

Strange as it seems, *The Wall Street Journal* had kept a polite distance from Wall Street ever since the forties. This was true both in the literal sense—the paper had not had an office actually located on Wall Street since the years of Dow and Jones—and in a figurative one. The *Journal* management tended to look at Wall Street as a teeming thoroughfare of greed, the province of schemers, shameless promoters, and their lackeys. The *Journal* would always chronicle a major Wall Street scandal. Ed Cony, for example, had distinguished himself once again in the early sixties writing about corruption among officials of the American Stock Exchange. But apart from scandals and crises, *Journal* reporters did not mingle much with the Street. When Warren Phillips was managing editor, he would glance out his office window in the direction of Wall Street and Broad, remarking to someone he was about to hire: "We don't want our people getting too close to the people *out there.*"

The *Journal* had a good deal more to fear from intimate contact with Wall Street than the other way around. Once upon a time the newspaper and the Street had been on very intimate terms indeed. During the twenties the *Journal* had been a pliant trade sheet printing whatever fluff a friendly broker felt might levitate the price of a stock he owned. The newspaper usually had been happy to go along, provided certain people were clued in to the action. It had all ended in disaster for the paper, and, were standards lowered, no doubt such disaster might easily recur. Temptation always looms large on Wall Street, especially for newspaper reporters earning less perhaps than an energetic truck driver.

Kilgore's precursor, William Henry Grimes, had ended much of the double-dealing among the *Journal* staff, though not all of it. A reporter arriving in the late 1940s might still be asked by a salty old editor if he had bought any stock in the company about which he had written favorably. When the idealistic lad replied that he had not, the editor would be incredulous: "Why would anyone believe what you've written if you don't think enough of the company to buy some stock?"

Kilgore's major problem had not been eliminating the remnants of this behavior, but erasing the taint that decades of it had left behind. He had done so, in part, by allowing the *Journal*'s routine Wall Street coverage to become drab and pedestrian, even as the newspaper's business reportage became bright and exciting. Where stock and bond coverage once had taken up almost all of the *Journal*'s front page, Kilgore and his successors banished daily coverage to the inside pages, one page for bonds and another—the next-to-last page—for stocks.

No one could accuse the *Journal* of easy virtue any longer. Dow Jones & Company had very strict standards for employees. The company had a long-standing policy against employees profiting from inside or advance information, and Kerby and Phillips warned reporters and editors against even the appearance of impropriety. Dow Jones employees and executives were barred from serving as directors of any other company. They could not trade stocks on margin, borrow money from *Journal* advertisers, own stock in any companies they covered, or otherwise profit from inside information picked up on the job.

These rules were not just perfunctory. They were meant to insulate reporters from temptation, much as some religions make it a sin just to look at another man's wife. Neither people nor institutions are infallible, as the *Journal* was reminded occasionally in small but nonetheless painful incidents. In one such matter the *Journal* could claim perfect innocence. Thomas S. Lamont was a key vice-president of Morgan Guaranty Trust Company and the son of Thomas W. Lamont, once perhaps the most powerful man on Wall Street. In 1964 the younger Lamont had his bank buy stock in Texas Gulf Sulphur, of which he was a director. Two years later the Securities and Exchange Commission came down on Lamont and other Texas Gulf Sulphur employees with six-guns blazing. As it turned out, Lamont and the others had acted with advance knowledge that the company had made perhaps the largest ore strike of the century. There was no question that the bank had bought stock before news of the strike was out, but Lamont's culpability remained in doubt. He had instructed the bank not to buy stock until a time when he believed the Dow Jones ticker would be spreading the word across the country. Unfortunately the company had announced the news at a press conference in New York, then locked the doors so that reporters could not make their phone calls until they had watched a mostly superfluous half-hour slide show about Texas Gulf Sulphur's new discovery. At some point amid all the Kodachrome, Morgan Guaranty commenced buying stock. Lamont later tried to defend himself by asserting that he had been the victim of Dow Jones & Company's lassitude, a serious charge against the financial news monopoly. But apparently it had been Texas Gulf's own publicity machine that had kept Dow Jones from getting out the news before Morgan Guaranty exercised its buy orders.

Nonetheless, the Texas Gulf Sulphur affair held an important message for Dow Jones and the *Journal:* People would always seek to use the financial press, whether for profit or for self-protection. Lamont had tried to use Dow Jones as a scapegoat; others undoubtedly would try to use it as accomplice. The threat of contamination was a condition of proximity to Wall Street. In the 1960s—a time of unusual flippancy—that threat loomed larger than ever.

Through the late fifties the *Journal*'s daily stock market coverage remained the province of the redoubtable Oliver J. Gingold and his sidekick, Woody Norton, men of integrity. As Gingold neared eighty, however, his health was deteriorating. Gingold's "Abreast of the Market" column was now ghostwritten by younger men— John Allen, later of *The New York Times,* and after him Vic Hillery. Still, the column continued to carry Gingold's by-line until his death in 1966 at age eighty-four. Gingold sat in his wheelchair all day, sipping bourbon through a straw, watching the stock market tape, making an occasional phone call on a special light-weight phone, and retaining the last word on the column before it went to press. Norton worked on a small part of the "Abreast" column with its own small headline—"Purely Gossip" or some-times "Heard on the Street." As the headline implied, Norton's section was devoted to what Wall Street was talking about—why some stock had moved four or five points the other day or why it was going to be a good year for Firestone. Usually it was com-piled from newsletters, but it was the closest thing the paper had to real gossip.

When Ed Cony became managing editor shortly before Gin-gold's death, he felt the time was ripe to lift the *Journal*'s Wall Street coverage above the routine. At Cony's urging, Vic Hillery wrote more pointed columns, introducing the comments of a new generation of institutional money managers to replace the old brokerage gang Gingold had counted upon. Hillery's columns were an improvement, but there was a limit to the excitement one could generate in a column about yesterday's stock market activity. As the late A. J. Leibling once lamented, there are only so many ways to say that yesterday's stocks went up or down.

Cony's solution was to make a separate column out of "Heard on the Street." Though he probably did not realize it, the *Journal* had had a prominent daily column, "Broad Street Gossip," through much of the 1920s, but the column had not survived the sober years of the Depression. The idea of the new "Heard" column was to tell what Wall Street really was up to, what was going on behind all that blather about "trends being bullish" or investors adopting a "wait-and-see attitude."

It was a propitious time for such a column: As in the mid-twenties, Wall Street was nearing a crossroads. In the mid-sixties the financial markets were less and less dominated by individual investors and increasingly under the spell of large institutions— pension funds, insurance companies, and mutual fund houses. Not only that, the big institutional investors were abandoning bonds, their traditional safe harbor. McGeorge Bundy of the Ford Foundation had declared that bonds no longer constituted a "prudent" investment, and the flight to equities was on. Even as inflation, the Vietnamese war, and massive new social welfare outlays gnawed away at the stability of the U.S. economy, Wall Streeters plunged into the stock market with an abandon they had not shown in four decades. These were the "Go-Go Years," as chronicled by *The New Yorker*'s John Brooks, a time of dizzying overspeculation, when the heroes of Wall Street were hip young gunslingers who moved huge blocks of stock in and out of the market as though they were playing penny-ante poker. It was an exuberant era of new issues—new stocks thrust upon the public, sometimes with little more to recommend them than a spiffy-sounding name ending in "-tronics." No matter if the company had never shown a profit. Plenty of stocks traded at the breathtaking multiple of one hundred times annual earnings, the historical average for the price-earnings multiple being around fourteen. Like the late twenties it was a time that would end in great disillusionment.

Cony had no one on hand who could write a "down-and-dirty" column about Wall Street. The price that the *Journal* paid for its innocence regarding the Street was a degree of naiveté. *Journal* reporters could be tough and skeptical about Wall Street so long as they wrote about scandals or routine press releases, but no one knew what to expect when all those tipsters, self-promoters, and gossipmongers down there became important everyday sources. Accordingly the *Journal* reached out and hired Charles Elia, a veteran Wall Street correspondent then with the *World-Telegram and Sun.* Cony could hardly have done better. Elia (pronounced E-*lye*-uh) was worldly and wise, a man who could mingle with Wall Street without letting it sully him.

The Street had changed a good deal in forty years, but some of its ways are immutable. Back in the twenties critical information about a stock was whispered by one member of the club to another until, like a chain letter, it spread to the public beyond. As with a chain letter, the inside information benefited mainly those who heard about it early in the game, before the mass of investors jumped in and sent the price of the stock on a tear. This essential pattern remains. The only change has been in the nature of the information that can be used without breaking the law. The Securities and Exchange Commission's Rule 10(b)5 had long prohibited trading on inside information—that is, using significant company information to make a profit before the information becomes available to the general public. But hardly anyone on Wall Street paid much attention to the rule until the SEC demonstrated its seriousness in the Texas Gulf Sulphur case. Tom Lamont's prosecution provoked fear and trembling throughout Wall Street. Thereafter, everyone knew that the commission was dogging the footsteps of key corporate officials, bankers, and financial journalists. The SEC even went after printers who bought stock on the basis of information gleaned from the bulky prospectuses they prepared for brokerage houses and law firms.

Because of the law, certain things outside the legal definition of "inside information" became valuable Wall Street currency. Since it was illegal to trade on real inside poop, the opinions of respected stock market analysts frequently became the next best thing, a proxy for genuine knowledge. If a trader cannot trade on knowledge as to what is going on in the boardrooms of General Motors or Exxon, his best alternative may be to find out what the top analysts of those stocks *think* about them before the rest of his crowd finds out. Getting an early bead on key analysts' opinions, in other words, now provides some of the trading edge that inside information once supplied.

Put simply, the aim of Elia's "Heard on the Street" column was to disseminate analysts' opinions, to give the small-time investor in Omaha access to the same analysts' opinions as the man running a $300-million pension fund at Bankers Trust. It was a worthy goal, but also a risky one. Once it became known that the *Journal* was seeking the real skinny on the market, every sleazy broker in town was going to be palming off information for his own purposes—namely to run up some stock he owned or to run down some stock he had sold short. Maybe his information was good, but then again, maybe it was stale or just plain wrong.

Initially Elia had trouble getting cooperation from Wall Street. Analysts wondered why their customers should pay, say, $5,000 a year for research material if they could read it in the *Journal* for twenty-five cents. But Elia worked on the assumption that Wall Street was a tiny little village where, if two people knew a secret, five hundred other people surely knew it, too. He started by persuading brokers to give him research reports they received from various analysts. Pretty soon Elia's column acquired cachet. Analysts began volunteering their opinions, for they gained prestige when their names appeared in "Heard on the Street," and they could still advance the interests of top clients by telephoning them before they spoke to the *Journal*.

Soon the investment community figured out that there were infinite ways to turn the "Heard" column to one's own advantage. Feeding information to Elia could be highly profitable. If you knew Elia was going to quote your bullish opinion on some stock, you could then go and load up on it, knowing the column would probably send the stock up a bit, if only for a day or two. Elia, well aware of the dangers, would sometimes have to kill a column not yet out of his typewriter because by mid-afternoon he would hear that trading had already commenced on the basis of what people *thought* he was going to say. For dealers on the Street, Elia's column had become a tantalizing piece of speculative meat, a fresh morsel served up every day.

"Heard on the Street" soon became too much work for one man. Elia needed a partner, and he got one, a tiger of a reporter

with more raw gumption than perhaps any three men in the
Journal newsroom. He was an old-time reporter of the Hecht-
MacArthur school, a very conspicuous exception to the reserved
Middlewesterner so typical of the *Journal* staff. He also seemed
the unlikeliest of men to become what the newspaper had always
shunned—a true media celebrity. Yet in a matter of months, that
is indeed what he became. His name was Dan Dorfman.

Actually it was Daniel Donald Dorfman, but he felt the allit-
eration sounded too comical. Like Elia, Dorfman had been at
the paper only a short time, having come there from the deceased
World-Journal-Tribune. New York bureau chief Bill Clabby picked
Dorfman to help out Elia, not because Dorfman knew anything
about the stock market—he didn't. He picked him because no
matter what assignment you gave Dan Dorfman, he turned in
explosive copy—sometimes a bit *too* explosive, as Clabby soon
discovered. Dorfman was the sort of man whom the *Journal* hierarchy probably never understood or really trusted. He was a
thoroughgoing eccentric. But for the late sixties on Wall Street,
he seemed just right—brash, scrappy, an aggressive reporter. By
the time Dorfman rolled the first sheet of paper into his typewriter, colleagues said, he was primed to kill.

A colleague once described Dorfman as everybody's younger
brother. In the Grade-B World War II movie, he was the short,
wisecracking paratrooper who gets ambushed in the first reel;
the rest of the platoon spends the next five reels avenging his
death. Externally Dorfman looked the part. He was five-foot-
seven with curly black hair, heavy-lidded eyes, and a little mustache. He was a bundle of nervous energy, but he disguised it
beneath a layer of clownish flapdoodle. He spoke machine-gun-
style in a horsey whine that sounded as though it really came
from some ventriloquist nearby. But Dan Dorfman was nobody's
fool. He would get on the telephone—which was where he did
his best work—and play that innocent-little-brother role to the
hilt. He would pose the most sensitive, embarrassing questions
in a tone of voice suggesting that he could not possibly understand the impudence of what he was asking. When the hapless
victim indulged him with a fragment more information than was
wise, Dorfman bore in like a kamikaze. As an interrogator he

had few journalistic peers. Colleagues would shake their heads in admiration, thinking that however likable Danny was, any executive who spoke to him a second time was certifiably crazy.

Dorfman not only looked and sounded different from other *Journal* reporters; he was different. For one thing, he had not attended any college anywhere except for a few journalism courses at New York University night school. He was born in Brooklyn in 1930, the son of a garment industry cutter. Due to his parents' divorce and his father's early death, Dorfman spent much of his youth in foster homes and in poolrooms, maturing by his own admission into a fairly successful hustler. "If the poolroom ever closed, eight of us would have been homeless," Dorfman once recalled. But his mother urged him to learn a marketable skill, so he enrolled in the New York School of Printing. Hating it there he escaped to the U.S. Army, where he started a small newspaper with some friends and began to see that reporting offered an alternative to the loathsome trade of printing. Out of the Army, Dorfman took a $38-a-week copyboy's job with Fairchild Publications, publisher of two formidable garment-industry trade papers, *Women's Wear Daily* and *The Daily News-Record*. Dorfman's grammar left a little to be desired, so he took a high school class at night to correct it. But for gathering information, Dorfman's pool-hall hustle was much better preparation than anything the Columbia School of Journalism could have taught him.

Dorfman might never have left Seventh Avenue except that Fairchild began to treat its ace reporter shabbily. In 1964, after going eighteen months with only a $5 pay raise, Dorfman jumped to the ailing but still great *New York Herald Tribune*. He arrived there with barely enough time to establish his reputation before the paper folded. Jim Bellows, the *Herald Tribune*'s ingenious young editor, asked Dorfman to write a five-part series on garment-district ethics, giving him ten days to finish. When Dorfman delivered the stories on schedule, Bellows rewarded him with a $50 bonus. More important, though, the stories gave Dorfman a name in New York newspaper circles. After the *Herald Tribune*'s demise, Dorfman worked briefly and unhappily at the short-lived *World-Journal-Tribune*, then went downtown to *The Wall Street*

Journal. Dorfman was thirty-seven when Bill Clabby hired him to cover the food industry, very old by *Journal* standards. He says he had to take a hefty pay cut. But Dorfman was finally in the right place.

Dorfman would recall that his greatest asset had been ignorance. A reporter who really knows his subject matter also is burdened with many preconceived notions, a serious handicap, since the best newspaper stories are those debunking the common knowledge. A reporter who is ignorant has no choice but to think through every issue anew, and perhaps in so doing he may see things others have overlooked. With Charlie Elia as his tutor, Dorfman would pore over the list of the previous day's most active stocks, a list printed in small agate type in each day's *Journal.* Elia told him that there ought to be an explanation as to why each stock on the list had moved up or down. If the explanation was not obvious, perhaps there was a good story there. One day Dorfman focused on a drug stock called Syntex, down eleven points the day before. He called a couple of brokerage people, and one of them murmured in an almost condescending way: "Jim Balog doesn't like it." Who was Jim Balog? An influential drug analyst at William D. Witter, as it turned out. It was a moment of epiphany. Wall Street had hundreds of these people saying they liked a stock or they didn't like it, and every time an important one hiccuped, he moved the stock market a little.

Elia was more than Dorfman's mentor; he was his hero. Elia was sagacious, courtly, and circumspect, yet skeptical. He wrote lucidly and treated people fairly, but he laid things on the line. Dorfman would have liked to be Elia, but he lacked the reserve. He had the jugular instinct and could rarely resist giving in to it. Once the natty Elia wore a black shirt to work, the sort that gangsters wear in old movies, and Dorfman had to have one, too. In fact, he had to have several. But somehow on Dorfman the black shirt looked different. On Elia it was a terribly subtle expression of individuality; on Dorfman it was like standing up to sing "The Internationale." He wore a decaying sports jacket and big, gaudy neckties along with the shirts. One day he went to a lunch with Thomas Murphy, chairman of General Motors, and he wore a flashy tie emblazoned with a picture of Mickey

Mouse. Murphy reportedly kept staring at the tie all through lunch, trying to divine its meaning.

Dorfman's great specialty, it developed, was not in chosing a wardrobe, but in puncturing the balloon of high-flying stocks just when they were most vulnerable. To the small-time stock players out in the sticks, this skill made Dorfman less of a peoples' champion than an all-around menace. He would get phone calls from people who were genuinely upset, saying, "You've already ruined my IBM; now you're after my Polaroid. Why can't you leave things alone?"

If stocks were vulnerable, it was hardly Dan Dorfman's fault. By 1968 Wall Street was frenzied. Not since 1929 had there been this sort of market speculation. Besides the hip young portfolio managers buying and selling millions of shares so fast it could make the brokers' heads spin, there were all the new issues, the absurdly high price-earnings multiples. There was Saul P. Steinberg trying to take over the behemoth Chemical Bank, and people like Meshulam Riklis and Charles Bludhorn trying to conglomeratize every company in sight. The stock market was one big, heaving bubblebath, and Dorfman had the knack of knowing precisely the moment at which an individual bubble was about to pop. He would find stocks that were so overblown that they had no place to go but down, and then he would delight in being the little boy who stuck his finger in them first. A column on Bio-Medical Sciences sent the stock down twenty-five points in a matter of minutes. Another one on mighty IBM caused an eleven-point drop. He wrote a column knocking the glamorous semiconductor industry that sent Texas Instruments down six and Motorola down seven.

Dorfman wrote positive things about stocks, too, and generally their prices did rise for a day or two afterward—but people would not remember him for that. His power to move stocks became enormous as his hit-man reputation grew. *Institutional Investor* studied Dorfman's column during the month of March 1973 and found that sixty-nine of the seventy-four stocks he mentioned in "Heard on the Street" had risen when the review was favorable or declined when it was negative. The movement in the stocks might be only temporary, but there was no denying that Dorfman's power was extraordinary. If, during the late sixties or early seventies, you were commuting to work on the Long Island Rail Road, you would see the same phenomenon each morning—row upon row of Wall Street men clutching their little Styrofoam coffee cups and, almost as one, opening the *Journal* to "Heard on the Street." If it was one of Elia's columns that morning, they would read carefully, respectfully. But if it was one of Dorfman's, the coffee would wait. They would clinch the paper a bit more tightly, bringing it closer to the eye. Often as not, a Dorfman column was going to puncture somebody's balloon, cost somebody some money. As far as Wall Street was concerned, this was juicier than any gossip column about Hollywood.

Dorfman seldom left the office. He had a local delicatessen send up tongue-on-rye sandwiches at lunchtime. But that made him no less flamboyant. He would place a phone call, a former assistant recalls, to Gulf & Western's Charles Bludhorn at 11 A.M., telling Bludhorn's secretary that he needed to speak to the tycoon at once. Then he would amble up to the news desk for a few minutes, instructing his assistant to page him as soon as Bludhorn called back. "A call for you, Dan," Dorfman's assistant would shout.

"Who is it?" yelled Dorfman.

"Charles Bludhorn."

"Charles Bludhorn calling *me!* Well, how do you like that?"

Once, in early 1973, Dorfman wrote a column saying that Bludhorn, perhaps the brashest of the conglomerateurs, was accumulating stock in A&P, the vast supermarket chain, in preparation for a possible takeover bid. A&P, eager to learn the source of Dorfman's information, quickly complained to the Securities and Exchange Commission's New York office, which agreed to subpoena Dorfman. The process server walked into the *Journal* newsroom and handed one subpoena to John Williams, who had also worked on the A&P story. Then the process server called out, "Where is Dan Dorfman? Where is Dan Dorfman?" Dorfman was in his usual corner, typing madly and pretending not to listen. When the process server approached him, still shouting, "Where's Dan Dorfman?" Dorfman says he pointed to an older staffer sitting at the opposite end of the room. The hapless process server stalked away, tripping over reporter Priscilla Meyer, who was doing her back exercises on the floor. Dorfman, meanwhile, escaped to the ladies' room, hiding there until he could slip out of the building unseen.

The excitement Dan Dorfman generated was not always amusing. He also incited tempers and tested the editors' limits. The news desk was full of men who could spot trouble at a glance, men who knew how to fend off lawsuits and homogenize each story into *Journal* style. None of the rules seemed applicable to Dan Dorfman. Charlie Elia's columns were so balanced and well reasoned that they barely needed editing. Dorfman's, by contrast, seemed about as restrained as a Molotov cocktail. Often Dorfman would drop his little bombshells on the news desk at ten minutes to zero hour, giving the editors no time to defuse them. Dorfman's tactics finally drove the news desk to take the only protective measure it could. The desk simply refused to handle Dan Dorfman's copy, no matter what time it was delivered.

By default, the job of editing Dorfman's columns fell to Bill Clabby. The New York bureau chief, in another life, would have been the very model of a Marine Corps master sergeant, yet even he could not always control the rambunctious Dorfman. Clabby admired Dorfman's energy and liked him personally. But Clabby frequently felt uncomfortable with what the industrious columnist wrote. The columns made news, no question about that, but news of a sort that was particularly open to manipulation. Like most highly aggressive reporters, he felt, Dorfman saw the world in black and white, without any compromising shades of gray. Moreover, Clabby thought, Dorfman harbored personal prejudices and tended to side with his best sources. Dorfman was tagged as a one-dimensional reporter. Worst of all, Clabby thought, Dorfman's information came from a narrow assortment of stock market people—"crapshooters." Many people on Wall Street knew—or at least thought they knew—who Dorfman's sources were, thus increasing the odds that people were going to learn to manipulate him.

Given enough time, Clabby felt, he could usually edit Dorfman's columns into something resembling fair balance, but what could he do when Dorfman threw in the next day's column at 3:45 P.M.? What Clabby eventually did in such instances was to open a drawer in which he kept a spare column by Charlie Elia.

Still, there were times when Dorfman made a perfect end run around the *Journal*'s defense. In July 1968 he interviewed Robert L. Vesco, perhaps the greatest financial con man of the era. Strictly off-the-record, Vesco told Dorfman that his company, International Controls, a so-called "junior conglomerate," had acquired a hefty amount of stock in Electronic Specialty Company, which was ten times larger than Vesco's own firm. But Vesco made no secret of wanting to take it over.

How much Electronic Specialty stock did Vesco have? Dorfman asked. Vesco refused to say, for that would only drive up the price of Electronic Specialty and make the takeover more expensive. On the other hand—and still *strictly* off-the-record—if Dorfman would care to guess that Vesco had *five* percent of Electronic Specialty stock, the financier would not *deny* it. Dorfman had a sensational column the next day on "rumors" of a possible Electronic Specialty takeover. The company behind the takeover attempt "was rumored to be" Vesco's International Controls, Dorfman reported, which, "according to brokerage house reports" already had about five percent of Electronic Specialty's roughly two million shares.

Soon afterward, Vesco demanded and got an audience with Electronic Specialty's chief executive. Laying a copy of Dorfman's column on the desk, Vesco noted the strength of his position. The five percent position in the stock described in *The Wall Street Journal* was something like having a full house in poker. Would the executive like to discuss the terms of Vesco's takeover? The unwelcome deal was completed within a year, even though Vesco's stake in Electronic Specialty at the time of Dorfman's column, it turned out, had been somewhat less than one-half of one percent. Vesco had used Dan Dorfman and used him badly.

Dorfman was used again when he wrote a column that was bullish on Brunswick Corporation and bearish on American Machine & Foundry, its rival in the bowling equipment business. The analyst who fed Dorfman the story went back to his office and told all of his friends to go short on AMF, touching off a major SEC investigation. God only knew how many similar incidents the commission never found out about.

In retrospect, Dorfman would complain of the tremendous difficulty in holding so much power and influence. "The column should have been read as just a point of view," he would say. "Instead it was read emotionally, as a reason to buy or sell. . . . I think I was fair. I went after the junk. I tried to equalize the situation for the little guy." But Dorfman was not really equalizing things for the little guy so much as he was sensationalizing. He both knew this and appeared to take pride in it. Up and down Wall Street, he was known as a man who broke stocks and crushed portfolios, and it was a powerful brand of celebrity. "I just wiped out $250 million in equity overnight," he reportedly crowed to a colleague after a column had appeared that was bearish on the American housing industry.

There was much more to be said for Dorfman's columns than the fact that they helped sell newspapers. They could point the finger at scurrilous Wall Street behavior in addition to acting as a catalyst for it. Once he wrote of insider trading activity in Liggett & Myers stock at the brokerage firm of Neuberger & Berman. Afterward Dorfman got a note from SEC Chairman William Casey saying: "Dear Dan: Just to let you know—We're on the case."

In the end Dorfman would leave the *Journal* under something of a cloud. The editors had basked in his celebrity for almost six years, knowing that the paper rarely indulged in such flamboyance before Dorfman's arrival. But they also sensed that Dorfman's style of doing things was a little dangerous, that his sources—creatures of that greedy, alien world called Wall Street—were perhaps a little too intimate with the reporter. It was the time of Watergate, after all, when all institutions were especially conscious of appearances, and the *Journal* simply would not risk a scandal of its own.

What almost certainly ended Dorfman's career at the newspaper was an incident that might have looked to an outsider like a payoff, but one that Dorfman insists was simply an inadvertent misunderstanding. The reporter was indeed on close terms with some sources. One of them, whom Dorfman later described as "maybe my best," was a broker with a small firm who, Dorfman explained, was having trouble raising enough capital to underwrite an initial public offering—a new stock. Sometime in late 1972 or early 1973, the broker credited Dan Dorfman with $500 worth of the new stock. Was it a favor to a good friend or a small payoff for some past favors? Dorfman insists that it was nothing of the kind. Dorfman's explanation is that he had lent the broker $500 to help with the initial public offering—though such ventures normally require millions in capital—and that, without his knowledge, the broker had used the money to buy stock on Dorfman's behalf.

Perhaps nothing at all would have surfaced under ordinary circumstances, but Dorfman knew that the Securities and Exchange Commission, suspicious about the process by which new stocks were being launched, had undertaken an investigation that was bound to turn up his stock ownership, so he felt he had little choice but to tell managing editor Ed Cony and New York bureau chief Bill Clabby. There was melancholy and anger on all sides. Dorfman complained that he'd been growing unhappy in his job for quite some time now and that his pleas for a job change had been ignored. But the paper could not risk a scandal. Dorfman resigned.

Dorfman left that spring to work for *Institutional Investor,* the magazine that had just featured his picture on its cover. The explanation given was that Dorfman had been taken with the publication while being interviewed for its cover article. Dorfman would soon move on to more visible platforms like *New York* magazine, *Esquire,* television, and his own nationally syndicated column. He would never recapture the power he had had at the *Journal;* how could he? But his fame and certainly his income would grow steadily. As for the *Journal,* it had been reminded that there were reasons it could not unleash a Dan Dorfman upon Wall Street, reasons it could not have the kind of intimate relationship with the people *out there* that it had had back in the twenties—not under any circumstances. The chemistry of the financial district was just too volatile for that.

CHAPTER 13

On the Inside Track

BILL KERBY SAT in Barney Kilgore's old ninth-floor office, just a few floors above the newsroom but really worlds away from the newspaper he had helped Kilgore create. Here was Jove atop Parnassus, a newsman turned publisher and chief executive, yet so removed from the real life of the *Journal* that reporters and editors scarcely knew he existed. Kerby was a kind and intelligent man but, unlike Kilgore, an introvert who seldom strayed onto the lower floors of the building. Kerby could still hurl down an occasional Jovian thunderbolt, though, and its effect might reverberate around the newsroom for years.

That is precisely what Kerby did in late 1969, when reporters were demonstrating in the streets, when the front page was drifting farther and farther afield from business, with stories about witchcraft in Manhattan; the human uses of a balm manufactured for cow udders; the plight of a small California town punished by sonic booms from Air Force jets; the private life of Martha Mitchell, wife of the Attorney General; the folk wisdom of humorist Art Buchwald; legal aid lawyers; a rural newspaper editor; the sudden popularity of reindeer meat; and organic farming. It went on and on.

In mid-December Kerby called Ed Cony to his office and told him that the paper had drifted too far from business coverage. "I don't know what you're talking about," snapped the pugnacious Cony. "Don't you like what we've done with the stock market page?"

Kerby had to admit that Dan Dorfman's column made pretty good reading. Maybe it was the front-page editor who was diverting the paper. No, Cony recalls insisting, there was nothing the matter with Paul Lancaster. "If anyone's to blame, I'm the guy. . . ." Kerby saw Cony's face turning white, a sure signal of Cony's mounting wrath, and quickly soothed him. It was all a question of emphasis, said the chairman reassuringly. And the two men agreed that perhaps they ought to take Paul Lancaster to lunch. Downstairs, Ed Cony advised the page-one editor to prepare for a rebuttal of Kerby's charges that the newspaper contained "too much froth." Lancaster boned up on several weeks' worth of back issues like a lawyer getting ready for court. He meant to show Kerby that the stories *Journal* reporters were producing were of such exceptional quality the paper *had* to print them.

They had no sooner sat down to lunch at Kerby's club than Kerby went on the attack in his quiet way. The chairman said he felt that Lancaster and others wanted to strip the paper of its business identity. Kerby was all for broadening the paper, he insisted—anything but " 'incidental rapes and small fires,' " to quote Barney Kilgore, "just so long as it has to do with how people earn a living and spend their money." But things were getting out of hand, Kerby charged, citing one front-page story that had just been published about life in a Scottish monastery. Lancaster was speechless. Of all the stories on Lancaster's front page that fall, the Scottish monastery story had been his favorite. Cony tried to stick up for his page-one editor, but Kerby seemed convinced that Lancaster had let the paper down. Accounts of the chairman's displeasure—especially with the monastery story— soon reverberated through the newsroom. The Green Berets, those ajudged the most talented writers and reporters, felt they, too, were under attack. A good many would depart soon, after being pushed into covering hard business news again for the ticker and the inside pages. Paul Lancaster felt pressured. The lunch left a sour taste with him. He would leave the paper within a year.

The *Journal* now embarked upon a long period of retrenchment. The rebellion against business was over, and now the pendulum would swing the other way, until the *Journal* was nearly in danger of becoming a pedestrian trade paper again. But the process would take several years.

Fred Taylor was forty-two when he replaced Ed Cony as managing editor in late 1970, a tall, big-boned man with a slightly glowering manner. He was aloof and self-contained, a man of sardonic humor who knew more about ballet and theater than about hog prices or steel production. Like Ed Cony, five years his senior, Taylor had worked at *The Portland Oregonian* before starting on the *Journal* copydesk. And like Cony—who was now on the executive floor—Taylor had begun with no intention of remaining at the paper for very long. He had wanted to cover sports or more exciting general fare and had had trouble imagining that he could find contentment as a business journalist.

Taylor was unusual in that he succeeded at Dow Jones without appearing to work hard. He was one of those men of powerful intelligence for whom hard work seems almost superfluous. Even the best writers ordinarily struggle at the typewriter, but not Fred Taylor. He seemed to set his keyboard on automatic pilot. A typical reporter sitting down to write a five-page story might use up ten or fifteen sheets of paper before he is done. Taylor rarely needed more than five, for he was highly organized, perhaps the rarest of qualities in a journalist. He had almost the ideal background for a managing editor, having worked on the front-page rewrite staff, covered labor and the Pentagon in Washington, and managed bureaus in Detroit and San Francisco. In addition Taylor had shrewd news judgment and rock-solid integrity. Shortly after Taylor became managing editor in 1970, Dick Rustin, a gritty reporter covering the securities industry, came up with a story about the New York Stock Exchange that detailed how exchange officials had misled Congress with an overly buoyant picture of the financial health of its member firms. Taylor wandered by Rustin's desk, looked over the story, and though it was late in the afternoon, ripped the next day's front page apart, inserting Rustin's story. Exchange officials were livid. Several came running over to the *Journal* newsroom demanding to know the names of Rustin's sources. Taylor stood solidly behind the reporter, offering only to run a story on an inside page detailing the exchange officials' objections. A month or so later, the exchange issued a press release confirming virtually all of Rustin's story, and Rustin, whose manner was normally as rough as the Brooklyn sidewalks on which he had grown up, walked into Taylor's office and thanked him profusely.

For all his intelligence and integrity, Fred Taylor was seen as uncommunicative. A reporter or subeditor who walked into his office with a question rarely escaped the sensation that he had intruded. Taylor was hard to know, a complex man who covered himself with a shell of privacy and went for months without expressing himself to key staff members. Bureau chiefs say they heard from him at infrequent intervals, if at all. Taylor made the perfunctory visits to the bureaus, as had managing editors since Kilgore's day. But Taylor did not seem to like mixing it up with the reporters. In this respect he was utterly unlike his predecessor, Ed Cony, who loved a good argument on almost any subject.

Fortunately the new page-one editor was adept where Taylor was not. Mike Gartner was a brash, cocky extrovert, just thirty-two when he won the coveted page-one job in 1971. He bubbled with ideas and seemed to energize the newsroom single-handedly. Gartner was a clever and commanding presence, a stocky blond man who was as natty in appearance as he was glib in office banter. A reporter would approach Gartner in need of reassurance about a somewhat iffy story proposition. Gartner would arch his brows and whisper a conspiratorial "Fantastic!" and the reporter would walk away brimming with confidence.

Gartner had been yet another of John McWethy's discoveries. McWethy, the *Journal*'s premier campus recruiter, had found Gartner on a trip to Carleton College in Northfield, Minnesota. Gartner came to work on the *Journal* copydesk in June 1960, full of puckish self-confidence. But Gartner's self-assurance seemed warranted. He had a very sure touch with a typewriter. After a short time he was shipped out to a cub reporting job in Chicago, the normal promotion route. To everyone's surprise Gartner more or less seemed to flop there. As it turned out, Gartner was not very good at doing anything routine.

Warren Phillips, still managing editor then, was sufficiently astute to recall Gartner to New York. Once back in a desk job, his ascent to the pinnacle of the rewrite team was threatened only by a romance with an attractive young copy clerk to whom Gartner became engaged. Phillips reportedly congratulated them both, then reminded Gartner of the company's long-standing nepotism rule forbidding both halves of a married couple from working there. Unfortunately, Phillips suggested, the future Mrs. Gartner would have to resign. Gartner considered the matter, then informed his boss that since he was the older, more easily employable of the two, he would resign instead of his fiancée. Phillips reportedly said nothing, disappeared upstairs, and returned with the news that the Dow Jones nepotism rule had been rescinded.

By 1971 it was clear that the *Journal* would have to promote Gartner or risk losing him, for he had already attracted tempting job offers from Time Incorporated, among others. Paul Lancaster stood in the way. The tall, courtly page-one editor was as gentle and reflective as Gartner was abrupt, but Lancaster did have a glaring liability—his dislike of business stories. And there was at least the suspicion that Bill Kerby did not much care for him. The subject of the notorious Scottish monastery story apparently still surfaced on occasion in the eighth-floor executive meetings.

When the eighth floor had anointed Fred Taylor as managing editor in 1970, it had been obvious that the executives expected him to move the *Journal* away from the soft feature and sociology stories of the Cony-Lancaster era, back toward more coverage of business and economics. The need was even more obvious by the following year, with the country in the grip of severe recession.

Taylor did not doubt that the eighth floor was right. He knew that the *Journal* had lost its ability to write about business and economics with an appreciable degree of sophistication. It had to become more hard-nosed. Yet Fred Taylor understood the subtlety of the task. He had a talented, enthusiastic staff, the best of whom had signed on precisely because of the newspaper's reputation for covering matters like civil rights and sociological trends. He himself had often felt that way. Indeed, covering business at the *Journal* had been branded a job for dullards through most of the sixties. The problem was to remedy the situation without ruining the paper's crispness and originality. He could not risk alienating the staff by changing the ground rules too briskly. Taylor would liken the task to turning around the *Queen Elizabeth II:* It had to be done very gradually, without loss of equilibrium.

Taylor's first move was to issue an edict: The front page would have at least one story about business or economics every day. The next big step turned out to be appointing Mike Gartner page-one editor, for Gartner did not share Paul Lancaster's aversion to business and seemed almost constitutionally incapable of producing a dull front page. Taylor was of two minds about displacing Lancaster. He liked and admired the man, as most everyone did. There was to be no outright demotion. Taylor asked Lancaster to accept a new position as "features editor" for page one, a job whose duties would prove so vapid that Lancaster soon afterward decided to resign. Taylor was visibly distraught to learn that Paul Lancaster was quitting, but he was hardly in a position to offer him a more meaningful job.

Fortunately Mike Gartner lived up to expectations. He could be enthusiastic about almost any kind of story but the commonplace. Like Cony and Lancaster before him, Gartner despised what were known as "barometric boxes," a hackneyed genre of story so named because one of the oldest front-page standbys was the almost perennial article about the cardboard box industry, holding it up as a "barometer" of the economy as a whole. Gartner insisted on the unexpected, whether the subject was business, politics, or, as in one case, a social history of the carrot. He printed stories about the international realignment of currencies, the perils of inflation, and President Nixon's gamble with wage-price controls. But he also made space for articles on the irresponsible behavior of business and the demise of the never-popular midi-skirt ("Back to Pork Bellies, WSJ" huffed *Women's Wear Daily* the next day).

Under Gartner the *Journal's* status as the leading financial publication began to right itself again. The atmosphere of the news department turned more ebullient than ever. Not only was the paper still sprightly and clever, but the real financial experts were once more honored and encouraged—Charles Stabler on banking, Dick Janssen at the Treasury Department, Lindley Clark and Al Malabre on macroeconomics. Richard Rustin's coverage of the securities industry was so enterprising that the lofty *New York Times* was impelled to lodge a complaint with the New York Stock Exchange, alleging that Exchange officials were denying the *Times* its fair share of information.

Under Gartner and Taylor the *Journal's* investigative reporting also bloomed anew. The paper broke the story of Equity Funding, the $120 million insurance swindle, then probably the largest single fraud in history; it broke the Home-Stake Production Company oil swindle, a $100 million tax shelter scam whose victims included scores of top executives, politicians, and celebrities; and it uncovered the story of Vice-President Spiro Agnew's illegal kickback arrangements, dating from his days as governor of Maryland. (Agnew called a press conference when he learned that the *Journal* was about to break the story, thus ruining the paper's exclusive.) These were heady times for the *Journal*.

Next to Gartner himself, the reigning hero of the news department was a man who almost never set foot in New York. He was the *Journal's* dashing young Asian correspondent, Peter R. Kann. Kann was another romantic figure, a blithe spirit from Harvard who had spurned the normal career path at the newspaper. He had opted instead for dangerous adventure in a far-off land from which he had turned out war dispatches of magnificent breadth and poetic sensitivity—all in the finest T. E. Lawrence tradition. Even allowing for the considerable mythology that enveloped him, Kann was a remarkable fellow. He was of middling height with thinning blond hair and sharp features. He was unfailingly polite without being formal, personally smooth without seeming unctuous. What made Kann so exceptional was a superabundance of charm. He knew how to flatter so subtly that people had no idea the effect was purposeful. Kann had the knack of making the one remark in a thousand that left new acquaintances utterly disarmed. And he had a deft, impish wit that allowed him to abuse any number of institutional rules without penalty. Kann was extraordinary—a curious combination of introvert and extrovert, a thoroughly likable fellow, great company in a saloon or a poker game, yet shrewdly unrevealing of his inner thoughts.

Kann grew up in Princeton, where Barney Kilgore lived, though neither he nor his family knew the publisher well. Kann's father, Robert Kann, was an eminent Austrian historian, a Jewish refugee who had gained appointment to Princeton's prestigious Institute for Advanced Studies. Attracted to journalism as a teenager, Peter Kann found part-time work at Kilgore's *Princeton Packet* picking up newsstand returns, typing up bowling league scores, and later reporting stories. Kann occasionally saw Kilgore emerge from his limousine, enter the little newspaper shop on Spring Street, roll up his sleeves, and proceed to set type for an hour or so with the men in back.

Early one fall before Kann returned to Harvard, he sat through opening day of a first-grade class in a Princeton school and wrote a story for the *Packet* from a child's perspective. Kilgore sent Kann a congratulatory note, and the following week Kann's story was reprinted on the front page of Kilgore's other pet newspaper, *The National Observer*. Kann was never aware of receiving any favors from Kilgore, but the publisher did drop a heavy hint that he should apply for a job at the *Journal* after finishing college. Kann, moreover, got a prized summer job with the *Journal* between his junior and senior years, though he applied for it without informing Kilgore.

Still, the *Journal* might not have hired Kann permanently had it known of all his extracurricular doings at Harvard. One of Kann's fellow *Crimson* editors, he recalls, made a hobby of swiping stationery from celebrated professors, then forging amusing letters with the help of cronies. Just after Kann's graduation in May 1964, Jawaharlal Nehru died in office, and *Newsweek* devoted its cover story to the meek new Indian prime minister, Lal Bahadur Shastri. By coincidence, Kann and his friends possessed a few prized sheets of stationery pilfered from the desk of John Kenneth Galbraith, economist and former U.S. ambassador to India. They concocted an overly clever letter mimicking Galbraith's baroque literary style and impugning the ability of the new prime minister to hold the country together. *Newsweek* eagerly printed the letter in its next issue, touching off a full-blown diplomatic incident. At the time Galbraith himself was secluded in his Vermont summer home, oblivious to the letter hoax. When the former ambassador finally got word of the letter, he demanded that the government launch an investigation. Kann and his friends had little choice but to confess the deed with multiple letters of apology. Luckily for Kann the *Journal* did not learn of the matter. Newspaper reporters have been fired for lesser pranks.

Kann joined the *Journal* that winter in the Pittsburgh bureau. A year later, after a brief hiatus in San Francisco, he was posted to Los Angeles, where the bureau chief, Mitch Gordon, had need of a junior reporter to take on some of the scut work.

Peter Kann had near perfect disregard for the conventional success track. Bureau chief Gordon was an agreeably tough character, a soldier of the old school who believed in order and decorum. He did not have much luck with Kann, who was uncommonly good at beating any system. A thoroughgoing dreamer, Kann had long entertained fantasies of becoming a foreign correspondent. Since there was a war in Southeast Asia, that seemed to Kann the place where he belonged. Kann asked Gordon if there was a chance that the *Journal* might send him there, but Gordon was hardly encouraging. The *Journal* had precious few men in Europe then, none at all in the Far East.

At that point Kann considered leaving the newspaper, but instead he decided to make one great push for the Asian assignment. After reiterating to Ed Cony that he badly wanted to go to Vietnam, Kann set out to prove that he could write dazzling international stories. The *Journal* had any number of petty jurisdictional rules, primarily designed, Kann thought, "to keep you from writing great stories." Kann got around them. He drafted a story suggestion about Mexico's opium-smuggling trail, purporting to know about a U.S. link that fed directly to Southern California. Actually, the Southern California connection was completely fictitious, a ruse to get around the Dallas bureau's exclusive rights to stories about Mexico. Kann needed six different signatures to get approval for the story, but eventually he obtained them. Once in Mexico he conveniently forgot about the California angle and wrote a colorful account of life in small mountain villages dependent upon the cocaine trade, contrasting their views with the futile efforts of wild-eyed Mexican Air Force pilots to incinerate the crop.

Soon afterward, in the spring of 1967, Fred Taylor, then Pentagon correspondent, returned from Vietnam and told his friend Ed Cony that it was high time the paper assigned someone permanent to the controversial war. In an inspired moment Cony phoned the relatively inexperienced Kann and asked if he still wanted to be the *Journal*'s man in Asia. Eight weeks later Kann landed in Saigon.

Peter Kann was personally disorganized, a notoriously poor speller who was all but incapable of arriving on time for appointments. In addition, he could be maddeningly absentminded. Once, he boarded an Army cargo plane for a trip to embattled Khe Sanh, a combat zone so dangerous that military pilots never switched off their engines while their ammunition cargoes were being unloaded there. They allowed just enough time for grunts to push out the freight, then turned around and took off again. Passengers would spill out of the plane as fast as their feet could carry them—anxious to get away from the volatile cargo. When Kann's plane pounced on the steel runway at Khe Sanh, everyone leapt for the door—except Kann, who reportedly sat deeply absorbed in a worn paperback copy of Alexander Solzhenitsyn's *The Cancer Ward*. A colleague shook him and shouted, "Let's get the hell out of here." Kann calmly closed his book, put it inside his pack, and disembarked as casually as if he'd been landing at La Guardia. There was no question that Peter Kann had a guardian angel somewhere.

As a journalist, Kann's saving grace was his unparalleled eye for detail. Kann was one man covering a war to which other newspapers and networks assigned teams of men. In *Journal* tradition he was free to ignore the daily war bulletins and strive for the flavor of the conflict. This he did like no other journalist.

Driving through the Mekong Delta in a battered Volkswagen, Kann found that natives were less in dread of the Vietcong than they were of a nine-nostrilled water snake reared, according to rumor, by a local necromancer. He saw a group of South Vietnamese infantrymen frantically hunting for their shiny new M-16 rifles when a party of U.S. visitors surprised them. He wrote about following a glad-handing U.S. Congressman, Joseph Y. Resnick of New York, on an official inspection tour. The Jewish politician told his military guides that he wanted to meet New York GIs, preferably Jewish ones, and got exasperated with rounds of military briefings. Kann caught him berating an Army protocol officer at Saigon airport: "You've nearly ruined my entire trip. . . . I specifically asked to see troops in the field. . . . I've seen pacification . . . I've seen refugees. . ."

Kann's swashbuckling reputation was finally cemented by his coverage of the 1971 civil war in East Pakistan, for which he won a Pultizer Prize. His articles were not analyses of grand political and military developments, but touching eyewitness reports that piled one small anecdote upon another, forming a collage of the war's incomprehensible horrors.

Kann followed the simmering conflict from mid-summer 1971 through early December, when open fighting erupted between the Pakistani and Indian armies. At that point the *Journal* executives in New York decided that Kann should get out for his own safety. Fred Taylor sent Kann a cable on December 6: "Your stories unarriving here. Situation looks dangerous. Suggest you depart immediately." But Kann's marvelous stories eventually did arrive. Like Edward R. Murrow in London thirty years earlier, he described watching the bombing of Dacca from a hotel rooftop. His only response to Taylor's departure order was a one-word telegram that read: "What?"

Taylor cabled again on December 8: "Get out of Dacca before it's too late." Kann wired back: "Cable urging me leave Dacca unarrived. Sorry." In his diary, reprinted in the *Journal* a week later, Kann wrote:

> A half-million or so Bengalis probably died in last nine months; another 10 million or more trapped in misery of border camps. What makes a few hundred Western lives so valuable?

On December 10 Taylor sent a third cable: "Depart Dacca at once. Regards Taylor—Cony—Phillips—Kerby, New York." Three days later Kann's answer came back: "Who Taylor— Cony—Phillips—Kerby? Guy has funny name. Cheers, Kann— Kann—Kann—Kann." In his diary Kann wrote:

> City completely still as if some epidemic had suddenly wiped out all living things except the black crows hovering everywhere. Of course, the only epidemic is fear. . . . We awoke to the noise of C130 transports circling overhead. Looks as if evacuation flights for women and kids really are coming in. If the planes are leaving, this diary may leave with them.

Kann's diary left Dacca, but not Kann, and on December 14 Taylor cabled his correspondent for a fourth time: "Catch plane immediately. I am serious. Your life perhaps not in jeopardy, but job is." Kann wired back: "Will catch plane out. Which way Dacca airport, please?" Kann did not actually leave Dacca for another week, after wiring Taylor: "Get feeling you perhaps want me to depart Dacca. Will do immediately. Incidentally, war ended over weekend. Kann."

Compared to Peter Kann, Larry O'Donnell, the Detroit bureau chief, was a man of determinedly unadventurous ways. To Gartner and others in his privileged circle, O'Donnell was a plodder. He was a bland-looking man with sand-colored hair and puttyish features. People who met O'Donnell found him wholesome and inoffensive, friendly as a puppy, and given to homey exclamations like "Golly!" and "Gee whiz!" He was excessively self-deprecating in conversation, giving the impression of harmlessness and naiveté. But there was more to O'Donnell than met the eye.

O'Donnell's background was distinctly uncolorful. He grew up in suburban Scarsdale within a devout Catholic family, and he took an early interest in newspapers. O'Donnell had wanted to go to college at the University of Missouri, famous for its journalism school. Instead he bowed to his father's wishes and entered Holy Cross, a Jesuit school, where the required curriculum included courses on Thomism and epistomology. No one could know how much theology O'Donnell actually absorbed there, but people who knew him in later life would often describe him as a "village priest," "a Jesuit," meaning that he had a Churchlike belief in order and hierarchy.

O'Donnell graduated from Holy Cross in 1957, having been editor of the weekly college newspaper. He spent six months in the U.S. Army Reserves, then went to work for *The Wall Street Journal* under the charge of the venerable bond editor Pat Carberry, whom O'Donnell would later credit with teaching him to respect numbers. "The whole story was in the fourth decimal," O'Donnell discovered. After nine months with Carberry, O'Donnell became an assistant to George Church, then textiles editor. Church was only a few years older than O'Donnell but infinitely more experienced. And while O'Donnell would turn out to be a capable reporter, his writing would be considered by many, at best, pedestrian. Since the young Holy Cross graduate preferred sticking to hard business news, his halting prose was invariably given over to the literate Church for transfiguration. Off and on for a decade, George Church was O'Donnell's personal mentor, as well as his personal rewrite man.

As a cub reporter Larry O'Donnell seemed fresh-faced and eager, perhaps a little too naive. He had a well-hidden tough streak, though. He went to a corporate meeting early in his career and rose to ask the president to clarify something he had said. "If I had known there was a reporter here I would never have made that statement," the executive reportedly protested. O'Donnell surprised people at the *Journal* by quoting the man to that effect in the next day's paper. O'Donnell was never as guileless as he seemed.

After two years O'Donnell was assigned to cover the real estate industry, a subject no other major newspaper really followed. O'Donnell soon came across a major story—the pending collapse of perhaps the greatest American real estate tycoon, William Zeckendorf Sr., builder of the United Nations headquarters and myriad urban renewal projects. O'Donnell covered the unraveling of Zeckendorf's affairs for nearly five years. He discovered that because shares in Zeckendorf's company, Webb & Knapp, Inc., were publicly traded, the tycoon had to file documents with the

New York Stock Exchange detailing the financial arrangements for his new ventures. The documents showed that Zeckendorf was taking out loans at ever increasing interest rates, a sign of a mounting liquidity squeeze. By 1964 Zeckendorf was selling off chunks of his own stock in the corporation to keep it afloat and making his celebrated remark: "I'd rather be alive at twenty percent than dead at the prime."

O'Donnell continued to ride the story for another full year after the company's bankruptcy in 1965. Then, though real estate and textiles were almost the only subjects O'Donnell had covered, his reward for the Zeckendorf story was one of the most prestigious assignments that the *Journal* had to offer. In 1966 Ed Cony took O'Donnell aside and asked if he would like to become the newspaper's Detroit bureau chief.

O'Donnell's initial reaction to the offer—or at least his recollection of it—was curious. He told Ed Cony that he was not at all sure he was really cut from managerial cloth, that he was not sure that taking such a demanding job would be fair to his family. He and his wife had had four children within five years, after all. Throughout his career O'Donnell always would take pains to sound humble. And now, instead of instantly accepting this plum assignment that all but guaranteed him a gilt-edged future at the *Journal*, O'Donnell told Ed Cony he would have to think about it for a while. His deliberations about the promotion lasted only a day or two, though. Bill Clabby, the New York bureau chief, took him out to lunch and reportedly told him that only a jackass would turn down the Detroit assignment.

When Larry O'Donnell took over in Detroit in 1966, the bureau's fondest tradition still lay in publishing pictures of the new car models before the auto companies were ready to unveil them—the game that had begun with John Williams' great coup in 1954. It was far easier to get hold of the pictures than in Williams' day, but the project still required ingenuity, since other publications were now competing for them as well. The *Journal*'s ace reporter in Detroit was Jerry Flint, who was powerfully disappointed at not having gotten the bureau chief job himself. One of O'Donnell's first tasks when he got to town was to help Flint with the story that went along with the sneak-preview car pictures

Flint had pirated. O'Donnell was examining one of the pictures
with a magnifying glass, observing the minuscule changes from
the previous year's model. A slightly new slope to the bumper
was really the most obvious difference, for unlike in the industry's
heady times after World War Two, Detroit could no longer afford
to make sweeping changes every year or two. Cars began to look
more and more alike, year in and year out. O'Donnell recalled:
"I asked myself: 'Is this a sexy new car?' No, it was just a new
car. Why were we bothering with this stuff?" And after Flint departed for *The New York Times*, O'Donnell decided to discontinue
the ritual, much to the disappointment of former Detroit correspondents, who considered the new-model pictures important,
not just because of consumer interest but also because of *Journal*
lore.

The other tradition O'Donnell inherited from John Williams
was that of spurning advances from Detroit's omnipresent public
relations men. In 1954 Williams had gone to Detroit with instructions from Henry Gemmill not to attend any off-the-record
briefings and to avoid all the other pack-reporting exercises that
seemed to have made the Detroit press corps a captive of the
auto industry. Over the years Williams' success at remaining independently aloof had hardened into an institutionalized hobby
of baiting PR men, an office contest to determine which man
could remain most morally pure while serving his time in this
industrial Sodom.

Larry O'Donnell was nothing if not incorruptible. He found
the proffered gifts and favors of publicity men "ethically repug-
nant" and lost no time in demonstrating his ability to don the
hair shirt. O'Donnell forbade his men from the old practice of
taking home new cars from manufacturers on the pretense of
test-driving them. Henceforth, if a *Journal* reporter wanted to
try out a car, it had to be done at a company test track. He rein-
stituted the old John Williams rule of shunning local press club
affairs, though the club was a gathering place for major industry
figures.

And he enforced the old prohibition against taking gifts from
the industry by personally setting a perfect example of rectitude.

Once, an industry PR man reportedly sent an expensive case of whiskey to his home, and O'Donnell's wife mistakenly threw out the card. O'Donnell doggedly tracked down the donor and sent back the booze. On another occasion a PR man is said to have sent him an elaborate basket of fruit, cheeses, and ham at Christmas. O'Donnell reportedly put the basket under a table near his desk for all the staff to see and left it to molder there for a while. Then he called the publicist and, without explaining, asked him to come down to the *Journal* office in the Detroit Bank & Trust Building. The PR man arrived in short order, probably expecting that O'Donnell was about to consult him on some matter that would doubtless redound to his client's advantage. Instead O'Donnell rose and pointed indignantly to the ripening fruit beneath the table. "Would you carry that thing out of here?" he demanded. O'Donnell's bureau was consistently rated the most ornery one in town, and O'Donnell, reclusive and untouchable, was proud of the fact.

O'Donnell was hardworking and conscientious in the extreme. He made his men double-check everything and pushed them to unusual lengths to get the other side of the story. When a man or a company stood to be damaged by an article, the reporter in O'Donnell's bureau had to do more than just attempt to reach the victim for fair comment. If the man was out of town, one had to send telegrams, track down his lawyer, leave messages all over. O'Donnell was not merely fair; he was scrupulous.

And yet, through the late sixties, both in Detroit press circles and in the *Journal's* New York newsroom, Larry O'Donnell evidently had a spotty reputation. His writing had always been plodding, say editors, and he was considered a by-the-book sort of bureau chief. He was the kind of man who reportedly read handbooks on how to manage people and seemed to take it all literally. The stories that came out of his bureau—even the better ones—tended to be of the nuts-and-bolts variety. Rarely was there a page-one leader out of O'Donnell's bureau that surprised or delighted, the criticism went, and this was particularly dismaying to the page-one editors because the Detroit bureau contained some of the very best young men at the newspaper. It had some wonderful talent—Jerry Flint, Walter Mossberg, Norman Pearlstine, a succession of others—but O'Donnell kept a tight rein, even on his senior men. Many of them bristled.

Everyone in O'Donnell's bureau had his assignment, and if the assignment was to cover Chrysler Corporation, the reporter was expected to stick to Chrysler Corporation, even if curiosity might have led him to some potentially interesting idea involving Ford or General Motors. People in the bureau saw O'Donnell as a humorless bureaucrat enamored of order and hierarchy. He had a nervous laugh, and the air around him was heavy with tension. He worked endless hours and displayed the workaholic's telltale distrust of subordinates. If a reporter seemed to linger too long over the morning papers, O'Donnell would clear his throat audibly and give a disapproving look. He seemed dreadfully afraid of slipping up on a routine story and willing to forgo the exciting in order to safeguard the ordinary. When General Motors held its annual meeting to announce earnings, O'Donnell sent three or four men—four-fifths of his bureau—to race up and down the corridor on behalf of the news ticker. O'Donnell kept his reporters' noses to the grindstone. After they handed in their stories, he reportedly would make them churn out revision upon revision, never really explaining why they were necessary, except with some maddeningly vague declaration, such as: "It doesn't quite get to the substance" or "This needs a lot of work!"

Life with O'Donnell was so terribly frustrating that some say they began pleading with New York for transfers. O'Donnell clearly intended to be personable and decent, but his warmth often seemed more doctrinaire than real. He went to church regularly, took in waifs and runaways now and then, and made every gesture to be kind. But he made his staff miserable. One of those who most disliked working under O'Donnell was George Nikolaieff, who felt that his bureau chief was simply unwilling to let any reporter do really fulfilling work. Nikolaieff begged the company for a transfer to New York, believing, among other things, that the future of his marriage might depend on it. But he heard nothing. Then one night Ed Cony, the managing editor, came to Detroit for a routine visit. Larry O'Donnell threw a cocktail party at his home in one of the plainer sections of Grosse

Pointe. After a round or two of drinks, Nikolaieff found himself chatting with his tormentor in a corner. As Nikolaieff recalls it, O'Donnell, having no idea how much Nikolaieff loathed working for him, decided to let the young reporter in on a secret. Six months earlier, O'Donnell whispered, the New York bureau had called to request that Nikolaieff move back East. "I told them to forget it," O'Donnell reportedly said with a smile. " 'This guy has just barely unpacked his bags in Detroit; don't bother him.' " The worst of it, said Nikolaieff later, when recounting the story, was that O'Donnell had undoubtedly thought he was doing him a favor. Serving one's time in a gritty town like Detroit was, at least to O'Donnell, the way to succeed at the *Journal.*

CHAPTER 14

"I Just Went Wild Over that Curve!"

JUST WHEN THE *Journal* management began reining in reporters, forcing them to attend more closely to business in the trade paper vein, rather than spending their time writing about obscure monasteries and striptease queens, the opposite was taking place on the editorial page. The news pages were being hauled down to earth, but the opinion page was about to soar.

The *Journal* editorial page already held a unique place in American journalism as the quintessential defender of free enterprise. It was a cherished institution among conservatives, almost their daily bugle call. Most newspaper editorial pages, one might argue, are vestigial organs, remnants of the time when publishers first tried to refrain from gaudily splashing their views all over the front-page news columns. Relatively few people bother to read them nowadays, partly because the number of big-city newspapers has shrunk and the survivors' biases have become so familiar—and partly because editorialists seem to have so much difficulty these days working up a compelling sense of

238

indignation. Editorial writing may be a vanishing art. The average opinion page, once a proud, influential voice in the community, has become toothless and predictable, a handy place—often as not—for employing the controlling family's ne'er-do-well nephew or in-law.

Not at the *Journal*. Perhaps because it increasingly expressed a minority point of view in a country marching steadily to the left, the *Journal*'s editorial page found it easy to be indignant. But under the guidance of Vermont Royster, the page's boss and spiritual patriarch, indignation was couched in such reasonable terms that the paper's editorials rarely seemed tedious or predictable. What tempered them was the curious tone of optimism that Royster brought to the normally pessimistic conservative outlook. In the long run, Royster seemed to say, things would probably turn out fine. "After all," he once pointed out, "the Dark Ages only lasted five hundred years."

After Royster's official retirement in 1971, the editorial page began an important transformation. Always before it was the loyal opposition—wry, courteous, cognizant of the limits of its power. Now it became more militant, more brassy and adventurous. And with the election of Ronald Reagan in 1980, it accomplished something unparalleled in the annals of modern journalism. It fostered an entirely new economic philosophy—a *radically* new economic philosophy—that became for a brief time at least the prevailing economic doctrine of the White House. Not since the Hearst papers sent the United States charging up San Juan Hill had there been so visible a tie between the expressed opinions of a newspaper and the consequent deeds of the U.S. government.

Supply Side Economics was, practically speaking, invented by *The Wall Street Journal*. The movement began with a few obscure economists venting some unorthodox ideas, but it was the *Journal* editorial page that collected their thoughts, combined them into a politically palatable package, and attached a label. It was the *Journal* editorial page that actually went out and found politicians to espouse Supply Side, an altogether unorthodox string of circumstances quite unlike anything that the publication had ever previously attempted.

The critical thing about Supply Side—the linchpin of Ronald Reagan's domestic platform in 1980—was that it amounted to an intellectual rebellion against the anointed fraternity of professional economists. For years the high priests of economics had managed to persuade the general public that they knew precisely what they were talking about, even if the unindoctrinated layman hadn't a clue. Privately, the best of them might admit that economics was no more a real science than psychology or sociology, but merely an ongoing attempt to quantify the amorphous. Publicly, however, they spoke with impressive certainty, couching their predictions in the sort of Delphic ambiguity that virtually guaranteed they could never be entirely wrong. With Supply Side Economics, the *Journal* was not merely taking on its usual enemies—liberals, organized labor, etc.—but the whole field of academic economics as well. It was a swashbuckling act carried off by two men, Robert L. Bartley, chief of the *Journal*'s editorial page, and Jude Wanniski, his associate from 1972 to 1978.

Bob Bartley was one of those remarkable discoveries of John McWethy, the *Journal*'s Chicago bureau chief, who spent much of his time prowling Midwestern college campuses in search of talent. McWethy found Bartley in obscurity—obscurity even by Middlewestern standards. He was editor in chief of *The Iowa State Daily*, the campus newspaper of Iowa State University, the state agricultural school in Ames, not to be confused with the University of Iowa in Iowa City, one of the country's great centers of learning. Bartley had grown up in Ames, the son of a veterinarian on the ISU faculty. He was obviously smart enough to attend any college in the country, and certainly he was worldly enough. When the Ames high school principal outlawed the wearing of Bermuda shorts, Bartley, as editor of the school paper, wrote a blistering editorial concluding: "We fail to see what is so esoteric about the knee." He matriculated at Iowa State not because he aspired to be a farmer—one had to own land for that—but because the tuition was a bargain $54 per quarter, and he could save more by living at home. While Bartley's upbringing was not underprivileged, it was, in the best sense, *un*privileged.

At Iowa State there were three possible majors besides agriculture—all of them in fields vaguely related. There was business administration, psychology (here the connection was indeed vague), and journalism, which was essentially intended to train county agriculture agents to publicize improved farming techniques. Bartley chose journalism by process of elimination and duly became the apple of the faculty's eye. As it turned out, learning was quite possible under the circumstances—a surprise to outsiders, Bartley asserts, only because Midwestern small-town culture is so poorly understood. "The reason we have not had a Midwestern literature, perhaps, is precisely that the Midwest was too American, that it saw no reason to explain itself." But, of course, there was one great newspaper that reflected Midwestern sensibilities, *The Wall Street Journal,* and after earning a quick master's degree in political science at the University of Wisconsin and spending six months in the Army, Bartley fortuitously found his way there.

McWethy put Bartley through the usual first-year obstacle course in Chicago, concluded that he had promise, and sent him on to Philadelphia, a smaller bureau where, he thought, Bartley had a better chance of finding his wings. At that point Bartley veered away from any of the usual success paths for reporters. He wrote to Lindley Clark, then in charge of the *Journal*'s editorial page features, and volunteered to contribute book reviews. Impressed with Bartley's work, Clark suggested to Vermont Royster that they invite him up to New York as a summer fill-in on the editorial staff. "But I don't know how to write editorials," Bartley warned. Replied Royster: "It's just like writing book reviews, except you don't have a book." With Bartley, however, Royster would not always have the last word.

There was never much doubt that Bartley was Royster's protégé. Royster found him "brash . . . We had to squelch the hell out of him." But then Royster liked brashness in young people. Diffidence got you nowhere in his book. As Royster recalled, Bartley at first viewed the editorial page as too conservative, in need of "liberal enlightenment," but then again, Royster often would say things like that just to provoke people. Calling Bob Bartley a liberal was a bit like calling Mao Tse-tung a capitalist-roader to his face. An intense, ruminative man, personally reserved and uncomfortable with small talk, Bartley later admitted to having been "a bit caught up in the Kennedy glamour: you know, 'French food and intellectualism to the world.' But I was never exactly a liberal. I thought some of our editorials in 1964 were simplistically conservative. We were supporting the tobacco industry on the cancer issue, which seemed like an unnecessary burden."

Bartley's reassessment of the Kennedy glamour stemmed from the pressing issue of the mid-sixties, the Vietnamese war. He had supported the Kennedy Administration's role in the coup against Ngo Dinh Diem in 1963, but in retrospect it erased his faith in Kennedy foreign policy. Bartley would remain hawkish on the war because he believed that the United States was obliged to keep its commitment. But he was not at all content with the way in which the commitment had been made.

Though Vermont Royster retained the title of editor in those days, he was actually a senior executive of the corporation, occupying an office on the eighth floor. The daily operation of the editorial page was in the hands of Joe Evans, who years earlier had been Warren Phillips' predecessor in London. Like Royster, Evans was a gentle conservative, a graceful writer possessed of a style that was at times indistinguishable from Royster's own. As pedagogues, however, the two men exhibited real differences. Royster was a born teacher, a master of the Socratic method, who would sit at Bartley's desk crushing out one cigarette after another, dissecting his work clinically. When Royster left, Bartley would count up the number of butts on the linoleum to assess the damage. A three-butt session—about forty-five minutes' worth—wasn't really too bad, he felt. Then Bartley would look back at his excoriated copy and realize that while Royster had ripped through every other word or so, he had left no suggestions whatsoever as to how the editorial might now proceed. Evans was more Solomonic. During the morning skull sessions, he was open to argument as to what position the page should take on virtually any issue. Once he decided he didn't like an editorial, however, he simply went to the writer and told him what to write. The page did not look much different under Evans than it had under Royster, but the young writers deprived of Royster's tutelage were unquestionably the poorer.

Bartley would be the last of the great editorial writers trained by Royster, and though he would never acquire his master's graceful way with images, the learned air of gentleness, he would digest just about every other trick in Royster's repertoire. Royster had a set of guidelines for young editorial writers. He would tell them that in the first half of the editorial—the first column—you would lay out the argument for the opposition, "give the devil his due," then you would use the second column to demolish those points one by one. Bartley was a wizard of the game, but instead of conceding a point now and then, as Royster did, he would steamroll the opposition, debating points, it seemed, out of sheer bravado rather than necessity.

During the late 1960s controversy over the Vietnamese war was heating up on the editorial page, just as it was in the newsroom and in America at large. Each morning the writers would gather around Joe Evans' desk and fight for the soul of the editorial page. Bartley quickly emerged as the most hawkish and as the most effective debater. Bartley, moreover, was the most ardent defender of President Nixon, then under attack by liberals and intellectuals on all fronts. Sounding a bit like the President himself, Bartley would argue that the trouble with the country lay in too much permissiveness. How could these people, the liberal academics, expect the country to heed their advice when they couldn't keep control of their own universities? As for Vietnam itself, he wisecracked: "When winning the war didn't work, everyone decided the problem was that U.S. society was too immoral." After one editorial that was perhaps too nakedly pro-Nixon, Royster wandered into the editorial office and delivered a rare kind of warning to his star pupil: "Bob, I liked your editorial today, but there was one problem."

"What?" said Bartley, his voice faintly aquiver.

"You never want to get us that much in bed with any Presidential Administration. You never know what's going to happen."

In 1968 Royster finally decided that the paper should come out against the war. The resulting editorial was not a tirade against U.S. involvement in Southeast Asia; it simply said that the war was not worth winning at any price, that the U.S. should prepare for defeat. But once the *Journal* had turned on the Vietnam issue, Royster began to worry that Bartley was getting restless. The great debate was clearly over now; the paper had stuck its flag on the beachhead of the anti-war movement. Where did that leave Bartley? Anyone who knew him sensed that what drove this intense, brainy Middlewesterner was not ego or power-lust so much as a compelling fear of boredom. Royster's solution was to ship him off to Vietnam, to Hong Kong, and to Japan in the name of furthering his education. Vermont Royster was clearly enamored of young Bartley and did not want to lose him.

Bartley actually had not wanted to go to Asia. He wanted Washington, instead. "Oh, God," moaned Royster, sensing that putting Bartley in Washington would be like throwing a cat into a tub of cold water. But after Bartley returned from Vietnam, he kept nagging about Washington, and finally Royster relented. He had not been happy with the editorial copy coming from the Washington bureau anyway. Neither Alan Otten nor Henry Gemmill had been able to supply opinion columns that really satisfied him, for good reporters often have difficulty squelching their sense of impartiality long enough to write a good, stinging editorial. At least with Bartley, Royster knew he was going to get some provocative copy from down there.

Bartley arrived in the *Journal*'s Washington bureau in December 1970, the only person there who was not under the thumb of bureau chief Otten. The friction between the two was never subtle. Bartley insisted on going his own way, calling up sources at the Treasury Department, the Pentagon, and anyplace else he chose. In Otten's view Bartley was screwing up regular beat reporters' vital contacts wherever he went. "Get this son of a bitch out of here," Otten reportedly told Royster. That winter Royster announced he was retiring to Chapel Hill, leaving Joe Evans in sole command in New York and Bob Bartley to fend for himself in Washington.

Bartley hated Washington, just as Royster had known he would. He found the place narrow and stifling, a "company town" intolerant of dissent and hostile to intellectual ferment. "You meet too god-damned many journalists there!" he exclaimed, and the insularity he experienced was certainly real. Washington is the great den of pack journalism, a place where a reporter quickly learns the futility of deviating from the story line that all others are writing. Editors across the nation will read the front pages of *The New York Times* and *The Washington Post,* and their inevitable impulse is to wonder why their own Washington reporters did not get the same thing as those two august publications. Safer to plow the same furrow and sprinkle the same manure. Bartley was most struck by the oddity that the single most influential journalist in town was someone whose stories almost no one in Washington ever saw. This man was the late Peter Lisagor of the *Chicago Daily News,* whose importance stemmed from his knack of placing the key question at major press conferences, the answer to which would dominate the headlines in most major papers the next day.

In the early seventies, well before Watergate, the Washington press was openly hostile toward Richard Nixon. The reasons were many: reporters' liberal inclinations, Nixon's attempts to scale down the entrenched government bureaucracy—always the reporter's best source of information—and, no small factor, the President's reciprocal loathing for newsmen. Bartley was a Nixon partisan, and though such feelings did not constitute a capital crime, in the highly politicized mood of the journalism fraternity, they made him an outcast. In his isolation Bartley began casting about for other, congenial spirits. He made some interesting friends, like George Will, then an aide to one of the more obscure U.S. Senators—Gordon Allott of Colorado. And Bartley focused much of his energy upon defense policy, where he was more likely to encounter conservative-minded people. Among those he cultivated was a fellow journalist who had written a pro-Nixon column called "The Big Risk for Peace," supporting the controversial Safeguard antiballistic missile system. The man was Jude Wanniski, and he worked for the *Journal*'s sister publication, *The National Observer,* in nearby White Oak, Maryland.

It was no coincidence that Bartley and Wanniski should come to know one another as a result of their mutual admiration for Nixon. Wanniski, after all, was named for the patron saint of lost causes. As disagreeable as Nixon might have seemed to others, Wanniski loved him just for being unpopular. Loyalty to the little guy was deep in Wanniski's nature. In fact, what had made him a good reporter, perhaps a great one, was his passion for siding with the underdog. The more bruised and battered someone seemed, the more Wanniski liked giving sympathetic aid and comfort. He was a profound romantic.

Jude Wanniski was a coal miner's son, a dark-complexioned man with a large frame and rough peasant features. In manner and in speech, he was a dead ringer for a union organizer and a man who later inspired George Will, paraphrasing Macaulay, to say: "I wish I were as confident about *something* as he is of *everything*." A mass of contradictions, a right-wing populist, a creative and highly persuasive ideologue, Wanniski was flamboyant to the point of inviting ridicule. His first appearance at Dow Jones & Company had been on a day in 1962 when he drove up to the *National Observer* offices in suburban Washington in a silver Buick Riviera convertible, wearing mirrored sunglasses and a gold lamé sports coat, with his wife—a leggy former Las Vegas showgirl—seated next to him. Yet Wanniski yearned to be taken seriously. During the House of Representatives' Watergate proceedings in 1974, Wanniski would agree with Republican Congressman Charles Wiggins of California that their duty lay in defending President Nixon to the last. Thus, just a few days before the discovery of the "smoking gun" tape recording that finally proved the President's culpability in the cover-up scandal, Wanniski published a slightly farfetched explanation of how the President *might not* have known what his morally misguided aides were about. He was apparently the last journalist from any prominent publication to plead the President's innocence.

Jude Wanniski also stuck out from the journalistic crowd because he had a plan for himself. Most newspaper reporters stumble through their careers clutching at opportunity, wondering where life will lead them. Wanniski had his life laid out. Everything made sense; everything pointed toward some rational scheme of order. He wrote a book—really a Supply Side call-to-arms—called *The Way the World Works*. The title alone spoke volumes about Jude Wanniski's character.

Both his father and his maternal grandfather, men of nearly the same age, were anthracite miners in Pottsville, Pennsylvania.

There the similarity ended. His grandfather, active in dissident Lithuanian groups, was a committed Communist, he says. The father was more passive, an America-firster who put his faith in the flag and the United Mine Workers. The grandfather had nothing but contempt for the union, and if anyone asked why, he would scornfully explain: "Because John L. Lewis always called his strikes in the *summertime*." The disagreement between the patriotic father and the Marxist grandfather went beyond unionism, of course. The grandfather was skeptical of authority and ignored the fact that the FBI often hovered around the immigrant groups he was involved with. The father was horrified, refusing to let his children go near their grandfather's political gatherings for fear that the taint of Communism might some day haunt them. The father was ambitious for his children, and to make sure they did not follow their forebears into the coal mines, he moved the family to Brooklyn, which back then had a reputation for a superior public school system.

Wanniski grew up with a profusion of political instincts. Like his family he recalls being violently opposed to Joe McCarthy and to Richard Nixon for his role in the witch-hunts. In a high school history class one day in the early fifties, a teacher named Martin Wolfson entered the room, shut the door, and drew the curtains. "Is anybody coming?" Wolfson whispered conspiratorially, his black mustache twitching. "Today's lesson is: Communism isn't all bad! That's enough. Open the door!" Wanniski would remember being shocked and thrilled. Wolfson, he thought, was vindicating his grandfather. The next day, when a classmate reported Wolfson to the principal, the teacher acquired the status of a permanent hero in Wanniski's canon, along with Pete Reiser, a Brooklyn Dodger outfielder who was forever slamming himself against the left-field fence in Ebbets Field in futile attempts to take home runs away from the despised New York Giants.

Wanniski spent two years at Brooklyn College studying natural sciences at the urging of his high school advisers. Then he transferred to UCLA, switched into political science, and stayed on for a one-year master's degree program in journalism. Upon graduation he was offered a job as assistant to the city hall re-

porter at *The Los Angeles Mirror* at $83 a week. "All that time and
$83 a week to learn to be a city hall reporter," thought Wanniski.
He declined the offer and instead picked three cities where he
wanted to work—Anchorage, Las Vegas, and Honolulu, all three
boom towns with internationally known datelines. He decided
that he would spend precisely one year working in each place,
then move on to greater fame and glory.

Wanniski hitchhiked to Anchorage in the spring of 1959 with
$150 in his pocket. *The Anchorage Times,* it turned out, didn't need
any new reporters; neither did the rival *Daily News.* Desperate,
Wanniski offered to work free for a month. The *Daily News* took
him on, and over the next thirty days Wanniski garnered, by his
count, thirty-three by-lines. Admiringly the paper gave him a
salary of $115 a week to stay on. In the space of a year, Wanniski
did nearly everything it was possible to do at the little paper. He
wrote a magazine column, wrote theater criticism, and covered
city hall and crime. (" 'Killings,' " he recalls. "Always 'killings,'
never a 'murder,' even if the gun was still smoking in the Eskimo's
hand when they led him from the bar.") And after exactly 365
days, he left. He did not go to Honolulu. He had a job waiting
there, but could not afford the plane fare. He went to Las Vegas,
got turned down by the *Sun,* but obtained a promise from the
competition, the *Review Journal,* that he could have the next job
that fell open, provided he was willing to take a pay cut. He was.

After his 365 days in Las Vegas, Wanniski, now twenty-four,
was preparing to leave for a job with the *Honolulu Star-Bulletin.*
He would stay at the *Review Journal,* he told editor Bob Brown,
only if he could cover every beat on the paper, one month at a
time. Brown, amused by the idea, agreed, and Wanniski stayed
on for a second year, after which he demanded his own column.
"You're too young," Brown insisted, but eventually the editor
gave in. It was 1962, and two important things happened to Jude
Wanniski that year. The first was that Bill Giles came through
town signing up stringers to contribute to the new *National Observer.* The second was that Richard Nixon, beaten in the Presidential race two years earlier, suffered a second, more humiliating defeat in the California gubernatorial election. Wanniski,
a long-time Nixon hater, wrote a column criticizing the former
Vice-President, but Editor Brown, who had met the man on sev-

eral occasions, took Wanniski to task. "You know," he told the young columnist, "Nixon isn't all bad."

"My God," thought Wanniski. "That's Martin Wolfson talking!"

The conversion from Nixon-hater to ardent admirer was almost instantaneous. Wanniski went to the library and read *Six Crises.* He "got to like Nixon's globalism. Here I'd always seen him as 'Fortress America,' wanting to seal off the rest of the world, but I found he had the same impulses towards the family of man that I did. He viewed the Communists as people to be dealt with—like spoiled children. . . . I became a full-fledged Nixonite."

Two years later Brown resigned as editor of the *Review Journal,* reportedly in a dispute with the publisher. Wanniski called Giles at the *Observer* and said he was in desperate need of a job. And that was how, several weeks later, Wanniski, with his Las Vegas bride, came roaring up to the *Observer* offices in his flashy convertible and the gaudy attire of a casino pit boss. The reception was chilly, especially from the *Observer*'s established political writers, James Perry and James Dickenson, who did not know quite what to make of this Brooklyn cowboy. Wanniski was certainly no threat to them. He was assigned to write for the inside of the paper, which automatically relegated him to a lower caste than Perry and Dickenson, front-page men all the way. Nonetheless, Wanniski recalls feeling lonely and unwelcome.

He was sitting in the *Observer*'s small employee canteen some weeks later. A few tables away Bill Giles was chatting with a thin, swarthy stranger, a Latino from the looks of it. "Jude," Giles called out, "come over here and meet Juan Felipe." At least, that is what Wanniski *thought* Giles said.

Wanniski gathered from their brief conversation that this man Juan Felipe was a new Latin American correspondent, and he was anxious lest the poor fellow feel as unwelcome as he did. "Tell you what, Juan," said Wanniski, clapping him solidly on the back, "let's you and I have a drink together later on." Juan Felipe nodded stiffly.

Wanniski strode back to the *Observer* newsroom. "Hey," said someone. "Guess who's in Bill Giles' office. Warren Phillips!"

Thus does Wanniski recall his introduction to the company's future chief executive.

Wanniski sits over lunch at the Spring Brook Country Club near his home in Morristown, New Jersey, on a dull November day in 1981. The dining room has a great, wide window overlooking what must be a difficult tenth hole. He is telling the story of his journalistic career, which is unusual at every turn. "I'm the guy who goes out and gets laughed at," says Wanniski, by way of explanation. Life has thrust him into roles that would make most people squirm, yet Wanniski professes contentment and relishes describing himself as an idealistic bomb-thrower. "I've always been uncomfortable with any role other than maverick," he insists. "I *like* to take the unpopular position."

Out on the golf course, a long row of ducks flies overhead, aligned in an asymmetrical "V." Their grace is too stunning to ignore, particularly since the conversation, like the autumn sky, has taken on a slightly melancholy cast. Once Wanniski's attention is called to the ducks, his eyes lift from the silverware, flirt with the birds momentarily, then seize from them an explanation. "Did you ever stop to think," he says, "that when ducks fly in a 'V' there is really a kind of voting process going on? They have a collective notion of where they are going, and they will pick a lead duck and follow him as long as he flies a straight course. But when the lead duck veers off, he loses their confidence. The line shifts to a new vortex; they follow a new leader."

Wanniski may have been the butt of jokes among the *Observer*'s big-league political writers, but Bill Giles, a bit of a street-fighter himself, was an admirer. The editors had to watch Wanniski's copy carefully, for his strong personal predilections had a habit of creeping in, Giles recalls. Still, there was no denying Wanniski's creativity. He had a way of thinking in terms of anecdote and metaphor; he knew how to grab the readers' attention; he was relentless in his search for the novel idea. Wanniski liked to spot politicians before their time and shower attention on them. Hence, in the mid-sixties he began arranging off-the-record dinners for his editors and colleagues with still relatively unknown senators like Edmund Muskie of Maine and George McGovern of South Dakota. Wanniski had not been hired as a star columnist. He was assigned to write a modest digest of Capitol Hill news for page two. But Wanniski invariably gravitated toward controversy, especially toward issues where President Nixon's prestige was on the line.

In February 1971, a time of sputtering economic frustration, the Nixon Administration unleashed its annual economic forecast, which was quickly denounced by the economics profession as hopelessly optimistic. The White House forecast said that the Gross National Product for the year would come to $1.065 billion, some $20 billion higher than the consensus opinion. At the Joint Economic Committee hearings on the forecast, Senator William Proxmire asked Office of Management and Budget director George Shultz just how his department had arrived at its "ten-sixty-five" figure when everyone else was saying "ten-forty-five."

Sir, said the budget director, we have a different way. And he proceded to outline an unorthodox method of calculating GNP that had been developed by his chief economic aide, a thirty-year-old prodigy named Arthur B. Laffer, who had accompanied Shultz to Washington from the University of Chicago. Art Laffer was a short, pudgy, cherubic man, utterly unschooled in the wiles of Washington and candid to a fault. Until his "ten-sixty-five" GNP forecast came to the fore, he had been on his way to a superlative academic career. A ranking scholar at Yale and top graduate student in economics at Stanford, Laffer had taken only three years to obtain a tenured spot in the economics department of the University of Chicago, arguably the most prestigious economics faculty in the country. Suddenly he was a target of ridicule, with antagonists ranging from the liberal eminences of economics—Paul Samuelson, Walter Heller, John Kenneth Galbraith—to his conservative colleagues back at Chicago. *Business Week* lambasted him with a cartoon showing the young Chicagoan at the controls of a Rube Goldberg contraption labeled "Laffer Money Machine." The magazine smirked: "Sure enough, $1.065 billion does come out of 'Laffer's money machine.' But it is the result of such a strange mechanism that the model has become, if anything, more controversial than the forecast. . . . [It] has something in it to offend everyone."

Laffer had hardly done anything to deserve such a shellacking. "I am anti-forecast, as is the entire Chicago school," he asserts. "But there is nothing wrong with checking probabilities. We merely took figures reflecting what Herb Stein [chairman of Nixon's Council of Economic Advisers] had used in figuring an 'optimum feasible path.' It wasn't really a prediction; it was an assumption. But I did believe in it."

No sooner had George Shultz's testimony concluded than Art Laffer's telephone began ringing with calls from the press. A reporter from *The Washington Post* got to him first, he says, and Laffer told the reporter that the economic model to which Shultz referred was really just a simplified thing—for internal office use mainly. The interview appeared in the next morning's *Post* with not quite the spin that Laffer had intended. The story seemed to suggest that Laffer had set out to devise an economic model for forecasting the GNP that would be sufficiently simple for *even* his boss George Shultz to understand. Feeling more and more like one of Franz Kafka's victims, Laffer decided he would give no more interviews.

As page-two political columnist for *The National Observer*, Jude Wanniski hardly had much access to the OMB Director or the Secretary of the Treasury. Yet the story of the moment was the attack on the Nixon Administration's economic forecast, and Wanniski could not bear to sit on the sideline. He made a call to Art Laffer, the young White House economist under so much pressure, and Laffer's secretary told him to go away. Wanniski did not go away. He kept hounding Laffer until, after the immediate furor blew over, Laffer agreed to have lunch. In fact, the anguished economist was relieved to be able to tell someone his story, even if Wanniski, sitting in a little sandwich shop near the Executive Office Building, could barely understand a word of what Laffer was saying. But they became friends, and they kept on lunching. Wanniski, who knew nothing of economics, says he began to call Laffer to ask "stupid questions"—"What's the law of supply and demand?"—that he would never feel comfortable asking other experts. And Laffer says he was thrilled to talk to someone who "wasn't there to maul me."

There was, as yet, no such creature as Supply Side Economics. There was just Art Laffer talking and Jude Wanniski listening. Laffer held a gaggle of unorthodox views that were at variance from both the liberal disciples of John Maynard Keynes and the conservative monetarists, whose Mecca was Laffer's University of Chicago. Lord Keynes had been the first to articulate the government's responsibility for moderating the painful cycle from boom to bust, a pendulum that seems to have swung from time immemorial. Lord Keynes' prescription for alleviating severe economic depression was to stimulate the economy by putting money directly into the hands of consumers through government employment programs. Writing in the midst of the Great Depression, Keynes concluded that there was simply no other way to revive the moribund level of business investment without prolonged economic suffering. Keynes' *General Theory of Employment, Interest and Money* did not concern itself much with the evils of inflation that might ensue from too much government pump-priming—for at the time inflation was hardly a pressing worry, quite the opposite. But in the post-war era, with the problems of the Depression far behind, Neo-Keynesians discovered an inverse relationship between inflation and unemployment: When one is high, the other is low. And so in times of rising unemployment, the standard liberal remedy became the elixir inflation—until in time it got out of hand.

Monetarism—the conservative orthodoxy of the 1970s—is just the opposite of government pump-priming, a bitter medicine that could only be administered by a stern economic disciplinarian. In essence, the monetarist theory holds that if only the government will maintain a sound currency and restrict its own spending, the economy will cure problems like unemployment and inflation of its own accord.

Art Laffer adhered to neither of these philosophies. Indeed, he says he had no sweeping theory of his own, just a good many insights about tax rates and incentives. And Laffer had other ideas which surfaced that August, when President Nixon, desperate to do something about inflation, imposed temporary wage-price controls and ended the right of foreign governments to exchange dollar holdings for gold. The official price of gold, fixed at $35 an ounce since the Bretton Woods conference of 1944, was now allowed to float. For the first time since the Depression, U.S. citizens were permitted to own gold for investment purposes.

Laffer and Wanniski had lunch at a French restaurant off La-
fayette Square. "What's important about all this?" Wanniski asked.
"The press will say that the main thing is the wage-price freeze,"
he recalled Laffer answering, "but really it's the closing of the
gold window."

"What's the gold window?" asked Wanniski. " . . . What's it
mean?"

"Put it this way," said Laffer. "From now on it's not gonna be
as much fun to be an American."

In December Joe Evans died of a heart attack at age fifty-two.
Warren Phillips called Vermont Royster down in Chapel Hill to
discuss Evans' successor. The logical heir to the editorial page
was the mild, scholarly Lindley H. Clark, Jr., the man who, coincidentally, had converted the editorial page to monetarism in
the early sixties. Clark, who held a master's degree in economics
from the University of Chicago, was a thoroughgoing professional. He had served for five years as the *Journal's* page-one
editor before moving over to the editorial page in 1961 to write
on economic affairs, and he did so with utmost clarity.

At the time when Clark arrived in the editorial department,
the page still clung to old-line conservative views—a balanced
budget, fixed currency exchange rates, a return to a *pure* gold
standard, and stable prices. When Clark asked Royster what he
should write editorials about, Royster would answer: "Attack inflation." Royster's page was going at the Federal Reserve ham-
mer-and-tongs for permitting inflation, then hovering between
one-and-a-half and two percent a year. The diplomatic Clark introduced his monetarist ideas very gradually—floating exchange
rates; steady, controlled growth of the money supply; no return
to the gold standard. "It all sounds logical," Evans would say with
a nod, "but how come all those bankers out there disagree?" Ultimately Clark prevailed and made the *Journal* editorial page the
voice of monetarism, much as Bartley and Wanniski would later
make it into the voice of Supply Side.

Royster and Phillips both admired Clark. There was no question that he was in line for Evans' job, no question that he de-
served it, and yet they thought he was perhaps *too* scholarly, too

mild. They would prefer to choose someone who might make more waves, someone with a touch of Royster's asperity. There was no one who approximated that description but Bob Bartley, thirty-four, Royster's favorite, still down in Washington making Alan Otten's blood boil. If they gave Bartley the page, Clark would undoubtedly want out, they thought. So might younger men like David Anderson and Edwin MacDowell, Bartley's regular debating adversaries in the morning sessions with Evans. Despite the likelihood of these defections—all of which came to pass—Phillips phoned Bartley and gave him the job. The first person Bartley told about his promotion was his wife, Edie. The next call he made was to George Will, whom he asked to join him. Bartley knew he was going to need some new writers. Will declined, citing his Senator's forthcoming re-election campaign. Bartley's third call went to Jude Wanniski. "But I don't know how to write editorials," said Wanniski, with the same uncharacteristic modesty that Bartley had expressed to Royster eight years earlier. Bartley's answer: "All it takes is arrogance."

Bartley and Wanniski moved to New York concurrently, living at the St. Moritz Hotel while their wives—Wanniski had by now remarried—packed up affairs in Washington. The two men spent immoderate time together, eating supper in the hotel dining room and taking long walks afterward as far south as Union Square. Their heads were full of ideas on nearly every subject under the sun, ideas that would not square with any existing political camp, liberal or conservative.

One thought Wanniski had was that the editorial page of the *Journal* behaved as though it were ignorant of the power it possessed. A newspaper with a daily circulation of 1.3 million, read by the most influential people in the country. Wanniski thought, my God, *The Wall Street Journal* editorial page. . . . They've no idea of the power. . . . And Bob Bartley was apparently thinking the same thing.

Bartley had not hired Wanniski to write about economics, but rather about Washington politics. Wanniski's desk was adjacent to Lindley Clark's, and the learned Clark still wrote nearly all the economics editorials. But Clark apparently could not get over his disappointment at having been passed over. After several weeks Clark was permitted to return to the newsroom as a special economics correspondent, leaving Bartley's page devoid of a resident economist. Wanniski meant to fill the gap. Though he himself was an amateur, he had a good friend who was a bona fide expert, and they spoke on the telephone at length every day.

Life had not been kind to Art Laffer. He had returned to his teaching post at Chicago at the same time Wanniski was moving to New York. But back in Chicago the faculty made him more miserable than ever. The memory of the embarrassing "ten-sixty-five" prediction had faded in Washington, but it glowed brightly in Chicago. Laffer was learning that no politics were as vicious as the academic brand. That summer the University of Chicago economics department had sponsored a lecture by the esteemed Paul Samuelson of MIT entitled, "Why They Are Laughing at Laffer." As if in passing, the great Samuelson had noted: "Doctor Laffer . . . but I am premature; he's *not* a doctor. . . . " Whatever else Samuelson had had to say that evening was anticlimax. Was it possible that Arthur Laffer—this living blight on the Chicago economics department—did not even have his Ph.D.?

It was not only possible; it was true. Laffer, who had won tenure faster than anyone else in the department's history, had not quite completed requirements for his doctorate at Stanford. It was something Laffer had occasionally joked about. He had never gotten around to making some pedestrian revisions in his doctoral dissertation, so he had never actually received his degree. Now it was no laughing matter. Laffer says he made the revisions in a matter of three weeks and quickly got the degree, but not soon enough to stop the Chicago faculty from forming a committee to investigate the possibility that he had deliberately misled them. The committee found no evidence of deception, but the ostracism was almost total. He was not invited to seminars or parties; most of the faculty would not speak to him; and he despaired of ever getting his research published. Though Laffer remained popular among students, he was ostracized by the Chicago faculty. Not for another five years would he depart for the University of Southern California and begin to rebuild his life. In the meantime Laffer had virtually no outlet for his ideas, apart from his daily talks with Jude Wanniski.

Wanniski would tell Laffer about the major news events each day—Laffer rarely read the papers—listen to his reactions, then argue his ideas at the next morning's editorial conference. When the United States devalued the dollar in early 1973, the consensus view among economists seemed to be that the act would add one-half to three-eighths of a percentage point to that year's Consumer Price Index, the most closely watched inflation monitor. Parroting Laffer, Wanniski insisted that it would add five percent. The others on the page laughed at him.

One of Wanniski's early questions to Laffer back in 1971 had been, "Who is the greatest economist alive?" Laffer had answered not with a familiar name like Friedman or Samuelson, but with an unknown, Robert Mundell, an early mentor of Laffer's at Chicago who had written an important textbook, *International Economics*, in 1968, then faded into obscurity at the University of Waterloo in Ontario. Wanniski did not meet Mundell until he and Laffer attended a conference in May 1974 at the American Enterprise Institute in Washington, where Mundell was delivering a paper on global inflation. It was a timely issue, for the oil price shocks of the year before had driven worldwide inflation to scary levels.

Mundell is a squat man, somewhat baby-faced, with a mop of prematurely gray hair and a slurred manner of speech—an unprepossessing figure, it would seem, except among economists. In any case, Wanniski was enraptured by him. Rather than arguing for a tax hike to cure the ailment of inflation—the conventional wisdom of the moment—Mundell wanted a stimulative tax cut à la John Maynard Keynes. Inflation, he argued, could be contained by tight monetary policy. Wanniski's populist imagination was on fire. He was used to hearing Laffer espouse the same global conservatism, but here was Mundell, agreeing with Laffer's internationalist outlook and yet advocating a domestic tax cut, the ultimate in liberal economics. "A strange triangulation was occurring in my mind," he recalled. "I was bursting."

Laffer had much the same reaction to Mundell's speech. He thought that perhaps Mundell was right, that the income tax might be crippling economic incentives so severely that a tax cut, rather than simply spurring consumer spending and making inflation worse, might actually boost production sufficiently to reduce inflation and offset any losses to the Treasury.

The three men dined together that evening, and Mundell went further. Unless the government enacted a tax cut of at least $10 billion that summer, Mundell insisted, the automobile industry would suffer an egregious depression in the fall, and the rest of the economy would "fall off a cliff" in January. Unemployment, Mundell predicted, would reach a horrendous eight percent, and the next year's budget deficit might be $70 billion. Wanniski remembers looking at Mundell and Laffer and observing how coldly mesmerized they were by these numbers. "Where they saw numbers, I saw people, and I felt sick to my stomach. I was in possession of awful, terrible wisdom that no one except us had. I asked them how they sleep at night? They told me all they could do was come up with ideas; they couldn't live them. But I *had* to live them or else go crazy. At that moment, I became a true zealot."

The next three years would nearly ruin Wanniski's second marriage, he recalls. His second wife, Christine, a childhood sweetheart, could not understand what drove her husband. He had a manic side she had never glimpsed before. Wanniski slept fitfully, lost interest in anything extraneous to Mundell and Laffer, cut off all social life. He was in the grip of a new religion, and he dedicated himself to converting *The Wall Street Journal.*

Returning from the Washington conference, Wanniski rushed in to his friend Bartley and said, "Bob, we need to push for a big tax cut." Bartley was incredulous. What on earth was Wanniski talking about? And Wanniski had to confess to himself that he simply hadn't the words to explain what Mundell and Laffer were thinking. Though he ranted about the tax rates and incentives and gold-backed currency, no one listened. Wanniski was becoming such a pest on these matters that at last Bartley had to silence him so that others could do their work. He wryly issued a fiat: "No discussion of international exchange rates until after the three p.m. deadline."

That fall Dow Jones chairman William Kerby wrote his only editorial piece anyone could remember, sending it to Bartley "for consideration." Bartley read Kerby's article and, not too surprisingly, deemed it worthy of publication. Kerby's message: Americans had to bite the bullet and accept a tax increase. The column nearly drove Wanniski crazy. He frantically telephoned every high-level contact he had made in the Ford Administration. He called Secretary of the Treasury William Simon, White House economics advisors William Seidman and Alan Greenspan, and finally White House Chief of Staff Donald Rumsfeld. He told each man that the Republican Party was going to take a bath in the mid-term elections with a platform based on President Ford's "WIN" buttons ("WIN" being an acronym for "Whip Inflation Now") and a five percent tax hike. "You've got to press for a tax *cut*," Wanniski pleaded. They listened to Wanniski briefly and dismissed him—all except Rumsfeld, Wanniski says. "Who else believes this?" asked the Chief of Staff. "Just me and two economists, Robert Mundell and Arthur Laffer."

"Arthur Laffer!" Rumsfeld reportedly shouted. "Arthur Laffer is a genius!" Though most of the press had long forgotten Art Laffer and his "ten-sixty-five" prediction, Rumsfeld apparently had not. In late 1974 the Commerce Department had just completed final statistical revisions on the Gross National Product for the year 1971. Wonder of wonders, because of the year's unexpected burst of inflation, Laffer's seemingly absurd forecast of $1.065 billion had turned out to be almost exactly right, one of the most accurate GNP forecasts ever recorded. "Get Laffer down here," ordered Donald Rumsfeld.

Laffer came to Washington in December, a month after the elections in which the Republicans suffered epic defeat. Rumsfeld was unavailable, but he dispatched an aide, Richard Cheney, to meet with Wanniski and Laffer. The trio met for drinks and dinner at a restaurant near the White House. It was a historic meeting, but not for reasons anyone else could have predicted. As Winniski recalls the evening, Laffer, a man of uncontrollable energy, simply talked too fast to be comprehended by anyone not already versed in his views. As the meeting wore on, it became obvious that Cheney did not understand. In a fit of exasperation, Wanniski recalls, Laffer grabbed a paper cocktail napkin and sketched a simple graph on it—a bell-shaped line that Wanniski would enshrine as the "Laffer Curve"—which showed how in theory two different tax rates might produce the identical amount of revenue for the government.

It was no great feat really, merely a quick way of demonstrating the principle of diminishing returns—that in theory a lower tax rate *could* generate as much or more tax revenue than a higher rate, which is something every first-year economics student learns. The "Laffer Curve" itself was elementary economics. What was radical was the assertion that the United States was already past the point of diminishing returns in its tax policy—far to one side on the curve. The evidence behind this theory invited further dismay from the economics profession, for it was largely empirical. Quite clearly, a good many people in upper income-tax brackets spent an unhealthy amount of time figuring out how to cut their taxes—time better spent, from society's point of view, plotting ways to simply make more money.

Years later, after Laffer and Wanniski had had a falling out, Laffer would insist he could not remember the cocktail napkin incident. Neither could Richard Cheney. Yet Jude Wanniski, a born genius in the art of publicity, would never forget it. "I just went wild over that curve," said Wanniski. And so would the electorate six years later, after Wanniski had made the "Laffer Curve" a household phrase. The curve was scientific-looking evidence that there was nothing wrong with the U.S. economy that could not be cured by a big, broad tax cut. The economics establishment jeered.

So far Wanniski had only one convert to his cause—another noneconomist, who would turn out to be more influential than he imagined. Wanniski spent substantial time in Washington throughout 1974, often lunching at the American Enterprise Institute, a conservative think tank. One of his frequent brown-bag partners there was Irving Kristol, among the most provocative writers on religion and sociology and later the high priest of what became known as Neo-conservatism. Kristol was another novice on the subject of economics, but he thought that Wanniski made great sense. And he was not one to worry about Wanniski's lack of proper credentials. "The problem with modern economics," he would explain, "is that the field has become so conceptually abstract in an effort to mimic natural sciences that it has lost touch with the real world. Economics has become highly mathematical, but the truth is, Keynes, Marshall—all the great economists—were suspicious of mathematical economics. They believed the precision was illusory."

That November Kristol took Wanniski to lunch at the Italian Pavillion in New York and asked him to write a lengthy article for his magazine, *The Public Interest,* on the subject of the press corps' economic ignorance. Wanniski rejected the idea, saying that it was unfair to assail the press when it simply reflected the ignorance of the economics profession itself. Okay, said Kristol, then why not an article about the economics profession itself? This Wanniski would do, and a few months later Kristol published the piece, "The Mundell-Laffer Hypothesis: A New View of the World Economy," the blueprint for the as yet unnamed Supply Side movement. Not many people read *The Public Interest,* but those who do tend to be influential. One devoted reader in 1974 was a man named Jeff Bell, aide to perennial Presidential candidate Ronald Reagan of California. "That was the breakthrough article," Bell says of Wanniski's *Public Interest* piece. As Bell prepared Reagan's program for the 1976 campaign, he tentatively penciled in a proposal for a monumental tax cut. The tax cut proposal never surfaced in Reagan's '76 campaign; it was too farfetched for campaign manager John Sears. But the idea simmered beneath the surface. Four years later it would boil to the top.

Meanwhile Bartley's resistance to Wanniski's ideas was thawing. The *Public Interest* article not only enabled Wanniski to put his musings into words, it helped forge agreement between Mundell and Laffer where they had never quite come to terms. Wanniski, Laffer, and Mundell dined frequently at a pub near the *Journal* office, and Bartley began joining them.

Bartley's slow conversion to Supply Side coincided with the mounting financial travails of New York City, which was on the verge of bankruptcy throughout 1975. Improbable as it seemed for an upstanding corporate citizen of lower Manhattan, the *Journal* suddenly appeared to favor civic default. Indeed, Bartley and his staff appeared to fervently hope for bankruptcy, which they saw as a way of publicly vindicating their theories about excessive taxation.

They were disappointed, for the city heroically staved off financial collapse, but Wanniski was writing a series of articles on another subject—petroleum allocation—that would prove out many of Mundell's ideas in the arena of foreign exchange. With the first winter primary elections approaching, President Ford was on the verge of signing a bill to extend oil price controls. Though price controls may be contrary to laissez-faire Republican instincts, the President was persuaded by advisors that without regulation, the price of Number Two heating oil would quickly rise by seven cents per gallon, thus sending his re-election chances up in smoke. Wanniski debunked the theory, using Mundellian logic to show that the U.S. oil price already *was* the world price, and that decontrolling oil would ease the contortions in America's fuel allocation system, making petroleum more available to the public with no appreciable rise in price. This time Wanniski was right, as Ronald Reagan's decontrol of oil prices in 1981 would demonstrate. But in 1975 Ford and his aides found the advice altogether too risky.

Like Wanniski, Bob Bartley had no formal background in economics, but he did have unflagging respect for rational argument, and to him, Wanniski's reasoning sounded more and more compelling. "In college," Bartley later told an interviewer, "I had a bacteriology teacher who gave me a great insight into life. He said that if you were transported back into time and met Pasteur and Koch, you'd probably think they were just like a lot of other nuts—except they were right."

In 1975 Bartley attended a Washington seminar, where he met Buffalo Congressman Jack Kemp, a former professional quarterback who had his own odd ideas about cutting taxes. The two men chatted amiably in Kemp's office. More than anything, Bartley was impressed by the pictures on Kemp's wall. One showed Buffalo quarterback Kemp sitting mud-soaked and weary on the bench, the very picture of dejection after being carried off the field unconscious in a loss to the Jets. Another showed quarterback Kemp stooped and cringing with San Diego end Ernie Ladd, six-foot-eleven and 330 pounds, stretched full-length in the air above him and about to land. It would have been impossible for Bartley to see such pictures without thinking of Jude Wanniski. Back in New York Bartley reportedly told his friend: "You'd better get by and meet this guy Kemp; he's quite a piece of horseflesh."

Wanniski was skeptical. But Irving Kristol had also been impressed with Kemp, and he, too, prodded, saying that Kemp was unhappy because the media were not paying any attention to him. Finally, in January 1976, Wanniski was walking through the cavernous Rayburn House Office Building when he noticed Kemp's office door. The publicity-hungry Congressman welcomed the journalist, and they disappeared into Kemp's office for a talk that took up the rest of the morning and the afternoon, and continued till midnight at Kemp's house, through a supper of macaroni and cheese. Kemp and Wanniski made a natural team—the politician and the publicist.

After January 1976 Wanniski and Laffer would come to dominate Kemp's statements on economics, and with an attractive politician articulating their views, the two men suddenly found Bartley giving staunch support as well. It was far more seemly for the *Journal* to endorse the views of a bright Republican Congressman, after all, than to endorse identical views held by no one in particular except an inexpert member of the paper's own editorial page and his friend, the former laughingstock of Washington.

The ball was rolling. The Wanniski-Laffer movement had everything but a catchy name. That problem was solved in November 1976. At Warren Phillips' suggestion, Bartley had established a Board of Contributors, a collection of provocative writers from varying political camps. One of them, former Nixon economics advisor Herb Stein, wrote a column attacking supporters of the tax-cut idea as a bunch of "supply-side fiscalists," criticizing their lack of concern for monetary policy and inflation. Wanniski disapproved of Stein's orthodox conservatism, but he had to admit that the professor had a way with words. He seized Stein's phrase, lopped off the cumbersome "fiscalists," and dubbed the ideas espoused by himself and his friends "Supply Side Economics." Stein probably would never forgive himself.

Bartley's editorial page was firmly behind Kemp and his tax-cutting program by late 1976. The country's most prestigious financial newspaper was giving the Supply Side argument so much attention that, far from sounding radical, it began to sound like the accepted norm in conservative economics. Walter Heller, chief economic aide to John F. Kennedy and an unstinting liberal critic of Supply Side, was bowled over by the *Journal*'s role. "The editorial page was a rocket booster for Supply Side theory," says Heller, himself a regular *Journal* contributor. "Supply Side was hatched, incubated, nurtured and given wing there with every possible opening. There was an absolute campaign to put it on the map."

Late in 1976 Jude Wanniski took a leave of absence from the *Journal* to write his book, *The Way the World Works*, under a grant from the conservative Smith Richardson Foundation. The book, published the following September, was a somewhat tendentious economics primer, laying out the rationale for Supply Side. Yet one had to admire the sheer agility of Wanniski's argument. Like an acrobat defying gravity, he seemed to balance nearly all of recorded human history upon the fine point of taxes and related work incentives. When taxes were increased, civilization palled; the vandals took over and revolutions broke out. When taxes were cut, everything flourished. In one of the book's high points, Wanniski connected the birth of Jesus Christ to a general tax reduction effected by Augustus Caesar. Wanniski obviously could not brush his teeth in the morning without pondering the effect of tax rates on his ablutions. Indeed, someone in the *Journal* editorial office remarked upon the proliferation of prostitutes around Times Square, and Wanniski reportedly chortled: "They're there because of the tax system."

Long before finishing his book, Wanniski was functioning as an unpaid member of Congressman Kemp's staff. At the 1976 Republican National Convention in Kansas City, Wanniski helped Kemp try to negotiate with representatives of candidate Ronald Reagan, offering to swing delegate votes from western New York away from Gerald Ford in exchange for Reagan's endorsement of a tax cut. The deal never got off the ground, but Kemp made a stirring speech to the convention, saying: "Let the Democrats continue to be the party of big spending. We are the party of less spending and lower taxes." The speech evidently made an impression on Reagan. In a syndicated newspaper column written just after Ford's defeat in November, Reagan came out for a large cut in income taxes.

Before the '76 convention Kemp had championed an array of tax cuts for business dubbed the "Savings and Investment Act." After the election, however, he changed tactics, opting for a broad assault on personal income taxes. His aide, Paul Craig Roberts, an economist from the University of Virginia, drafted a bill that called for a thirty percent across-the-board cut in marginal tax rates. The bill was introduced in the Senate by William Roth of Delaware, who insisted on inserting a three-year phase-in period for the tax cut. The controversial Kemp-Roth Bill was considered lunacy by most of the economics establishment, but politically it was cotton candy. The Republican National Committee endorsed the bill enthusiastically, and by 1978 nearly all of the party was behind it, thanks in part to the ground-swell popularity of California's Proposition 13, a property-tax-reduction referendum that arose almost spontaneously, spurring talk of a nationwide "tax revolt."

Wanniski was now spending more and more time with Kemp. In the process he had managed to unseat Bob Bartley as the *bête noire* of the *Journal*'s Washington bureau. Fred Taylor, now managing editor of the *Journal*, got word that Wanniski was working politicians all over Capitol Hill, saying: "Here's my program and you ought to support it." Taylor explains: "Our reporters would show up in a Congressional office, and the man would say, 'Oh, yeah, Jude Wanniski was just in here from your paper telling me about Supply Side Economics. I think it's a bunch of crap, but how can you ask me what I think about it when I know that you've already made up your minds?' " Actually, some Congressmen reportedly complained to *Journal* reporters that Wanniski had gone further than that. They said he was twisting arms, suggesting that the *Journal* would support them editorially if they went along with Kemp-Roth and attack them if they didn't. The fury mounted. Warren Phillips took the bureau out to dinner one night and is said to have inquired, somewhat routinely, if there was anything he could do to help things function more smoothly. "Fire Wanniski," came the plea from one end of the table.

Phillips did not intend to fire Wanniski, whom he says he considered an original thinker. But when word reached New York that Wanniski had given a rousing speech at a Republican fund-raising event, Phillips and Bartley agreed that they had to warn him to desist from further political entanglements. Wanniski agreed. But his political passions had grown beyond control. In mid-1978 Phillips' deputy, Ray Shaw, was standing in a New Jersey PATH train terminal when he saw Wanniski distributing campaign leaflets for Jeff Bell, then running against incumbent Clifford Case for the Republican Senatorial nomination. "I figured that if Bell didn't win, there was no way Supply Side would go anywhere, and there would be no way to avoid global depression and war," Wanniski explains. Bell did succeed in wresting the Republican nomination from Case but then lost the general election to former basketball star Bill Bradley. And Wanniski lost his job at the *Journal.*

Things did not end there. Wanniski went on to a lucrative consulting business in which he was free to maintain a political profile. Bartley replaced him with another ardent Supply Sider, Paul Craig Roberts, the man who had drafted the original Kemp-Roth Bill.

Bartley's editorial page continued to push Supply Side, as Bartley, Wanniski, Kristol, Kemp, and Laffer remained an intimate circle. It soon became evident that Ronald Reagan would be the Republican Presidential nominee in 1980. Kemp had given early indications of running, too, but Reagan dissuaded him, assuring the young Congressman that he had also caught Supply Side fever. As friends of Kemp, Wanniski and Laffer went to Reagan's home for three days of briefings in early 1980. Recalls Wanniski: "I went into it skeptical if he'd know what we were talking about. . . . He was one hundred percent Supply Side. He loved the stuff. It was total unity. I came away thinking, 'This is the candidate.' "

Bartley's page stopped short of endorsing Reagan's candidacy point-black. The *Journal* criticized the Reagan campaign as the work of a "political packager" and predicted that unnecessary compromises would "cost him the ability to govern in a way that will make a real difference to the future of society." At the same time, though, Bartley's editorials savaged the opposition, leaving little question which candidate the paper preferred. Of Edward Kennedy he wrote:

> . . . so far as we can see he has never led anything except maybe a regatta off Hyannis. He was elected to the U.S. Senate at the age of 30 thanks to his brother the President and his father the millionaire. He has spent 16 years in the Senate championing such perennial losing causes as national health insurance and various anti-trust brainstorms. While this of course endears him to the left, it also leaves his legislative career devoid of substantive accomplishment.

And of President Jimmy Carter:

> Mr. Carter has been a weak leader because, far from being out in front of the people, he has had to be led kicking and screaming to go in the directions the nation needs to go and wants to go.

More than anything Bartley's page remained faithful to the spirit of Supply Side, much as Kemp and Wanniski attempted to hold the future President's hand to the flame. Reagan would espouse Supply Side sentiments at one moment, but at the next he would reveal an interest in controlled monetary policy and a balanced budget—ideas that smacked of irredentism. Each time, recalls Wanniski, "We would call Kemp and scream, 'Deviation! Deviation!' And he would call people [in the Reagan campaign] and scream 'Deviation!' " Though Wanniski no longer worked for Bartley's page, strong intellectual ties remained. Bartley's own analysis: "Jude taught me the power of the outrageous."

With Reagan's election the *Journal* editorial page found itself in the unfamiliar and uncomfortable position of having backed the winning horse. Reagan not only professed to be a Supply Sider, he also took a hard line on relations with the Soviet Union and on the need for a rapid defense buildup, two positions for which Bartley had pushed aggressively. Down in Chapel Hill, Bartley's old mentor, Vermont Royster, could only sigh at the *Journal*'s infatuation with the new President. His feeling was that a newspaper should never be "in bed" with any administration, a point he had made to Bartley hundreds of times. But then Royster would shrug. "Protégés have a way of running away from their patrons, just like your children."

Perhaps it was fortunate, from the paper's point of view, that President Reagan soon fell from grace as a Supply Side purist. Initially the President had appointed three top Supply Siders to key positions, Paul Craig Roberts as Assistant Secretary of the Treasury for Economic Policy, and Norman Ture, another of Kemp's economic consultants, as Under-Secretary of the Treasury for Tax and Economic Affairs. The third and most influential Supply Sider was Budget Director David Stockman. But once a modified version of the Kemp-Roth Bill had been passed, the Reagan Administration's Supply Side ardor seemed to cool. Stockman was the first open defector. In a much publicized article that appeared in *The Atlantic,* he professed to the heretical view that Supply Side was no more than a disguise for a "hoary old Republican doctrine" of trickle-down economics—a "Trojan Horse" to facilitate tax cuts for the wealthy.

The most critical element in the Supply Side theory had always been its emphasis on economic incentives. The crucial distinction that it made was between *average* tax rates and *marginal* tax rates. Supply Siders had been relatively unconcerned with average tax rate, the overall proportion of one's income that is siphoned off by taxes. Their passion was for cutting marginal rates, the amount of tax that would be owed on the next additional dollar of income should the individual decide to put in the effort necessary to earn it. For Wanniski and company "the margin" of incentive took on a mystical sort of significance, and they spoke of it in terms reminiscent of the Holy Grail. "Adam Smith wrote about the 'higglety-pigglety' of the market place," says Wanniski, "but you can simplify any puzzle by looking at 'the margin.' Change *always* occurs on 'the margin.' " And it was the unique, magical powers that flowed from "the margin," Supply Siders believed, that would lift the economy from the woeful difficulties of the preceding decade. The most pressing question, naturally, was just how long the rehabilitation would take. Wanniski gave an interview to *The Village Voice* claiming that the results would be immediate: "One of the first insights I had was when I asked Laffer, 'How can these incentives be instantaneous? Won't we have to wait three years for them to occur?' Laffer said, 'How long does it take you to reach over and pick up a $50 bill in a crowd? Aah! That's how quick it is. If the incentive is there, the production is there.' "

But the Kemp-Roth tax cut did not produce immediate benefits. Instead the nation plunged into prolonged recession, and the President seemed more and more inclined to old-fashioned remedies—strict monetary policy, budget restraints, even some tax *increases*. The Supply Siders in his administration blustered and were ignored. Both Roberts and Ture were allowed to resign after a year or so in office with little regret from the Oval Office. Stockman, by contrast, was kept on even after he had renounced the faith, for the President seemed to prize his budget prowess more than the spiritual commitment of the others to Supply Side.

While both the public and the President seemed to grow skeptical of pure Supply Side doctrine, the true believers, led by Wanniski, raised a clamor that the tax cuts had not worked because they had not been accompanied by a return to the gold standard, a point on which they had been curiously silent during the campaign. But in their crusade for a quick return to the gold-backed dollar, the Supply Siders were utterly unpersuasive. "Presumably, if we went back on the gold standard and *that* didn't work," joked William S. Ruckeyser, managing editor of *Fortune,* "they would say it was because we didn't seed the clouds." The extreme Supply Side became so isolated in its beliefs that by late 1981 Robert Mundell would declare that there were only four "real Supply Siders" left—himself, Wanniski, Laffer, and Lewis Lehrman, a Neo-conservative businessman running for the New York governorship.

Bartley never endorsed this cabal in its plea for a new gold standard, but his page did remain faithful to the tax cut long after the philosophy had lost its patina of fashionability. At a convocation of *Journal* management and staff that November, one of the reporters asked Warren Phillips if he thought the newspaper would suffer a loss of credibility if Reagan's Supply Side program fizzled. Phillips nodded at Bartley and reportedly said: "I'll let Bob answer that." And Bartley snapped back: "Of course it will suffer!"

"Well," said Phillips dryly, so that no one could be sure whether or not he was peeved with Bartley, "if that should happen, I'm sure that the editorial page would explain that the program simply hadn't been implemented with the purity we had recommended."

CHAPTER 15

Creative Tension

IF THERE WAS one event that signaled the end of the Kilgore era—for Kilgore's spirit enveloped the newspaper for years after Barney Kilgore's actual death—it was the near-fatal accident that John McWethy suffered while driving from St. Louis to the University of Missouri in late 1971. The Chicago bureau chief was on his way to a recruiting session when he dozed at the wheel during a treacherous Missouri ice-rain that glazed the road almost imperceptibly. The rented car swerved into a ditch and turned over, pinning McWethy's neck beneath the roof. He was pulled out of the wreckage alive but permanently crippled from the neck down.

The Wall Street Journal was still a paternalistic institution then. The managing editor, Fred Taylor, sent McWethy a telegram that read: "We didn't hire you to hop, skip or jump. We hired you for your talent in judging stories and people." After a ten-month convalescence, McWethy returned to the office in Chicago and stayed on for another seven years, until he turned sixty-five. He remained actively in charge, a likable man with no trace of bitterness.

Nevertheless, the accident marked a kind of turning point for the *Journal.* It ended McWethy's recruiting activities and with them the newspaper's long-standing preference for bright, eager young people fresh from Mid-American colleges. John McWethy had been perhaps the *Journal*'s strongest proponent of reaching out to the heartland, where cynicism remained rare and the work ethic more or less intact. McWethy had gone to great lengths to hook the young men he wanted—not with money, for he was a notorious tightwad, but with tireless correspondence and salesmanship. He had been among the last disciples of Kilgore, and the fruits of his ministry had been people like Mike Gartner, Bob Bartley, Bill Clabby, and dozens of others.

After McWethy's confinement, the paper tended to hire more experienced journalists, especially from other Eastern publications. When it did hire directly from the campus, it often went for Ivy Leaguers. Soon the *Journal*'s recruitment practices were much the same as those of *The New York Times, The Washington Post, Time,* and *Newsweek.* Its distinctive Midwestern character faded. Women were admitted to the newsroom in growing numbers, as was true at most other papers. The newer staff members were smart and ambitious, perhaps more so than ever, yet they were different from their predecessors. The new *Journal* reporter was more worldly, knowledgeable about matters like remuneration and status, uncomfortable with the anonymity and scut work that had always been staples of life at Dow Jones & Company. N. R. Kleinfield, part of a mass exodus from the *Journal* to *The New York Times* in the early seventies, left behind a remark that would be heard around the *Journal* for years to come. "There are only two things that the *Times* can offer me that the *Journal* can't," Kleinfield is said to have declared, "—fame and money." Over the next decade the *Journal* gradually would increase staff salaries to the point where senior people made about as much as their counterparts at the *Times.* Individual fame, however, would remain elusive.

For all of the *Journal*'s accomplishments, the newspaper would miss out almost entirely on the two biggest stories of the seventies—the Pentagon Papers and Watergate. The problem was not so much that other newspapers had these stories first—for *The New York Times* broke most of the Pentagon Papers and only *The Washington Post* had Woodward and Bernstein. The problem was really that the *Journal*, whether out of arrogance or impotence, continued to ignore the stories when they preoccupied the nation. Other publications at least caught them on the rebound, reporting on the monumental news that the *Times* and *Post* were making. The *Journal* inexplicably did nothing. In fact, it was Bob Bartley and Jude Wanniski, with their sometimes strained efforts to defend President Nixon editorially, who represented the *Journal*'s only substantial reaction to the Watergate scandal.

Of the *Journal*'s almost nonexistent Watergate coverage through President Nixon's resignation in 1974, Fred Taylor said: "My only defense was that I got no pushing from our people in Washington. I read the *Post* with fascination, but I couldn't make sense of Watergate. I couldn't believe Nixon could be that stupid, and none of our sources seemed to be worth a damn." *Journal* executives also blamed the limitations of the paper's front-page format, which had served so well for so many years. Whatever its virtues, they insisted, the front page of the *Journal* was no place for articles that could not at least pretend to be definitive. For the most part the excuse rang hollow. The true problem was what it had been so many times in the *Journal*'s past—especially times when the pendulum began to swing away from general news coverage and back toward business routine. The true problem was that the newspaper simply lacked the resolve to tackle great historic events. The *Journal* had performed admirably in Little Rock in 1957 but had given short shrift to the growing drama of the civil rights movement as it exploded violently in the 1960s. It had covered the Vietnamese war, perhaps the seminal American event of the late twentieth century, with one man, Peter Kann, writing feature stories. Now it utterly ignored one of the great political crises of modern American history.

The New York Times also felt badly outdone by Woodward and Bernstein, but it reacted appropriately. The *Times* went out and hired a bevy of the very best investigative people it could find. Within a matter of months, the *Times* had broadened the scope of the Watergate story well beyond where *The Washington Post* had taken it. *The Wall Street Journal,* with the largest staff of national reporters of any newspaper, with nearly limitless financial resources available to the news department, with the capacity to handle complex financial scandals, surely the *Journal* could have done something about Watergate. Instead, to the dismay of most staff members, the news columns barely mentioned the scandal.

Whatever the reasons for this stupefying omission, the ultimate cost would be heavy. After Watergate other publications redoubled their investigative reporting, sometimes going to extremes and blowing penny-ante exposés out of all proportion to their importance. *The Wall Street Journal,* curiously, went to the opposite extreme, curtailing its investigative efforts until they were nearly nonexistent. The paper carried few investigative stories of heavy consequence after the mid-1970s. An outsider might have surmised that the *Journal* no longer felt up to competing with newspapers like the *Times* or the *Post,* that it no longer wanted to expend the time and money that investigative stories generally require. But those were not the true reasons the *Journal* shrank from the prospect of greatness. Sadly, in the late seventies the *Journal* became a paper of limited aspirations.

The initial problem was Mike Gartner's abrupt departure in 1974, for he seemed to take the newspaper's sense of daring along with him. The front-page editor who seemed to personify the hopes of so many reporters decided to accept the editorship of his hometown papers, *The Des Moines Register* and *Tribune.* Warren Phillips reportedly tried to keep Gartner with promises that he would be the *Journal*'s next managing editor, perhaps something more. But Gartner, thirty-five, would not be deterred. He went back to Iowa, a hometown boy who had made good in New York, then returned to his Midwestern roots, much as Casey Hogate might have liked to do.

The *Journal* had an abundance of bright, deserving people. For some reason, though, it could not find one to replace Gartner, who had been so much more than just page-one editor. With Gartner gone, the paper's fire abated and a chill set in. "I don't know what it was about Gartner," Ed Cony lamented much later. "A lot of us get carried away with the idea of saving the world. We forget that the main point of newspaper work is that it's supposed to be more fun than selling soap flakes." Gartner, of course, had been more than someone who had fun at his job. He had been, like Ed Cony, a bit of a dreamer, a man who aspired to some hazy and indefinite notion of greatness and inspired others to go along. Now, with Gartner gone and Cony upstairs, it seemed that there was no one left like that in the newsroom. There was a vacuum in leadership that no one had expected, that no one knew how to fill.

Fred Taylor was nearing what ought to have been the last phase of his term as managing editor when Mike Gartner, his obvious successor, resigned. Taylor's weakness, those around him felt, had always been uncommunicativeness, and now it became worse. With Gartner gone, Taylor seemed all the more reclusive. He seemed to long for the executive position with which ex-managing editors invariably were rewarded.

In the eyes of the staff, there were now two main contenders for Fred Taylor's job, both young bureau chiefs—Herb Lawson in San Francisco and Bill Blundell in Los Angeles. Each had spent time on the front-page desk, managed a major bureau, and proved wonderfully adept at working with younger staff members. Both were protégés of Ed Cony. Their taste was for stories that surprised, amused, and enlightened. But while Blundell, Lawson, and most other bureau chiefs ran their bureaus in a somewhat laid-back, improvisational style, trying to generate mainly investigative pieces and amusing features, Fred Taylor was changing the rules in New York, moving the paper back toward harder coverage of business and economics. The eighth-floor executives under Warren Phillips seemed to swing farther and farther away from the Ed Cony school of journalism—rightly so, perhaps, in view of the 1973 Arab oil embargo and the severe economic shocks that followed. It ought to have been a matter of fine-tuning, really, but Blundell, Lawson, and most other bureau chiefs never quite got the message. In large part they didn't get the message because Fred Taylor hardly ever spoke to them.

After Mike Gartner's departure, Taylor needed an assistant, someone he felt was "methodical and solid" to help edge the paper back toward harder business coverage. Among the major domestic bureau chiefs, almost the only man with demonstrated dedication to nitty-gritty business coverage was Larry O'Donnell in Detroit, the bureau long considered the stiffest test of a man's mettle. The Detroit staff still thought him peculiar, but Larry O'Donnell had tamed their egos and given them a measure of *esprit.* His men no longer yearned to write great trend-setting stories like the reporters in New York and California. Instead, they thought of themselves, quite proudly, as trenchmates in the inglorious but worthy cause of smoking news out of the auto industry. They did not dream of winning the Pulitzer Prize; it was enough to supply two of the top five items that day in the front-page news digest. Larry O'Donnell had apparently succeeded in lowering their expectations and getting important work out of them.

O'Donnell moved back to New York in 1974 to become Taylor's assistant, having accepted the job with characteristic self-efface-ment and a grim determination to make good. He worked tire-lessly, firing off volleys of suggestions, impressing nearly every-one with his earnestness and his zest. He hovered, nitpicked, and drove people crazy with incessant instructions. A rewrite man would just be donning his coat to go home when O'Donnell would appear with a list of fifteen or twenty objections requiring another hour or two of work.

Perhaps knowing that Fred Taylor's reclusiveness was a prob-lem, O'Donnell began sprinkling laudatory memos around the news department—so generously in fact that they quickly became a devalued currency. While no one really disliked O'Donnell, a lot of people didn't take him seriously at first. The staff rated him a zealous beginner. Outside New York the senior bureau chiefs tended to ignore him completely.

O'Donnell's promotion automatically made him a candidate for managing editor, but at first neither he nor anyone else ac-tually expected him to get the job. Nonetheless, it gradually be-came clear that he was Fred Taylor's choice. On an autumn day in 1977, Ed Cony, now an executive on high, announced that Fred Taylor would become executive editor, always an ill-defined title, and that O'Donnell—to no one's great surprise—would take his place as managing editor. "You could have pushed me over with a feather," said O'Donnell of his own reaction.

In Larry O'Donnell the newspaper got a managing editor committed to industry news, a man so enamored of the smoke-stacks of Detroit and Pittsburgh that he would lash out at young reporters who requested assignment in London or San Francisco. Even O'Donnell's friends were shocked by his appointment. "In-dustrious mediocrity" was one top executive's assessment. An-other news executive snickered: "I guess all of the good people had left." O'Donnell struck nearly everyone as a peculiar choice to be top editor of *The Wall Street Journal,* arguably the most in-fluential newspaper in the country. *The New York Times* had A. M. Rosenthal, once a Pulitzer Prize-winning correspondent in Eastern Europe and a celebrated metropolitan editor. *The Wash-ington Post* had Ben Bradlee, maybe the most dynamic editor of the era and one of Washington's great power brokers. Larry O'Donnell's credentials consisted of some aggressive coverage of William Zeckendorf's collapse, eight years as a Detroit bureau chief, and three more years as Fred Taylor's assistant. He seemed a man of neither demonstrated brilliance nor broad culture. In fact, his normal reading—even as managing editor—consisted of only the *The Wall Street Journal, The New York Times,* and *Na-tional Geographic,* plus a few Catholic publications. He said he had no time for more. O'Donnell's distinguishing qualities were te-nacity and toughness.

The *Journal's* new managing editor soon embarked upon his maiden tour of the U.S. bureaus. There was nothing diplomatic in his manner. He was openly zealous, a fundamentalist preach-ing the new dogma of hard business coverage. In San Francisco O'Donnell booked a private restaurant room, and when the ap-pointed evening arrived, with bureau chief Herb Lawson very much in attendance, O'Donnell reportedly commenced his ser-mon while pre-dinner drinks were being poured. Not once that evening did he brook interruption. There was no joking, no gos-sip, no stroking.

Speaking in a low, flat monotone, O'Donnell accused them all of letting the newspaper down, of growing lazy, self-indulgent, and indifferent toward the *Journal's* true mission as the leading business newspaper. Lawson and his men had felt their main job was to produce work that was imaginative and informative, stories that were memorable and entertaining. But O'Donnell charged them with pursuing such stories mainly for personal glorification. All that would have to stop, he insisted. They would have to learn to be more on top of the news; they would have to make the *Journal* more of a *news*paper. There would be more emphasis on the nuts and bolts, less on the bizarre and irrelevant. In effect, what O'Donnell was telling them was to lower their own ambitions, precisely as he had done with his staff in Detroit.

David McClintick covered the publishing and movie industries for *The Wall Street Journal.* Though he normally worked out of New York, he was in Los Angeles when O'Donnell's promotion to managing editor was announced. He was working on an article profiling Columbia Pictures Industries, which was on the verge of releasing the most costly movie in history, *Close Encounters of the Third Kind.*

McClintick had been one of the *Journal's* most successful investigative men throughout the early and mid-seventies. His most memorable story to date: the Home-Stake oil swindle of 1974, a fraudulent tax-shelter scam whose victims had included scores of celebrities and wealthy professionals. He had also been the first to spell out the collapse of National Student Marketing Corporation, and he had unveiled the questionable tax dealings of ITT and others. In sum, McClintick's credentials as an investigative reporter were sterling. Now McClintick's instincts told him that he might have stumbled across one of the best stories of his career.

Two months earlier Columbia Pictures Industries had suspended its studio president, David Begelman, pending the outcome of a company investigation of certain "unauthorized transactions." The general suspicion was that Begelman's transgressions were probably no worse than expense-account padding. But McClintick had learned that the studio president's indiscretions included some rather serious acts of check forgery and embezzlement. More intriguing still, Columbia Pictures was about to reinstate Begelman as studio president, despite full knowledge of his misdeeds.

McClintick strode into the New York newsroom early on Sunday, December 18, 1977, and outlined the story for Mack Solomon, the deputy page-one editor who regularly presided on Sundays. McClintick urged Solomon to run the story in the next morning's *Journal* because Alan Hirschfield, president of the parent Columbia Pictures Industries, was going to issue a press release making Begelman's return as studio president official. The press release would say that Begelman had sought "therapy" for emotional problems responsible for his errant behavior and that the company was therefore satisfied that he was fit to be president again. Skeptical of such company rhetoric, McClintick proposed writing the story not as a heavy exposé, but as a Hollywood soap opera, replete with a cast of ingenues, such as actor Cliff Robertson, whose name Begelman had forged. Solomon nodded his approval, and McClintick sat down to write the story.

Larry O'Donnell phoned the office late that morning, as he usually did on Sundays. When Solomon told him about McClintick's Hollywood saga, O'Donnell ordered the story killed. The managing editor had a vague distrust of McClintick that apparently went back a couple of years, to the point when he first discovered the reporter was writing a book in his spare time, a book about the Home-Stake oil swindle. At most publications editors delight when a staff member publishes a good book, but not O'Donnell. O'Donnell emphatically disapproved of reporters who wrote books. Indeed, he disliked any display of ego or ambition that was independent of the *Journal,* for he felt that the time and energy men devoted to such things was somehow stolen from the newspaper, no matter if the extracurricular project was squeezed into vacations and off-hours. O'Donnell coined a curious phrase for what was troubling him about McClintick. He accused the reporter of having "a mental conflict-of-interest," meaning that McClintick was guilty of being interested in something other than *The Wall Street Journal.*

After finishing his talk with Solomon, the managing editor spoke directly to McClintick. First of all, he reportedly told the reporter, "I never believe a press release until I've seen it." Second, he was opposed to airing someone's psychiatric difficulties in print, despite the possibility that David Begelman had sought psychotherapy mainly to head off serious criminal charges. Furthermore, though O'Donnell had not seen what McClintick was writing, he did not much care for the droll approach that Solomon had described. Last, O'Donnell reportedly told the now astonished McClintick, the Begelman affair did not seem particularly important. The movie industry was a fairly minor one in the large scheme of American business, and Columbia Pictures was not even the largest movie studio. Why couldn't McClintick spend his time on matters of more consequence?

David McClintick tried to argue. His information about the next day's press release had come straight from the top of Columbia Pictures Industries. Begelman's psychiatric troubles seemed to him like an obvious ruse. Columbia Pictures was a large corporation, listed on the New York Stock Exchange, with thousands of shareholders, and here the company was reinstating a studio president who had committed a number of possible felonies. How could anyone call this story inconsequential? That the affair revolved around Hollywood, he felt, made it all the more compelling.

But O'Donnell would not be moved. Maybe there was a legitimate news story in this Begelman thing, he reportedly conceded, but it hardly warranted space on the front page of *The Wall Street Journal*. Really, it was a personnel matter. O'Donnell instructed McClintick to wait for the next day's press release, then to write a straightforward account for the "Who's News" section, a digest of corporate promotions and job appointments that regularly runs on an inside page.

McClintick was seething, but he did as he was ordered. His Begelman story ran on Tuesday, December 20, in the "Who's News" section on page twenty-five. That morning someone telephoned Cliff Robertson and his wife, Dina Merrill, in their thirtieth-floor apartment at the United Nations Plaza, calling their attention to the "Who's News" section of *The Wall Street Journal*. When Robertson saw it, his jaw probably fell open. Cliff Robertson was the man who had first blown the whistle on Begelman, his one-time agent. After receiving a tax form from Columbia falsely stating that the company had paid him $10,000 for work never performed, Robertson had gone to considerable trouble to unravel the mystery. When the actor had turned up evidence of a Begelman forgery, he had kept urging police to take action, but to no avail. Robertson was furious at seeing Begelman get off scot-free. And now, adding insult to injury, in the first public airing of the matter, *The Wall Street Journal,* of *all* publications, was burying the scandal, hiding it deep inside the paper. Was some sort of conspiracy afoot? Miss Merrill picked up the telephone and called an old friend, Katharine Graham, chairman and publisher of *The Washington Post.* "Cliff has a story to tell your newspaper, Kay," said Robertson's wife.

The *Post* ran its first Begelman story on Christmas day 1977. Soon afterward Dan Dorfman wrote a Begelman piece for *New York* magazine, and the press orgy began. "Hollywoodgate" became the subject of cover stories in *Newsweek* and *The New York Times Magazine.* It was on the front pages of all three New York newspapers, as well as in the gossip columns. But for a solid month, *The Wall Street Journal* printed nothing else on the matter. McClintick, stung and demoralized, finished up his profile of Columbia Pictures with little enthusiasm. The managing editor seemed to have it in for him. The day after McClintick's Begelman story had run on the "Who's News" page, he recalls O'Donnell sending him an insulting little memo asking if he were *sure* he had adequate sources vouching for the Begelman check forgeries—as though McClintick were some cub reporter who might not understand the importance of such things.

McClintick finished his story about Columbia in mid-January, but it lay around the front-page desk until it finally ran on January 30. By this time the *Journal* was far behind on the Begelman story and the rest of Hollywoodgate. In fact, it was the last important newspaper to weigh in with a major article on the subject. It ought to have been the first. David McClintick was still seething. In his view Larry O'Donnell had not only been insulting, he had committed the unpardonable sin of blowing a terrific story for no good reason. Trying to contain his anger, McClintick typed out a lengthy memorandum criticizing the paper's mishandling of the Begelman matter and asking O'Donnell to decide what further coverage, if any, he desired. McClintick thought his memo judicious and well reasoned, but then again, a sober, detached staff member might not send a memo to the managing editor reminding him of the sizable blunder he had just made.

Perhaps what McClintick wanted was an apology, maybe a confrontation. In any case, from O'Donnell's office came neither mollifying words nor angry ones, but rather a frosty silence that lasted six full weeks. Then, at the urging of the New York bureau chief Stewart Pinkerton, O'Donnell at last assented to a meeting with McClintick. The managing editor reportedly greeted the reporter in a pleasant manner, saying in effect: "Well, you asked for this meeting. What was it you wanted to discuss?"—as though he had not the slightest idea what was troubling the reporter. McClintick reminded him of his memo, of the points he had raised in it about the paper's handling of the Begelman affair, and of the questions he'd raised concerning further coverage of Hollywoodgate.

Now the superficial pleasantness apparently vanished from O'Donnell's manner. He was stony and imperious, speaking in the low, flat monotone that he used when asserting authority. The real problem O'Donnell reportedly began, was that McClintick had procrastinated with his profile of Columbia Pictures. That was why the *Journal* had performed so poorly with the Begelman story. McClintick protested. His story had been ready weeks before it finally ran. O'Donnell's accusation was simply unfounded.

O'Donnell paused, then shifted the line of attack. "You're out of line to question me about this," he is said to have told the reporter. The managing editor of *The Wall Street Journal* didn't have to answer to his underlings. "Besides," O'Donnell reportedly went on, "your overall rate of production hasn't been up to snuff in the last year. . . . I'm going to put a clock on you. . . . If your productivity hasn't picked up by Labor day. . . ." That was all. O'Donnell dismissed McClintick curtly, but McClintick turned before he reached the door and stammered: "I think you owe me an apology."

"Do I?" O'Donnell reportedly said, barely looking up at the man. "Well, I don't know what it is that I should apologize for, but if it will make you feel better, I'll say 'I apologize.' " O'Donnell made it clear then that he did not want McClintick pursuing the Begelman story or, in fact, any other story relating to Hollywood scandal. Explains O'Donnell: "Here was a guy asking for a broad charter to pursue the Begelman story, and his *track record* wasn't that good, not over the last couple of years anyway. I might have been happy to give the story to someone with a better track record." But it was preposterous for him to deny McClintick's reportorial accomplishments: They were outstanding by any measure.

The dispirited McClintick lingered at the *Journal* through the following spring, growing increasingly depressed. Finally he brought himself to quit, having contracted to write a book about the Begelman matter and the whole question of movie industry ethics. The book, entitled *Indecent Exposure,* turned out to be a frothy mix of boardroom drama and Hollywood decadence, a virtuoso demonstration of behind-the-scenes reportage. McClintick's manuscript was so hotly anticipated that even before publication in the summer of 1982 there was a black market for its galley proofs in and around Hollywood. The book's cover dotted beaches and patios around the country all summer long, and after months on the best-seller list, it left David McClintick wealthy and famous beyond the typical *Journal* reporter's dreams. McClintick had had his revenge, but O'Donnell spoke of the reporter in retrospect with unrepentant disdain. The more undeniable McClintick's success, the more O'Donnell seemed to disparage him.

O'Donnell's behavior grew more and more curious. He dealt with the two star bureau chiefs by demoting Blundell in Los Angeles and forcing Herb Lawson to resign. Unlike the O'Donnell of old, who had written memos on every subject under the sun, the managing editor now told close associates he was concerned lest any signal he gave be "over-interpreted." He preferred not to put things in writing but to let his thoughts drift down to the staff in the form of rumors. When O'Donnell did post a note congratulating someone for a story, it was often worded as an insult to everyone else. He would say, on one occasion: "It just goes to show how you can write a good story without going on and on," or "Why can't we have more like this one every day?"

Once, after the newspaper had given blanket coverage to an important business development, O'Donnell posted a note that defied the staff's comprehension. It said: "I'm not writing another complimentary note. I've written too many lately, and you all will get swelled heads. You understand my position, don't you?"

The physical size of the newspaper had always been a subject of concern. The people who ran Dow Jones knew that among the *Journal*'s greatest attributes was its compactness. Once the paper had become solidly profitable, Barney Kilgore had fought against the urge to let the paper grow—from thirty-two pages to thirty-six, from thirty-six pages to forty, and so on. But the newspaper had to grow—to accommodate more stocks being traded, more news being generated, and more advertisers trying to get their messages before the public. In June 1980 the *Journal* took the monumental step of adding a second section. (Within five years it would consider adding a third.) The decision was based almost entirely on advertising considerations, but nonetheless, it added much more news space and created the need for new columns and areas of coverage.

The additional pages vastly expanded the size of the managing editor's empire. To deal with all this growth, O'Donnell felt he had little choice but to forge a newsroom bureaucracy of subeditors and administrators. He felt the managing editor of the paper could no longer indulge in making routine, day-to-day decisions. Accordingly O'Donnell reportedly passed the word that he would no longer have an "open door policy." In case the staff missed the message, he had a bank of three offices erected in front of his own, obscuring the reporters' view of him. And he began to create a large number of new middle-management jobs, three assistant managing editors, an assistant to the managing editor, sundry assistant New York bureau chiefs, a "spot news" editor in charge of routine corporate developments, sub-assignment editors, and more. In Fred Taylor's time and before, the authority of the newsroom had rested in only three men—the managing editor, the page-one editor, and the national news editor. Now, however, there were so many petty baronies and subdivisions of power that it was difficult to tell where one editor's authority ended and the next one's began.

The bureaucratization of the news department in the late seventies and early eighties did have some advantages, as most bureaucracies do. It was committee journalism rather than individual effort, and the result was a more consistent, homogeneous product. The new subeditors probably did get reporters to work more efficiently, pushing them to write more numerous stories and making sure they attended to industries they might formerly have neglected. And the new middle management took a good deal of the work load out of the managing editor's office, settling routine disputes and deciding which stories merited more attention than others.

Yet few people seemed happy with the new setup—not the reporters, not most of the newsroom bureaucrats themselves, and not the Dow Jones news executives watching from on high. For one thing, as the number of fiefdoms and feudal baronies increased, so, too, did the news department's internal politicking. Rather than answering to just one or two masters, a reporter now had to satisfy several. For the first time political cunning became somewhat essential to one's survival there.

An example was Dick Janssen, the *Journal*'s top man on international finance, who had been bureau chief in London before O'Donnell took over. O'Donnell sent veteran Washington correspondent Alan Otten to replace him, bringing Janssen home to New York as the new subeditor in charge of financial news—the banking, brokerage, and insurance industries. Janssen had plenty of intellectual background for the job but was apparently woefully unprepared in the art of office infighting. The *Journal* had always prided itself on being free of office politics, but in the new bureaucracy of the newsroom, a man's responsibilities were seldom well defined. In fact, they were often deliberately vague. Part of Larry O'Donnell's strategy seemed to be allowing room for some to grab more power while others lost it. O'Donnell said he did not believe in simply "giving people power." He openly preferred the "creative tension" approach—pitting several people against one another in an area in which any one of them might wrest a smidgen of authority, watching how they bloodied one another in the process.

In Janssen's case none of the financial writers in New York

was told to report to him. Their nominal boss was still Stew Pinkerton, the New York bureau chief. Janssen found that he simply had to insert himself into the process, riding herd on those staff members whose beats most logically fell under the heading "financial." Inevitably there was friction. One day an older reporter flew into a tizzy after Pinkerton and Janssen gave him conflicting instructions. Janssen and Pinkerton were discussing the incident calmly when O'Donnell strolled up and amiably asked the two what they were "plotting." When the reporter's consternation was explained to him, O'Donnell declined to intervene. "I don't care *who* he thinks he works for—at least for a while," said the managing editor. Maybe a bit of uncertainty was just what the reporter needed, suggested O'Donnell.

Shortly thereafter Dick Janssen went down to Philadelphia to attend a day-long conference. While Janssen was away, the New York bureau chief took action that, in effect, amputated Janssen's authority with a quick, surgical stroke. Pinkerton posted a notice declaring that henceforth, all New York reporters—financial people included—would report directly to him. When Janssen returned to the office the next day, staff members rushed up to ask if it were true that he was leaving the paper. Janssen had had no plans to that effect, but soon he did indeed depart for *Business Week.*

The new politics of the news department spread to distant bureaus as well. In the past bureau chiefs had considered themselves more as practicing journalists than administrators. Now their roles changed. The new generation of bureau chiefs saw themselves, first and foremost, as production managers. Chicago vied with Los Angeles and the others to see how many more stories its staff could produce. Quality was less important than quantity. The bureau chiefs had always kept track of how much individual reporters produced, but now they also kept tabs on one another, worrying that some rival bureau chief might score more points in New York by getting extra production from his staff.

Not surprisingly, the civility of the bureau chiefs seemed to deteriorate under the pressure. In previous times dismissals at the *Journal* had been relatively civil. The bureau chief took the young reporter aside and explained that things just were not working out. There was time allotted for the employee to line up a new job and to leave with a fair amount of his dignity intact. But in the O'Donnell era, cruelty became fashionable, for it was a badge of a bureau chief's toughness. One major bureau chief became notorious for reducing women reporters to tears by berating them in front of colleagues. Another became known for his ability to humiliate reporters into resigning, thus avoiding the need to pay severance. He used what was called "the death desk," set in a windowless corner. The bureau chief would install his prey there and blitz him with tedious, mind-numbing short news assignments.

It was not just the ambience of the *Journal* that was changing, but the paper's character as well. From a newspaper that once set trends for the entire news industry, it now became a publication that tried to emulate others. Many sensed that the touchstone of excellence within the *Journal* newsroom was now *Business Week,* a more specialized publication that had never aspired to the *Journal*'s mass appeal. *Business Week,* along with its sister business publications put out by McGraw-Hill, seemed to become the most frequent target of *Journal* recruitment raids, for O'Donnell wanted reporters who already were experts, not more people fresh from college and full of literary pretensions.

The *Journal* had a network of low-level spies at *Business Week, Forbes,* and *The New York Times* so it could be forewarned of what the competition was about to print. Such petty espionage was hardly unique in journalism, but still, in the *Journal*'s case it was unorthodox. It was hard to imagine men like Henry Gemmill really caring what other publications printed.

O'Donnell's main goal apparently was to make sure the *Journal* was on top of breaking news developments the very next day, just like any other newspaper. And he wanted to blanket a big event with second-, third-, and fourth-day stories, just like other papers. There would be no more waiting a day or two in order to write the quasi-definitive piece that really told readers what was going on. The managing editor insisted that the paper could perfect "the fast turnaround" and do it without sacrificing fine writing or thoughtfulness. O'Donnell was now flogging the bureau chiefs to make their staffs produce more stories, and inevitably there was less regard for quality. The *Journal* could and did learn to get on top of news faster, but in the process it was becoming a deadline-dominated paper whose stories were less and less different. Until now no paper had really rivaled the *Journal* front page in thoughtful writing or in careful analysis. The reason was the Kilgore legacy: the idea that the *Journal* would always remain a "second newspaper," one to which people turned after reading their hometown paper. As a corollary Kilgore felt that the *Journal* had to offer a quality and variety of information unavailable elsewhere, and this he accomplished by lavishing extraordinary time and energy on page-one stories. It was impossible to speed up the process without sacrificing something, even with whole teams of extra editors. There were certain things that could not be accomplished by committee.

Morale was in a dismal state, despite the fact that the *Journal* now paid its staff quite well. Many who had worked for the likes of Ed Cony, Fred Taylor, and Mike Gartner longed for the old days, feeling that they now labored for a newspaper stubbornly preoccupied with the routine. The paper's grand tradition of detaching a relatively new person to work for weeks to develop a big story seemed all but gone. Few people wanted to risk a project that might consume more than a week or two. The problem was not laziness, but fear of failure. The management kept careful track of each person's quantitative output. To spend excessive time on a story that might fizzle no longer seemed feasible. "I can tell you," said one of the paper's most distinguished reporters, "that front-page stories now get written on the basis of five telephone calls, where they used to be written on fifty."

If there was decay in the quality of the newspaper, its most serious manifestation was perhaps the diminished commitment to investigative reporting. The *Journal* seldom came up with ground-breaking stories anymore, a serious defect in a paper of the *Journal*'s size and standing. The last Pulitzer Prize for investigative work had been in 1967.

The managing editor was aware of the problem, though he hardly seemed alarmed by it. If the investigative machinery had grown rusty, he asserted, it was because reporters no longer dared take risks. O'Donnell seemed oblivious to his own culpability in the matter. "It's what's wrong with this business and what makes for pack journalism," O'Donnell continued. "What's missing is that go-where-the-story-is attitude. We're all too afflicted by middle-class comforts. Everybody! Everyone wants an interesting job, a fulfilling marriage without compromises, a house in the country, and they want it all at once." He might well have been right in his general diagnosis of American society, but one whiff of the tension in Larry O'Donnell's newsroom dispelled any notion that the reporters at the *Journal* had grown lazy or complacent.

When despair blankets the world, people naturally put their faith in Heaven. So, too, did many of the *Journal* staff believe that relief would come from the executive offices on high, where newsroom gods of another era, Warren Phillips and Ed Cony, tended to other matters—corporate affairs that seemingly had little to do with the newspaper. These hopes were not altogether rational, for the newspaper continued to grow and prosper under Larry O'Donnell's stewardship, as it had under every managing editor since Kilgore. Indeed, continuous growth in circulation and revenues now seemed like a law of nature at the *Journal*. In the first four years of O'Donnell's regime, the *Journal*'s circulation grew thirty percent, topping the two million level, thanks to the arrival of the post-war baby boom generation in America's managerial ranks.

Veteran staff members and even many of the ambitious young were nostalgic for the *Journal* of old, the newspaper of Kilgore, Cony, and Gartner that once had seemed so close to their ideal, but they knew that their sentiments might be immaterial from the corporation's point of view. They knew, deep down, that the *Journal* had such a hold on its readers that its quality might decline by half without any noticeable effect on the paper's financial health.

Almost no one knew what Warren Phillips thought of Larry O'Donnell's leadership at the *Journal*. As chairman of Dow Jones, Phillips remained as inscrutable as ever. Indeed, his attention seemed to be on other matters. In 1976 Phillips named Peter

Kann, one of the newsroom's great heroes, publisher of the *Asian Wall Street Journal*, an exciting new venture suggesting perhaps that Phillips' real interest lay in creating a global newspaper. But then he brought Kann back to New York, naming him a vice-president of the corporation and associate publisher of the U.S. paper in 1980. Unbeknownst to almost everyone, Kann and Phillips made concerted efforts to bring Mike Gartner back from Des Moines to take over the news operation. When Gartner refused, Kann went out and got his former Asian assistant, Norman Pearlstine, who had since gone to work for *Forbes* magazine. Pearlstine, who had once seemed to chafe under O'Donnell's rule in Detroit, was installed by Kann as national news editor in the spring of 1980, and the staff soon divided into factions—those who thrived under O'Donnell's burgeoning bureaucracy, and those who prayed that Kann and Pearlstine would usurp O'Donnell's position and somehow bring back the *Journal* of old. In September 1983 Pearlstine finally did inherit the job of managing editor, and O'Donnell joined Ed Cony and Fred Taylor, two other former managing editors, in somewhat vaguely defined executive positions.

There would be no resurrecting the days of Barney Kilgore. The *Journal* was too large and too complex for that. Kilgore's faith in Mid-America, in the intelligence, drive, and principle of the Midwestern college newspaper editor, was no longer a practical basis for staffing the newspaper. Pearlstine hired more and more journalists in their thirties and forties, people who commanded big salaries by newspaper standards, and people whose egos were already sufficiently well developed that there would be no subduing them.

Few people become journalists with the idea of getting rich. It is obviously the wrong profession for that. What they want, by and large, is a little glory, a place on the front page. And though the *Journal* has perhaps the most celebrated front page in American newspaperdom, it has but three front-page stories a day, five days a week, fifty-two weeks a year. Hardly enough to satisfy all the aspirations of some 540 journalists who were toiling at the *Journal* in 1985.

That is perhaps the most plausible explanation of how the

Journal's first real scandal since the days of C. W. Barron came about. Not since Dan Dorfman had the "Heard on the Street" column been a vehicle for any reporter's ego fulfillment. Tracking down the "stories" behind unexplained movements in one stock or another was considered dull work. None of the well-paid, experienced reporters on the staff wanted to do it. And so in late 1982, the *Journal* hired a news ticker reporter, R. Foster Winans, to do the job, paying him, at first, a little less than $30,000 a year and raising his pay a few months later to $610 a week. The salary, of course, was much better than one might have expected in an earlier era, but for a man in his early thirties with the most influential column in all of financial journalism, a man, it turned out, who was supporting his male lover, it was really not much remuneration. Nor could the *Journal* still offer the fun that Kilgore had promised, the thrill of being part of an enterprise striving for greatness. In all likelihood the *Journal* was about as great as it was going to get, and the fruits of that greatness went mainly to the stockholders, along with a select few journalists clever and fortunate enough to be on the fast track.

Winans was not one of that group, though he liked his work well enough, and one day, watching a vastly successful young stockbroker, Peter Brant, tee up on a Long Island golf course, it apparently occurred to Winans that wealth was a very attractive thing and that he wouldn't mind having a bit of it, too—just the reason people used to come to work at the *Journal* in the 1920s. "I'm a pretty unspectacular person," says Winans, trying to explain his actions long after he had been sentenced to eighteen months in prison. The crime was accepting money from Brant in exchange for tips as to the contents of forthcoming stock market columns. "I have a small circle of friends. I never saw a polo match or rode in a limousine until I came to *The Wall Street Journal*," he continues. "And I always adhered to the strictest possible ethics. But then I got to Wall Street, where what's *moral* is whatever you don't get prosecuted for! My personal finances were very bad, and Peter was a very charismatic figure. I added it all up, and I gave myself permission to be a bad boy. I thought there was no chance that the *Journal* would find out. I was wrong."

The *Journal*, as was surely necessary, defended itself not just in court but also on the front page, with an exposé of Winans that spared few details of his personal life. Then came an editorial called "Dirty Linen," in which the paper admitted its embarrassment and apologized to readers. "I've asked myself a lot of questions about the affair," said managing editor Pearlstine, a man who seemed naturally at ease in his powerful post and who earned generous plaudits from his staff despite the unmistakably corporate style in which he ran the newspaper. "The *Journal* has gotten a whole lot bigger. With the increase in size, was there maybe a kind of impersonalness that crept in? I don't know if I can answer that, really. I was one of Foster's biggest boosters. I thought he was a good reporter. . . . I thought he was underpaid, but I made it clear to him that over time we'd raise his salary. But every financial reporter faces temptation. . . . If an employee is determined to steal from you, there's not much you can do to prevent it."

In the end, it was hard to feel that the *Journal* had suffered much lasting damage to its reputation. If anything, the paper's vehement reaction to the Winans scandal demonstrated that it knew how intimately its success was bound up with its integrity. After all, the newspaper had died once a half century earlier when people realized that the *Journal*'s news columns in effect, had been for sale. Kilgore had merely attached the old paper's moldering name to an entirely new creation that was so ingenious, so absolutely right for the dawning post-war era that it would grow and flourish as no American newspaper ever had.

Kilgore's publication is now maturing, though no doubt its readership and influence will continue to grow. Will the *Journal*'s middle-age be the start of its decline? Seemingly not. The people who now run the paper appear to have learned just how delicate a task it will be to sustain the paper's growth without relaxing its standards or crushing its spirit. More than anything else, how long the *Journal* stays on top in American journalism will probably depend upon their ability to run an immense, powerful news empire with a measure of Kilgore's contagious enthusiasm.

Select Bibliography

Bartlett, Bruce. *"Reaganomics," Supply Side Economics in Action.* Westport, Conn.: Arlington House, 1981.

Bishop, George W., Jr. *Charles H. Dow and The Dow Theory.* New York: Appleton-Century-Crofts, 1960.

Bloom, Murray Teigh. "Everyman's Wall Street Journal." *Esquire Magazine,* November 1957.

Brooks, John. *The Go-Go Years.* New York: Weybright and Talley, 1973.

———. *Once in Galconda.* New York: Harper and Row, 1969.

———. "The Wall Street Journal Woos the Eggheads." *Harper's Magazine,* March 1959.

DeMott, John. "What Makes Danny Run?" *Institutional Investor,* June 1973.

Feemster, Robert M. "The Wall Street Journal, purveyor of news to business America!" A speech before the Newcomen Society in North America, 1954. Transcript in the collection of the New York Public Library.

Gartner, Michael, ed. *The Jilted Aardvark and Other Improbable Tales from* The Wall Street Journal. Princeton, N.J.: Dow Jones Books, 1970.

Gilder, George. *Wealth and Poverty.* New York: Basic Books, 1981.

Gingold, Oliver J. Interviewed in *Editor & Publisher,* November 24, 1956.

Hamilton, William Peter. *The Stock Market Barometer.* New York: Harper, 1922.

Kerby, William F. *A Proud Profession: Memoirs of a Wall Street Journal Reporter, Editor and Publisher.* Homewood, Ill.: Dow Jones-Irwin, 1981.

Jones, David R. *Origins of The Wall Street Journal, 1880–1902.* Masters dissertation in the Department of History, New York University, September 1961.

Laffer, Arthur B. and Miles, Marc A. *International Economics in an Integrated World.* Glenview, Ill.: Scott Foresman and Co., 1982.

Liebling, A. J. *The Press.* New York: Pantheon Books, 1975.

Loomis, Carol J. "The Story The Wall Street Journal Won't Print." *Fortune,* August 1971.

MacDougall, A. Kent, ed. *The Press, A Critical Look from the Inside.* Princeton, N.J.: Dow Jones Books, 1972.

————. "Up Against The Wall Street Journal." In *Stop the Presses, I Want to Get Off: Inside Stories of the News Business from the pages of More.* (Edited by Richard Pollak.) New York: Random House, 1975.

Miller, Norman C. *The Great Salad Oil Swindle.* New York: Coward-McCann, 1965.

Moffitt, Donald, ed. *Swindled! Classic Business Frauds of the Seventies.* Princeton, N.J.: Dow Jones Books, 1976.

Mott, Frank Luther. *American Journalism.* New York: Macmillan Co., 1942.

McClintick, David. *Indecent Exposure, A True Story of Hollywood and Wall Street.* New York: William Morrow and Co., 1982.

————. *Stealing from the Rich: The Home-Stake Oil Swindle.* New York: M. Evans and Co., 1977.

Nelson, Samuel Armstrong. *The ABC of Stock Speculation.* New York: 1934.

Noyes, Alexander Dana. *Forty Years of American Finance.* New York: 1934.

————. *The Market Place: Reminiscenses of a Financial Editor.* Boston: Little, Brown 1938.

Pecora, Ferdinand. *Wall Street Under Oath.* New York: Simon and Schuster, 1937.

Pound, Arthur, and Moore, Samuel Taylor, eds. *They Told Barron.* New York: Harper and Brothers, 1930.

————. *More They Told Barron.* New York: Harper and Brothers, 1931.

Pratt, Sereno S. *The Work of Wall Street.* New York: D. Appleton and Co., 1921.

Preston, Charles, ed. *The Best of The Wall Street Journal.* Chicopee, Mass.: Dow Jones Books, 1974.

————. *The New World of The Wall Street Journal.* New York: Simon and Schuster, 1963.

————. *The World of The Wall Street Journal.* New York: Simon and Schuster, 1959.

Rhea, Robert. *The Dow Theory.* New York: Barron's, 1932.

Royster, Vermont C. *A Pride of Prejudices.* New York: Alfred A. Knopf, 1967.

Senate Committee on Banking and Currency, *Stock Exchange Practices.* Washington, D.C.: The Library of Congress, 1932.

Sobel, Robert. *The Great Bull Market: Wall Street in the 1920s.* New York: Norton, 1968.

Talese, Gay. *The Kingdom and the Power.* New York: World, 1969.

Wanniski, Jude. *The Way the World Works.* New York: Touchstone, 1979.

Wendt, Lloyd. *The Wall Street Journal: The Story of Dow Jones and the Nation's Business Newspaper.* New York: Rand, McNally and Co., 1982.

White, Andrew Dickson. *Paper-money Inflation in France: How it Came; What It Brought; and How it Ended.* New York: Wall Street Journal, *ca.* 1940 (a pamphlet in the collection of the New York Public Library).

Index